TOWARD THE LIGHT OF LIBERTY

TOWARD THE LIGHT OF LIBERTY

*The Struggles for Freedom
and Rights That Made
the Modern Western World*

A. C. Grayling

WALKER & COMPANY
NEW YORK

Copyright © A. C. Grayling 2007

Published by Walker Publishing Company, Inc., New York
Distributed to the trade by Holtzbrinck Publishers

All papers used by Walker & Company are natural, recyclable products made from wood grown in well-managed forests. The manufacturing processes conform to the environmental regulations of the country of origin.

LIBRARY OF CONGRESS CATALOGING-IN-PUBLICATION DATA HAS BEEN APPLIED FOR

ISBN-10: 0-8027-1636-9
ISBN-13: 978-0-8027-1636-1

Visit Walker & Company's Web site at www.walkerbooks.com

First U.S. Edition 2007

1 3 5 7 9 10 8 6 4 2

Typeset by Hewer Text UK Ltd, Edinburgh
Printed in the United States of America by Quebecor World Fairfield

For Katie and Maddie

Liberty, next to religion has been the motive of good deeds and the common pretext of crime, from the sowing of the seed at Athens, 2,460 years ago, until the ripened harvest was gathered by men of our race. It is the delicate fruit of a mature civilization; and scarcely a century has passed since nations, that knew the meaning of the term, resolved to be free. In every age its progress has been beset by its natural enemies, by ignorance and superstition, by lust of conquest and by love of ease, by the strong man's craving for power, and the poor man's craving for food. During long intervals it has been utterly arrested, when nations were being rescued from barbarism and from the grasp of strangers, and when the perpetual struggle for existence, depriving men of all interest and understanding in politics, has made them eager to sell their birthright for a pottage, and ignorant of the treasure they resigned. At all times sincere friends of freedom have been rare, and its triumphs have been due to minorities, that have prevailed by associating themselves with auxiliaries whose objects often differed from their own; and this association, which is always dangerous, has been sometimes disastrous, by giving to opponents just ground of opposition, and by kindling dispute over the spoils in the hour of success. No obstacle has been so constant, or so difficult to overcome as uncertainty and confusion touching the nature of true liberty. If hostile interests have wrought much injury, false ideas have wrought still more; and its advance is recorded in the increase of knowledge as much as in the improvement of laws.

'The History of Freedom in Antiquity', Lord Acton
An address delivered to the members of the
Bridgnorth Institute, 26 February 1877

CONTENTS

Acknowledgements

My warm thanks go to my editors Bill Swainson and George Gibson, to Naomi Goulder for her excellent work on the references, to my assistant Florence Mackenzie, to Sophie Erskine for valuable endeavours in libraries in London and Cambridge, and to the always helpful librarians of the British Library, the London Library, Birkbeck College Library, the Warburg Institute, the Institute of Historical Studies of the University of London, and Senate House Library. Special thanks go to my friend Dr David Mitchell for his valuable comments on the manuscript. I have a debt of gratitude too to the scholars and historians, acknowledged in the notes, from whose work I have learned so much.

List of Illustrations

The Tennis Court Oath, Paris, 1789, by Jacques Louis David (*Musée de la Ville de Paris, Musée Carnavalet, Paris, France, Giraudon / The Bridgeman Art Library*)

Mary Wollstonecraft, by John Opie, *c.*1797 (*Private Collection / The Bridgeman Art Library*)

The Peterloo massacre, 16 August 1819 (*British Museum, London, UK / The Bridgeman Art Library*)

Chartist meeting on Kennington Common, London, 1848 (*The Royal Collection 2007* © *Her Majesty Queen Elizabeth II*)

Lord Acton, late nineteenth century (© *Bettmann / CORBIS*)

John Stuart Mill, 1870 (*Hulton Archive / Getty Images*)

A slave auction poster, 1829 (© *Wilberforce House, Hull City Museums and Art Galleries, UK / The Bridgeman Art Library*)

The infamous ship *Brookes*, showing how slaves were transported across the Atlantic under the Regulated Slave Trade Act of 1788 (*Library of Congress, Washington D.C., USA / The Bridgeman Art Library*)

A slave's punishment scars, Baton Rouge, Louisiana, 1863 (© *CORBIS*)

Abolition of slavery in the French colonies, 1848, by François Biard (*Photo RMN / Gérard Blot*)

Women's suffrage on the march in America, May 1912 (© *Bettmann / CORBIS*)

Emmeline Pankhurst arrested while trying to deliver a petition to the king in May 1914 (*Museum of London, UK / The Bridgeman Art Library*)

Elizabeth Cady Stanton, 1900 (*Time & Life Pictures / Getty Images*)

May Day rally of the Hitler Youth, Berlin Olympic stadium, 1937 (*popperfoto.com*)

A victim of Nazism in Bergen–Belsen concentration camp, May 1945 (*USHMM, courtesy of Madalae Fraser*)

The official inception of the United Nations, 1942 (© *UN PHOTO*)

Eleanor Roosevelt holding the 1948 United Nations Universal Declaration of Human Rights (© *UN PHOTO*)

An identity inspection by French troops in Algeria, 1950s (© *Archives Barrat–Bartoli / CORBIS*)

An apartheid protest in Durban, South Africa, 1986 (© *Reuters / CORBIS*)

Martin Luther King, 28 August 1963 (© *Hulton-Deutsch Collection / CORBIS*)

A black American takes her children to school in Nashville, Tennessee, amid protests from whites, 1957 (*Photo by John Malone, Nashville Banner*)

The World Trade Center in New York, 11 September 2001, as the second aircraft flies into the south tower (*Rob Howard / CORBIS*)

The first page of the 2001 US Patriot Act

Demonstrators protest against the Patriot Act, 2003 (© *Ramin Talaie/CORBIS*)

1

Setting the Scene

A T THE DAWN of the twenty-first century most people in the Western liberal democracies of Europe, North America and Australasia could reflect with satisfaction on at least one thing: that the history of their civilisation in the preceding five centuries had been such that ordinary citizens, men and women alike, have reached a position which at the beginning of that period was attainable by only a tiny minority of people: namely, aristocrats and senior clergy. In the year 1500 education, wealth, participation in political processes, the freedom and wherewithal to travel, and other opportunities and capacities which today's average Westerner takes for granted, were reserved to these few. By this measure alone one could justify what is sometimes called a Whig view of the history of the modern West, namely, that it displays progress – indeed, remarkable progress: a transformation for the better in the life of the common man. Add the many achievements of science, benign technology and medicine, and the justification for taking such a view increases.

And even when people cite major setbacks – such as the rise of totalitarian regimes in the twentieth century, responsible for frightful atrocities and terrible war – one can remain Whiggish by pointing out that the rest of the world, and principally the Western world, would not accept those regimes, and therefore opposed and defeated them – in the space of seventeen years in the case of Nazism, and seventy years in the case of Soviet Communism.[1]

Still, it does not do to get carried quite away by these thoughts. As the light of modern times grew stronger in Europe and the world it conquered from the sixteenth century onwards, so some of the shadows it cast grew deeper. The many negative aspects of colonialism and exploitation of the peoples and resources arrogated by European expansion constitute an ineradicable stain, despite the positive aspects that partially attended. Even as science and secularism grew, so the reaction to them at times waxed violent: the worst war in European history before the twentieth century – the seventeenth century's Thirty Years War – was a struggle of religion, capping nearly a century of religious struggles, in which the old ecclesiastical order fought to regain what it had lost to a diversity of new ones.

Grant the negatives and the shadows: it remains true that today's ordinary Western citizen is, in sixteenth-century terms, a lord: a possessor of rights, entitlements, opportunities and resources that only an aristocrat of that earlier period could hope for. This is the result of a singular process: the diffusion of what one might call enfranchisement. It consists in the increasing liberty of the individual, the growth of the idea that individuals have rights and claims, and that they can assert them even against the constituted authority of the land. In today's West a set of values is taken to constitute what a liberal democratic polity is, though in hard fact not all of these values are fully realised. Nevertheless they serve as defining aspirations. At the minimum they include individual liberty, privacy, free speech, due process of law and equality before the law, representative and transparent government, and a regime of equal rights and entitlements for all. In practical terms this is meant to imply such things as equality between the sexes, no discrimination on grounds of race or age, the vote for all adults, remedies for breach of rights, freedom of choice and action across a wide range of interests including whom to marry, whether to have children, where to live, whether to travel abroad or emigrate, and much more. They also involve the distribution of social goods such as education and health care, though in different liberal polities there is a broad range of opinion between those who think these goods should be justly distributed from a commonly financed pool, and those who think that it is the responsibility of individuals to provide them for themselves and their families. These are arguments about means: the principles and ends are the shared context of debate.

Yet getting to the position where these ideas are taken as common-places was very far from easy. When one thinks of what had to happen in order for the ordinary twenty-first-century Western citizen to attain the position he enjoys in these respects, the litany of achievements is impressive. First, the hegemony of a single church over the minds and lives of individuals had to be broken. Then absolute monarchy had to be challenged, and replaced by more representative systems of govern-ment with citizen participation. Both processes were occasionally revolutionary but mostly evolutionary, plagued by setbacks, made slow and difficult by the reluctance of both religious and temporal powers to give anything away. Many died in furthering these processes – in fire at the church's stake, in chains in royal dungeons, on the battlefield. Their story – the story of the price paid for what we have now – is central to what follows in these chapters.

As progress was made in these respects so the possibility of other advances grew. Education became more general, furthering the desire for more participation in political processes and more freedom to choose and pursue individual aspirations. Out of growing liberty came more desire for liberty, and alongside it grew concomitant aspirations: for the abolition of slavery; for rights for working people; for universal education; for the spread of democracy; for the enfranchisement of women; for universal regimes of human rights giving everyone the chance to choose their own lives and to achieve their own flourishing.

All this was impossible in 1500 except for that tiny minority of aristocrats and clerics. In the twilight of the feudal order people had a fixed place in a hierarchical structure, and very few escaped its restrictions. If anyone did so it was through a combination of excep-tional personal gifts and luck. Today, by massive contrast, living a life of freedoms and opportunities is the norm of expectation.

But – and what a but! – for how long will this remain true? For how long will Westerners continue to enjoy the hard-won liberties so long fought for, and at such cost? As the twenty-first century dawned the great achievement of the open liberal society was under threat, not as it had been at times during the Cold War (and even then, as we later discovered, more notionally than not), but because of terrorism, the related phenomenon of the resurgence of religious fundamentalism, and the retrogressive reactions of liberal societies to both. When the threat that liberal polities faced consisted of attack by enemy armies, the reaction was to have soldiers and nuclear weapons and fighter aircraft ready in return, and it was reasonably clear where lay the line in the sand which the enemy must not step over. That threat and that kind of preparedness were too familiar, alas, because of what modern war had become; it was for this that the world made its preparations, and, having done so, achieved a certain comfort and stability behind the ensuing armoured lines.

But terrorism is wholly different. It is insidious, secret, unpredictable, treacherous; it comes as much from within a given society as from outside it; it targets unsuspecting innocents in the course of their daily lives. It is crime on a monstrous scale, aiming at nothing less than mass murder and wholesale disruption of social and economic life. Moreover its association with strongly held religious belief complicates matters vastly, because whereas liberal societies are painfully anxious to respect the sensitivities of religious minorities, to show them a maximum of friendly and concessive tolerance, and thus to give them all the freedom they need to exist and flourish in their own chosen ways, those very freedoms allow the religious minorities to breed from among themselves, in their darker corners (the majority are surely horrified by what criminality comes from among their own), the very enemies, the paradoxical enemies, of the freedom and tolerance that first permits them to arise.

Perhaps worse still is what liberal societies might do to themselves in the face of this new and different threat. They begin, by small but dangerous increments, to cease to be as liberal as they once were. They begin to restrict their own hard-won rights and freedoms as a protection against the criminal minority who attempt (and as we thus see, by forcing liberty to commit suicide, succeed in doing so) to terrorise society. In a curious way, liberalism's efforts to restrict its own liberties are made according to the liberal principle that no minority must be singled out. Thus, even if it were known that all would-be terrorists spring from a small group within a small minority in society, it would be illiberal to impose restrictions just on them to protect the rest of society, on the grounds that this would be unfair and discriminatory. As a result society as a whole is brought under the liberty-restricting new regime.

In the United States the Orwellianly named 'Patriot Act', and in the United Kingdom moves to introduce identity cards, to restrict freedom of speech, to limit immigration, and to introduce longer periods of imprisonment without trial, are among the liberty-undermining measures that these states – both in the vanguard of the free world – have introduced in response to perceived terrorist threat. For observers of these moves, one of the most troubling things about them is their disproportion. When in 1940 Britain faced the imminence of invasion (and the actuality of daily aerial attack) by the might of the German armed forces massing just twenty miles across the English Channel, its government enacted some temporary security measures – *temporary*, note – such as identity cards and restrictions on the freedom of speech and the press. Now, in face of a far lesser threat, the greatest among the Western liberal democracies are enacting *permanent* legislation of even more draconian kinds.

The disproportion is explainable by a number of factors. The most dismaying is that the leaders of the Western liberal democracies do not much resemble those in office when many of the rights and freedoms that were threatened by Nazi aggression were younger and fresher, and understood to be precious in a way that they seem not to be to today's leaders. Today's leaders have grown up taking those freedoms and rights for granted, and are demonstrably not much interested in them any more; they find them an inconvenience because protecting them requires lengthier and costlier measures than they care to sanction. Alas, most of the general population either seem to share that indifference, or are merely ignorant of what is in process of being lost. The cliché – no less true for being one – has it that we only properly value things when they have gone: perhaps the day will come when both leaders and led wake to the carelessness with which they allowed a precious inheritance to slip from their grasp.

But in case they let that inheritance slip without anyone calling out to stop them, it is eminently worth reminding them of a large and significant fact: that the rights and liberties that have made every ordinary Western citizen the equal of a sixteenth-century aristocrat were very, very hard won. The great endeavours, the courage, the striving and the persistence with which, molecule by molecule, the rich and powerful had their fingers prised off their monopolies of power and their hegemonies over opportunity and freedom, constitute one of the great monuments of the human spirit. It is a story which has not so much been forgotten as never seen in its completeness. Each struggle for liberty led to the next; an inch of freedom here, an ounce of opportunity there, provided the chance for a next step upwards to further and different liberties, and to the securing of rights.

One way among many, therefore, of seeing the history of the modern West – the history of Europe and its world from the beginning of the sixteenth century – is to see it as a series of liberation struggles, transforming the remnants of feudalism into the liberal democracies which saw their greatest moment, and which enjoyed the warmest sunshine of their achievement as such, in the year that the Berlin Wall came down and the promise of the West flowed eastwards across its rubble – a blissful dawn, whatever subsequent years may have brought with them.

The point I urge in this book is that all the efforts towards securing the rights and freedoms we enjoy today (still enjoy, almost, although they are beginning to fray and diminish) cost blood, and took centuries. It dishonours those who fought for them to forget that fact now, and it does us no credit to be careless of what was thus won. My hope is that understanding what it cost – seeing our last five centuries as a continuously unfolding series of struggles to make ourselves free, to make us lords of ourselves – will summon resolve not to allow the erosion of our liberties in the spurious name of security, for as Benjamin Franklin said, 'he who would put security before liberty deserves neither'.

*

In the chapters that follow, therefore, I tell a story, one in which the history of the modern West is reconfigured as the tale of a long, tough, ultimately (but perhaps only temporarily?) successful struggle or interrelated series of struggles, aimed at the liberation of the individual. It is also a polemic, because that success is under threat. It is a true story, and a vitally important one, whose difference from the many other ways in which the history of the modern West can be recounted is that it offers a different perspective from what is standard – namely, the perspective of one whose business is philosophy, and who, in agreeing with the wonderful insight attributed to Thucydides that 'history is philosophy teaching by example', therefore sees the history of the modern West in terms of the evolution and application of a set of fundamentally important concepts that have shaped and directed an outcome, this outcome being the family of polities in which the concepts distinctive of contemporary liberal democracy hold sway.

This does not mean that I think contemporary liberal democracies perfect – far from it – or that the process by which their citizens' current circumstances evolved was always admirable – again, far from it – or that it did not too often generate its own opposites and oppositions which were sometimes peculiarly horrible (to repeat the salient examples: the Nazi and Soviet totalitarianisms). These are facts of the story too. But they do not change the essential insight that today's ordinary citizen has what once only very few highly privileged people had, and has it because much effort and blood secured it. In telling the story of this endeavour I count its cost; by counting its cost I hope to drive home the worth of what it achieved; by reminding ourselves of its worth I hope that we can be encouraged to fight to save it, for – to repeat, as one endlessly must – the process of losing our inheritance of liberty might have already begun.

In one way these chapters are a dialogue with the great nineteenth-century historian and thinker, Lord Acton, a champion of liberty whose thesis about its origins and growth I cannot fully share. This, to lay cards on the table straight away, is because Acton was a devout Catholic who saw liberty as a gift of Christianity. It is true that one of the first steps in modern times towards the freeing of the individual was the achievement of religious liberty and eventually toleration – a grim and sanguinary tale in too many of its aspects, though at last a noble one. But Acton, as I shall give reason for thinking, was wrong in his premise. He neglected the fact that whereas religious liberty was eventually wrung from the bitterly reluctant grasp of his own church in the endeavour which begins the great story of liberty, every next step taken by liberty's foot soldiers in all spheres, from science to the liberation of women's sexuality and fertility, was just as bitterly opposed by his own and other churches. His claim cannot thus be justified. In a way that must prompt all too familiar reactions from dispassionate onlookers, the history of liberty proves to be another chapter – and perhaps the most important of all – in the great quarrel between religion and secularism, for without the latter there would be (because there could be) no liberty at all. This too, therefore, has to be an integral part of the tale told here.

This tale is about the way profoundly important philosophical ideas drive history. There are two things to say about the relationship of philosophy and history as enquiries. Both are part of the quest to know and, which is a greater thing, to understand the human situation, and to profit by doing so. The profit to be taken lies in understanding ourselves and our own time, thus helping us to insights and to a sense of right proportion in things, and consequently to the best achievable management of ourselves and (jointly with our fellows) of our world.

The yield to be hoped from a philosophical examination of history is thus itself something philosophical: the recognition and articulation of an ethics (in the broadest, politics-including sense of this term) justified by what the past teaches.

What a philosophical view of history can aspire to is what the reassembler of a jigsaw puzzle achieves, namely, to make a coherent picture out of the pieces. As disputes among historians show, there are more ways than one of assembling the pieces of the past to give different and sometimes contrasting pictures of what happened and what it meant. The pictures go by the name of interpretations, and the plurality of them prompts some to think that they leave no room for truth. This is merely to misunderstand the various and complex nature of truth. But when a philosopher looks at the broad consensus of what historians relate of the past, he or she might have something to offer to the reflection which must always follow the primary task of historical scholarship. The search for meanings, for the sense of things, and most especially for the deep ideas that are the cogs driving history, is something to which philosophical reflection ought to be expected to contribute, not least because it is the nature and application of ideas which is philosophy's special provenance.

I do not mean to suggest that historians concentrate only on facts and not on their meanings; that cannot be so, because in one inescapable sense the meanings are the facts, and the practice of history comes down to their discovery and interpretation. Rather, I mean that there are certain ideas, philosophical ideas, whose place in the unfolding of the human story is so central and – even in their evolution – so persistent that it becomes a matter as much of fascination as of importance for the philosopher to trace their concrete realisation in the lives of people and societies. The ideas in question here are those of liberty and rights. By this historical examination of their unfolding and application their content is most clearly understood, and their formative influence best grasped.

There are various ways of explaining this thought more fully. One might be to employ Nietzsche's idea of a 'genealogy' of concepts, except that this involves too much suppositious reconstruction to be quite right for the task I undertake here. Neither do I mean to suggest that there is some great philosophical truth being revealed in the march of time, as the 'philosophical historians' Hegel, Marx, Spengler and Toynbee claimed. The very same ideas of liberty and rights that we now debate emerged in history in particular contexts, and much as one can best understand a human individual by knowing his or her biography, so knowing the biography of a fundamental concept or set of concepts helps to understand them too. This is a major part of the point in what follows.

Perhaps the best way to explain the project here is by analogy. Think of an anatomist demonstrating the structures of the body by dissection, laying bare and exhibiting the connections between muscles, organs, vascular system, skeleton and nerves. An historian of a given period must anatomise thus, in effect flaying the corpse of past time, unless he or she is interested in a particular aspect of that period – say, its military history (the muscles) or its economics (the vascular system). I see my task here as one of isolating and extracting a central nerve – the spinal cord, as it might be – whose animating ramifications consist in the successive widenings of various but related liberties, rights and empowerments of increasingly general classes of people approximately between the years 1500 and 2000, by which latter time the expansion had ceased and contraction had begun.

Among the many ways of giving an historical overview of Europe and its extension into the world, especially America, since 1500 is to focus either exclusively or in combination on the development of nation states, the rise of science, the decline of religion, the increasing destructiveness of military technology, the spread of constitutional forms of government, and more. Here I look at the same period from the point of view of the increasing realisation in practice of certain ideas – the philosophical idea of liberty together with its implications – as a result of hard effort, struggle and high human cost, and relate it to the danger it is now in.

This point is the conclusion of my argument. Shortly before the Czech Republic returned to its rightful place in the heart of Europe by joining the European Union in 2004, I had the honour of giving the keynote speech on 'the idea of Western values' to a conference organised in Prague Castle by the Office of the Czech President (Václav Havel) and the British Council. In the discussion afterwards a delegate stood up and made a comment, intended to be purely neutral, about the demographics of Europe. The native population of the continent is in decline, he pointed out, and the fastest population growth is taking place among immigrant communities, currently numbering about twenty million, and drawn mainly from Muslim parts of the world. By current trends the descendants of these immigrant communities will be in a majority in Europe in a relatively small number of generations' time. This (he continued) is just a fact of the dynamics of history, and in itself neutral. But let us suppose that the descendants of today's Muslims are loyal adherents to their ancestors' faith, and when they become the majority in Europe, choose to introduce traditional shari'ah law. Then the way of life of men and particularly women in today's Europe – twenty-first-century Europe – will seem an oddity, and a temporary one, in the history of the continent, because many of the liberties exercised by Europeans today, especially by women, are not acceptable to traditional Islam, and would not survive a change in religious and social climate.

And this – so the speaker concluded – should prompt a question: If we think that the values by which we in Western polities live today are right and good, what are we doing to entrench them against eventualities such as this?

Well, that is one way of dramatising the situation we face as we begin to descend the far side of a Parnassus whose summit – which I described above as having been reached in the year 1989, when the Berlin Wall fell – is accordingly behind us. Do we record the fact that the age of liberty might have passed its best point, after so brief a period of flourishing, or do we fight to keep all that the struggle to win it gained for us? One aim of this book is to show why we must answer the last question in the affirmative.

In tracing the rise and development of, and the current pressure upon, liberty and rights in the modern West, I take pains to describe the circumstances out of which the demand for them arose. The first great crack in the ice pack of illiberality came in the sixteenth century as a quest for religious freedom, and I dwell on that important story at length because it is the foundation for the rest. In order to appreciate the significance of the struggle for each form of liberty, whether of conscience and belief, of enquiry, of the person, or of political status, it is essential that we understand the situation of relevant unfreedom that preceded it.

The same applies to the correlative matter of rights. For example, the dire circumstances of labouring people in the industrial revolution necessitated the emergence of reformers and trades unionists; the bad press attracted by the latter in the United States and during the twentieth century in the United Kingdom obscures memories of child labour, dirty and dangerous factory conditions, poverty wages, and working days that ran from before dawn to after nightfall – conditions which courageous men and women impelled by humanitarian concern fought to change, often at great personal cost.

Most compelling of all, think of the Jews of Europe in the hideous Nazi period, herded into cattle trucks and carried away to be gassed or worked to death, or machine-gunned into pits they had been forced to dig. Think of their teeth and hair and spectacles piled up for recycling, think of the emaciated and bewildered barely alive prisoners found by Allied soldiers in concentration camps in 1945. These were the bleak and desperate circumstances that prompted the adoption of the Universal Declaration of Human Rights three years later, a fact evidently forgotten by those in comfortable academic studies who employ the casuistries of their trade to prove that the concept of human rights is empty.

Liberty and rights, then, are matters of very real, very deep, very important moment; they are life and death matters; they are crucial; they apply to each one of us – and we live in a time when they are under pressure. It is thus not just the getting of rights and liberties by our forebears, but also the reasons why they were needed, that I relate here.

There is a good reason why Lord Acton never succeeded in writing his great projected work on the history of liberty. It is that the project, if carried out in full and comprehensively, is so vast as to be incompletable (unless it were to take the dimensions of an encyclopaedia produced by a large team of expert contributors). Given the aim of my argument here, therefore, my choice has been to trace a very selective route along the central threads of the story, taking the Reformation as the appropriate point of departure for modern times. Many names, many considerations, many aspects have been left aside on purpose to keep the task clear and manageable, as their own experts will recognise; for whole volumes are devoted not only to the themes, periods and personalities discussed here, but even more so to those set aside.

Further, as this is a history of the fortunes of an idea and certain of its implications, it is not a history of events in the straightforward sense. For example, the American and French Revolutions were premised on the idea of liberty together with its implicated ideas of rights and representation, and are discussed from the point of view of their being endeavours to turn those ideas into concrete realities. But I do not rehearse the histories of the American and French Revolutions as such, and this applies across the board. Where historical and biographical detail is needed because it is unlikely to be familiar even in outline, it is given; the main framework of modern European and American history is otherwise presented through the fortunes of the idea whose history this is, and is otherwise assumed or alluded to.

One hopes that the distinction between a work of history and a work tracing the application of an idea in history will be clear: they demand different methodologies, and here it is the latter that is in hand. The main, centrally lying threads of the story of liberty choose themselves, and what is lost by selection is detail, not the thrust of the case.

In the first part of the book, up to and including Chapter 4, I focus attention on a small number of significant individuals, for in the early growth of modern liberty it was the contributions of men like Sebastian Castellio, John Milton, John Locke and others, that helped to articulate the drive towards liberties of conscience, thought and expression, which constituted the first steps towards more general liberty. In the second part of the book, from Chapter 5 onwards, when many individuals had become part of the swelling movement towards political and social liberties of connected kinds, I focus attention more on themes. The transition from individual thinkers in Part I of the book to collective thoughts in Part II of the book reflects the gathering success of the ideas of liberty and rights themselves. Thus the more generally these ideas came to be prized, the more generally people sought to see them realised in society and its institutions, and the less it was a matter of a relatively few courageous souls arguing for them.

I leave to the last chapter more explicit consideration of the meaning of 'liberty' itself, allowing the concept to evolve with the narrative of its history, as it did in fact. What its champions meant by it is more than clear enough in every case; it is defined by its lack, by the desire felt for it, and by the battles fought for it. People struggled and died for it, and though others have often enough done so on behalf of abstractions and even meaningless concepts, in the case of liberty something remarkable shines through: that its champions knew just what it was that they and the world lacked, and needed.

PART I

THE DEMAND FOR LIBERTY

2

The Reformation
and the Beginning of Modern Liberty

LORD ACTON BELIEVED that the struggle for religious liberty in the sixteenth century made a major contribution to the birth of liberty in modern times.[1] In one sense he was right, for without the Reformation the story of liberty might well be a shorter and more recent one. He saw this as a vindication of religion's claim to be a force for good in history. But another and more accurate way of looking at it is to see the effort made by a diversity of people to escape the hegemony of the Church as being, in truth, about many kinds of liberty, not just liberty of conscience and worship. This latter was a necessary first step, of course, for without the freedom to think for oneself in these matters there could be no chance of thinking freely on any other matter. But once individuals began to achieve immunity from punishment for taking a view different from prescribed religious authority, given that it concerned so serious a question as the destiny of their eternal souls, all else, step by step – albeit step by painful step – followed.

In this way it is hard to see, say, the Peasants' War of 1525 as the expression of no more than a pious desire by scarcely literate men to live by the gospel without the domination of priests. That indeed was one of their avowed aims, but behind the avowal lies the peasants' unmistakably worldly desire to get the priests – and their demand for tithes, their interference in all aspects of life, their control – off their backs. This is more than liberty of conscience; it is the aspiration to liberty as such.

That the struggle for religious liberty was a bitter and dangerous one scarcely needs saying, for men perished agonisingly in flames at the stake for pursuing it. But the very ferocity of the punishments made the arguments against religious intolerance sharper and more urgent in response, and once those arguments were out in the world, in print and in conversation, as thoughts and certainties in the minds of many, given that it was an era of such tremendous religious and therefore political upheaval, the diffusion of their influence throughout Europe was irreversible.

The seeds of the idea of freedom of belief, conscience and expression were of course germinating long before 1517, the year in which Luther nailed his theses to the church door in Wittenberg, thus lighting the touchpaper of the Reformation. The seeds of liberty were already present in classical antiquity, not so much discussed as assumed; for how could a citizen stand up and contribute properly to debate in the agora of Athens unless he were free to say what he thought? Admittedly, classical antiquity was an era of freedom only for the few – for the enfranchised, which meant adult male citizens – while the many, comprising women, children, slaves and other non-citizens, were anything but free. And even for the enfranchised few there were limits: Socrates was put to death on trumped-up charges of 'corrupting the youth of Athens' (by encouraging them to ask too many inconvenient questions) and disrespecting the gods.[2] Nevertheless, the idea of freedom of mind was implicit in the attitude of antiquity at its best and most admirable, and it was this that the humanists of the Renaissance recognised as, with equal parts of pleasure and enlightenment, they recovered the texts of the ancient authors.

One of the first fruits of this encounter was a change in attitude which, from our perspective, looks dramatic. Whereas the prevailing note of the Gothic imagination, indeed of the whole epoch that the Renaissance itself labelled 'the middle age' – that is, between the great ages of Greece and Rome and their own new dawn – had been one of renunciation for the sake of an afterlife, the humanists aspired to fulfilment in the present life. Where their medieval forerunners had published *contemptus mundi* works bewailing the wretchedness of embodied existence in the world, the Renaissance humanists applauded the dignity of man and the pleasures of the senses. Around them they could see artists producing portraits of mortal human beings, depictions of the nude, and landscapes in which the hunt, picnics, flowers and birds were the wordly themes. Poems to human love were published, and the literature of the pagan authors emulated, while all around a new urban civilisation was rising, beautified by architecture that celebrated proportions and symmetries that were not for the honour of God but for the delight of the human eye.[3]

Of course the Renaissance was by no means a secular age, and one instinct accompanying its relish of the classical authors was to assimilate them to the prevailing religious outlook. Accordingly, Dante's guide through hell was Virgil, as a proto-Christian not quite saved enough for paradise; Erasmus, doyen of the Christian humanists, so loved Cicero (in common with many in his time) that upon reading *De Senectute* he proposed naming him 'St Cicero'.

And the influence tended the other way too. Under the spell of the ancients many began to think that Christianity was not exclusive, but that the rich ethical doctrines of the pagan philosophers – in truth, richer and more detailed, more wide-ranging and more practicable, more in touch with human realities and possibilities than the narrow Christian morality – showed that there were universal principles that they and Christian morality shared, implying a more general, more inclusive outlook than was warranted by the strict exceptionalism of Christian doctrine ('I am the way, the truth, and the life; no one comes to the Father but by me') which entailed that there was no salvation outside the Church.[4]

But an even more significant aspect to humanism's endeavours was its free-handed attitude to historical enquiry. The rediscovery in monastery libraries of dusty ancient copies of hitherto lost texts and documents gave historical research a major impetus, whose results were of the first consequence. The Apostles' Creed was found not to have been devised by the Apostles themselves. The Donation of Constantine was exposed as a forgery. Many papal claims were revealed as resting on falsehoods and fabrications. Variations in biblical texts were discovered, with no certain way of choosing which was the truly authoritative version. Even worse, some texts were recognised as later interpolations, among them those of special theological significance for the Church's doctrines.[5]

This was not a situation one would expect the Church to tolerate, but for a while it did so – not out of love for liberty of thought or respect for knowledge, but out of indolence and a false sense of security, not least because so few people were literate, or, if able to read, educated enough to appreciate the significance of these researches. It was not indeed until the Reformation began in earnest that the incendiary character of these discoveries and speculations prompted a reaction from the Church, and by then it was too late.

In the first decades of the sixteenth century, in the lull between the Inquisition in Spain and Luther's Wittenberg theses, the prevailing spirit in educated Christendom was that of Erasmus, universally admired in Europe and widely influential. He combined the tolerance of humanism with loyalty to the Christian faith, and by embodying both was able to argue that matters of religious difference should be left not merely to general councils of the Church, but to the afterlife, when all such queries and doubts would be definitively resolved. He thought that theological disputes harmed ordinary Christian folk: 'The sum of our religion is peace and unanimity,' he wrote, 'and these can hardly stand unless we define as little as possible and in many things leave each person free to follow his own judgement.' This is advice that has since been assiduously followed in the milder forms of Protestantism, but although Erasmus was safe to articulate it before the violence of the Counter-Reformation began in earnest (following the Council of Trent in 1542), matters of definition proved to be the most explosive aspect of that tragic debacle. But the magic words had been spoken: 'free to follow his own judgement'. That very idea was too potent, too necessary in the context of the time to pass without response, both from those who thrilled to it and from those whom it filled with fear.[6]

The demand for liberty of conscience, as articulated in the words of Erasmus, was the chief response to the coercive imposition of its opposite. The first example of relevance to liberty's birth in the sixteenth century is the case of Torquemada, Grand Inquisitor in Spain at the end of the fifteenth century.[7]

Thomas of Torquemada was a Dominican friar who, ironically as the sequel will show, is said to have had a Jewish grandmother and was therefore linked to the *conversos*, the Spanish Jews who had converted to Christianity in their thousands during the fifteenth century. They had done so in order to avoid the wave of persecutions that broke over Spain in that fraught time, as the combined northern Iberian kingdoms fought to oust the Moors from the peninsula. For the Jews, memories of their forebears' expulsions from England and France were all too fresh – the former had occurred in 1290, the latter in 1306 – and fresh too were memories of the massacres of Jews carried out by Crusaders gathering to assert the supremacy of the cross of Christ not just over the Holy Land, but over a united and wholly Christian Europe. As the spearhead of this movement the Crusaders were in no mood to tolerate any non-Christian in their midst, and because the Jews lay closer to hand than the Muslim infidel, they too often received the first whetting of the Crusaders' blades.

In Spain the Christianising impulse that was aimed primarily at driving Islam out of the peninsula followed this pattern. Anti-Jewish sentiment was quickly inflamed by preachers as a side effect of the process, and this forced a dramatic choice on members of the Jewish community: convert, or leave. Mass conversions followed, perhaps the only example – and certainly the first – in the history of the Jewish people.[8] The effect of conversion was immediate: *conversos* were safe from persecution the moment they were baptised, because all their disabilities were dissolved by the holy water of the font. For those with the talent, money and capacity, conversion gave eligibility for public office, ordination into and eventual high office in the Church, and entry to and intermarriage with the nobility. And because there were many wealthy and gifted *conversos*, it was soon the case that they were at home in bishops' palaces and royal chancelleries, and few noble families were without *converso* relations.

Some historians speculate that all Spain's Jews might have become fully assimilated if this course of events had continued, but it is equally a matter of speculation whether conversion was invariably complete or genuine. Many Jews outwardly conformed to Christianity but secretly observed the rites and traditions of their ancient faith. Some might have mocked Christianity in private, and even desecrated its sacred symbols. Human probabilities would suggest this, even if some of the documents recording prosecutions by the Inquisition did not state as much. In sharp contrast, others among the *conversos* went to the opposite extreme by becoming zealously devout Christians, fanatical in their loyalty and observance, and therefore bitterly against fellow *conversos* who lacked their own warmth of conviction. If Torquemada was indeed from a *converso* line he fell into this latter category, and with a vengeance.

'Cometh the hour,' so the saying has it, 'cometh the man', and Torquemada was certainly the man for the hour that befell Spain. The Crusades had so polarised the faith communities then co-existing within the geographical boundaries of Europe that there could be no rapprochement, no live and let live, between Christianity and Islam as the fifteenth century drew to a close. For all the centuries of Moorish domination of southern Spain, Muslim, Christian and Jew had been able, by and large, to live in reasonable amity, mainly because it suited Caliphate politics not to stir trouble in the provinces. That time was past, and the Christian aim in Spain was now to make it a wholly and genuinely Christian space. Driving out or converting Muslims was therefore not enough; the same had to happen to Jews. But the conversion had to be real, not a mask of convenience, and evidence that it was this latter in too many cases prompted a zeal to flush out the hypocrites, and to test the orthodoxy of faith of those who claimed to be genuine. Torquemada felt himself to be the man for this task, and he had an instrument to hand for carrying it out: the Inquisition.

As a named office of the Church, the Inquisition had been in existence for two centuries before Torquemada's day.[9] Its antecedents were, however, ancient, dating its roots to the papacy of Valentinian I in the fifth century. Prior to that time Christianity had not been a persecuting faith; it had itself been a persecuted one, charged with 'atheism' by the authorities of Rome because of its refusal to honour the gods of the city and empire, so necessary for the maintenance of social and political bonds. By refusing to participate in the public rites, Christians seemed to the authorities deliberately provocative, because they rejected the ceremonies of citizenship and gave their allegiance to a ruler outside the empire – in heaven, as it happened, but therefore certainly outside the empire.

There were many different Christian sects in the early period, though, and when they came into contact there was often sharp conflict between them. Such were their differences and antipathies that if members of rival sects were thrown to the lions at the same time, they would separate to different parts of the arena in order not to be eaten by the same beasts.[10]

Nevertheless, from the outset of its official acceptance as the faith of the Roman Empire, Christianity was intended to be a tolerant religion; Constantine's Edict of Milan explicitly decreed as much. Likewise, some among the early Church Fathers argued against persecution as a resource for dealing with differences of belief and lapses from doctrine. In this the Church was repudiating some of its Old Testament roots, for the thirteenth chapter of Deuteronomy quite unequivocally voices God's command to put to death 'that prophet or dreamer of dreams' who 'hath spoken to turn you away from the Lord your God, who hath brought you out of the land of Egypt, and redeemed you out of the house of bondage.' The penalty for seducing any of the faithful to follow after other gods was death by stoning; the apostate was to be taken outside the camp and 'stoned with stones' until dead, and it did not matter (so Deuteronomy bluntly states) whether the person in question is 'thy brother, the son of thy mother, or thy son, or thy daughter, or the wife of thy bosom, or thy friend which is as thine own soul'. They are to be denounced and killed regardless, so exigent is the God of Moses for loyalty.[11]

If anything, the exclusivity and totality of the Christian claim on its votaries' allegiance was greater even than that of the equivalent Jewish claim, for the Messiah had come to them and was soon going to return, which made every demand, every necessity, a matter of urgency. Whereas the God of Moses had been jealous that his Israel should not go after other gods, for the early Church the choice they feared was between Mammon and God, the secular and the sacred, between Caesar and Christ, given that this world was not destined to last long. This in turn led to the view that the new Israel, the Church, was the only source of salvation; to wander outside it was to court eternal damnation. So the difference between the Christian and Jewish demand on the commitment of their respective votaries was not merely one of degree of exclusivity, but also of kind. In Judaism the crime was apostasy, that is, abandoning the God who had delivered Israel from the house of bondage in order to turn to other gods. For Christianity the crime was heresy, that is, incorrect belief, thereby going astray and leading others astray too. In this view lay the later justification for persecution, and for the form that punishment took, for it entailed that submission to Christ meant submission to an orthodoxy, which is to say: to the Church as the sole authoritative body. And it justified killing heretics to save them from getting further embroiled in a terrible sin, and from leading others into it with them.

Once anxieties about heresy and schism had begun to multiply in the early Church, its brief honeymoon of tolerance was over. There followed a rapid proliferation of laws against heresy, imposing punishments of exile, fines, confiscation of property, disqualification from inheritance, and very soon the death penalty. Manicheans and Donatists were the most persecuted in this early phase, but to begin with the death penalty was controversial. When Priscillian was put to death in 385, many Church notables – among them no fewer than three saints: Ambrose, Leo and Martin of Tours – condemned the Spanish bishops for ordering Priscillian's execution. St John Chrysostom said that it was an unforgivable crime to put anyone to death for heresy, and that it was enough to condemn heretics to silence and to disperse their congregations.[12]

Though these kinder views persisted for a time, they did not win the argument. St Augustine, Bishop of Hippo, was at first inclined to leniency in matters of heresy, but the Donatist problem in North Africa eventually hardened his views. It happened that he was told, by followers of that heresy who had been forced back to Catholic observance, that they had been kept under constraint by their Donatist clergy to prevent them from returning to the true faith. In response Augustine developed a theory of persecution premised on the idea that, because there is salvation only in the true Church, it is an act of love and kindness to force people to conform, and to punish lack of conformity. A good father prevents his son from picking up a snake, he said; a good gardener cuts off the rotten branch for the health of the rest of the tree.[13]

This last analogy proved to be a fateful one. Augustine was against the death penalty and did not mean the analogy to be taken literally. His successors thought otherwise.

By the tenth century AD executing heretics, typically by strangling and burning, was a commonplace. At first it was usually the temporal power which put heretics to death, but sometimes it was lynch-happy town mobs. At Soissons in 1114 and Cologne in 1163 mobs dragged accused heretics to their deaths against the wishes of the local clergy; but on many and probably most other occasions the clergy took the lead in prosecuting heresy, handing their victims over to the temporal authorities or the mob to be killed once they had reached a guilty verdict. This was the practice of that dangerous and seemingly irresistible zealot, Bernard of Clairvaux, in the twelfth century.[14] But by his time it was already common in such matters for churchmen to dispense with the help of the temporal authorities altogether, so that abbots and bishops often condemned heretics to death on their own warrant, and their own staff carried out the order.

These developments occurred independently of the growth of relevant canon law relating to remedies for heresy, which remained in an undecided state as to whether the death penalty should properly figure among the punishments. Room for controversy accordingly remained, and with it diversity of practice. Among twelfth-century princes who were adamant that death was the right sanction were Raymond V of Toulouse and Peter II of Aragon, and views such as theirs no doubt helped to settle the matter in favour of capital punishment. Less certain temporal princes were encouraged in such views in their turn by Pope Innocent III, who at the end of the twelfth century wrote to a number of them with a seemingly convincing argument that equated heresy with treason. If heresy is treason against the divine ruler in heaven, he argued, it should carry no less a penalty than treason against a mortal prince on earth. In this latter case the penalty is death; how could punishment for treason against God be less?

Out of these debates emerged, within decades, the very first efforts at an organised tribunal for repressing heresy. Some historians nominate the Council of Toulouse in 1229 as the moment when the Inquisition came into existence, but it was not until Gregory IX put the inquisitorial duties into the hands of monks, rather than leaving it to bishops and papal legates, that the Inquisition proper can be said to have begun. It was especially the mendicant order of Dominicans (the 'hounds of God') to whom Gregory entrusted the task, for they were the best educated and most disciplined of the orders, a fit instrument indeed for the work he assigned to them.[15]

In the late autumn of 1232 the Dominican monk Alberic began a tour of north Italy with the title *Inquisitor haereticae pravitatis*. His job was to enquire into the orthodoxy of views and practice of clergy and laymen alike. His method was to demand of all those in the parishes he visited that they should come forward and confess if they held heretical views, and he enquired into allegations of any irregularity, whether in belief or practice, made by the local clergy about their parishioners or one another, and by parishioners about each other and their clergy. Human nature and the normal resentments and frictions of life ensured that Alberic was not without work. Elsewhere – in the German states for a main example – some of his colleagues were swifter, harsher and more summary still, and their work quickly began to gather an ominous name.

The Inquisition had thus arrived; and it brought uneasiness, injustice and fear. It used techniques of mental and physical torture on accused persons and witnesses alike, with the official sanction of the Vatican. Some of its officers were assassinated by angry or anxious folk determined not to fall into its hands. Its history is not a happy one, and has been well told elsewhere; this is not the place for a detailed rehearsal of its story.[16] What matters here is one aspect of it that led eventually to a liberal reaction.

Technically the Inquisition related only to Christians, so Muslims and Jews were supposed to be exempt. In practice, however, votaries of either faith might find themselves in the Inquisition's hands if they harmed Christians or a Christian community, attacked the Christian faith, converted people away from Christianity, or returned to their original faith after having themselves converted to Christianity. Jews were at further risk for practising usury, which was a problem, since moneylending was in many places one of the few ways open to them of making a living, so either they put themselves in danger of the inquisitors, or they starved.

For all its bleak later reputation courtesy of Torquemada, the Spanish branch of the Inquisition had a faltering start. Historically the Iberian peninsula had been a theatre of many faiths, and indeed of alternative versions of them. Not only was it home to Jews, Muslims and Christians (the second and third of these groups living, in different places, safely under one another's dominion), but it had also been home to divergent forms of Christianity, both Catholic and Arian. In its early days in Spain the Inquisition was thoroughly disagreeable to the populace, a mob of whom murdered the inquisitor Fray Pedro de Cadrayta in 1233. Two years later the Cortes secured the agreement of the king to outlaw the use of torture by the Inquisition's officers, and in Castile and Portugal the Inquisition's remit did not run at all. If anywhere in Christian Europe seemed immune to the possibility of Inquisitorial excess (other than England where it never secured as much as a toehold, it was Spain. What irony this proved.

For most of the thirteenth and fourteenth centuries the Spanish Inquisition was accordingly a dormant institution, chiefly for the reason that there were few heretics within its jurisdiction. The main source of religious tension was a quite different one: the tragic ending of the mutual tolerance, indeed symbiosis, of the three major faiths. Tolerance had been the norm for so long that for many centuries Jews were admitted to high office in Christian parts of Iberia, and Muslims had lived there as freely as Jews and Christians lived in Muslim parts. Not that this was a fact viewed with tolerance anywhere outside Spain; successive popes decried this leniency, and as early as 1266 Pope

Clement IV exhorted King James I to expel the Muslims from his domains. Even earlier, in the eleventh century, popes and church councils alike had complained about Jews holding public office there. This earlier pressure had begun to bear ominous fruit by the first decades of the thirteenth century; in 1210 there were several clergy-encouraged and mob-effected massacres of Jews, and in 1276 popular sentiment against Jews was again fomented when Pope Clement IV followed his demand for the expulsion of the Muslims with a further demand that King James also expel all Jews.[17] Given these unhealthy precedents, it is no surprise that the fourteenth century saw increasing incidences of massacres of Jews, burnings of their property, and forced conversions: the age of tolerance was over.

For example, in 1301 at Valencia 11,000 Jews were compelled to accept baptism on pain of death. Elsewhere in that same year entire towns were burned to the ground and their Jewish populations slaughtered, so the Valencian option was a comparatively merciful one. Muslims were subjected to this treatment likewise, but with less ferocity, partly because they were fewer in number in the Christian domains, and partly because they did not carry the guilt of the Jews for 'the murder of God'. Eventually the volume of killings reached a limit; the sheer difficulty of massacring so many people meant that when Grenada was conquered and Aragon pacified, the choice offered instead to Jews and Muslims in those domains was typically between exile or conversion.

But these developments meant that by 1480, with Ferdinand and Isabella securely on the joint throne of a united kingdom, circumstances were ripe for the next step in the Christianising of the whole peninsula, namely, that of ensuring the completeness and thoroughness of Christianisation by checking that the *conversos* were sincere in their conversion. It would be intolerable if a dangerous fifth column of heretics were found to be lurking in the bosom of the people as a threat to their immortal souls. The desire to ensure purity of belief and purpose was a major part of Torquemada's motivation, and he intended to use the Inquisitorial office as his means.

But there was an additional component to Torquemada's aim. While

Jews remained in Spain there would always be the risk that they would reconvert even the most sincere *conversos*, and anyway as the people who carried the guilt for Christ's death they were a provocation and a scandal. For this reason Torquemada was determined to use the power of the Inquisition not only to purify the faithful, but to purge the infidel. Since technically its remit only ran to the former he needed to find a way to extend its authority. He saw that the popes in Rome were a lax Renaissance crew far more interested in the pleasures of this life and in other aspects of power politics than in the purity of Christianity – Pope Alexander VI, himself a Spaniard, had gone so far as to sign a treaty with the Turks against a Christian king of France. He therefore knew that they would be no help to him, and that he would require instead the imprimatur of the Spanish dual monarchs – the clever Isabella and the far less clever but pious and nationalistic Ferdinand. (It is sometimes pointed out that the stone effigies on their tombs indicate this difference: Isabella's weighty head pushes deep into the carved pillow, Ferdinand's lightly filled head makes scarcely a dent.)

Torquemada had become Isabella's confessor when she was sixteen and he forty-six. He understood her well; she was the kind of person for whom the bold and unusual stroke always seemed attractive, because she saw the potential if it succeeded, and was prepared to take risks. That is why she listened to Christopher Columbus and supported his scheme of sailing west across the Atlantic to reach the east, when everyone else thought he was merely mad. It is also why she listened to Torquemada, and supported plans for the expulsion of the Moors and Jews. Happily for Isabella and Torquemada, Ferdinand was of the same mind in this; he saw that if Inquisitorial investigations found that some of the wealthy nobles who were an obstacle to royal power were wanting in their principles or observance, not only would their influence be broken but their property could be distrained into the royal coffers. (He was intelligent enough when it came to money.) But this of course could only happen if the Spanish monarchs, not the pope in Rome, controlled the Inquisition, so Torquemada had no difficulty in persuading Ferdinand and Isabella to this course.

Torquemada's first task was to stop the process of conversion and assimilation, which had already gone very far, and to stir up renewed anxiety among Christians against both the unconverted Jews and Muslims and the *conversos*. For this he used the wandering friars, travelling instruments of propaganda whose preaching was the only means (apart from rumour) by which people in town and country outside the capital received information about great matters affecting the Church in the world. The friars were experts in inflammatory discourses and the stirring of intolerance; to them was added an informal cadre of young nobles called *familiares* who, in return for certain quasi-clerical immunities, shouldered the task of searching for and arresting suspected persons. The friars encouraged people to inform on one another, even children on parents and siblings on siblings. Soon enough the Dominicans had plenty of opportunities to set up a branch of the Holy Office wherever suspicions had been mooted. Every Saturday they would post sentinels on the roof of their lodgings to survey the town's chimney pots and note which among the putatively Christian households were not producing smoke, for these would be suspected of concealing hypocrite *conversos* observing the Jewish Sabbath.[18]

Seville was the first scene of Torquemada's activity, but he soon requested more general authority, and after a brief fracas with the Vatican (the pope refused to give Torquemada the powers he sought; Ferdinand threatened to withhold Spain's financial subventions to Rome; the pope backed down) he was appointed Grand Inquisitor of Aragon and Castile. That was in October 1482.

Torquemada's campaign began by following, at least for the opening salvos in a newly visited area, the precedent set by Alberic of Lombardy a century and a half earlier. The inhabitants would be exhorted to confess any deviations from orthodoxy, or to inform on that of others. A three-day period of grace was allowed for people to consider what to do. If within that time they confessed and accepted penance, their property would not be confiscated. Suspects were arrested, and if recalcitrant would be subjected to a variety of techniques designed to make them confess – there was no presumption of innocence in the proceedings. They would be questioned, imprisoned in chains in dungeons, then perhaps transferred to pleasant surroundings where friends visited to encourage confession, or spies were put with them to suggest unorthodoxies and to winkle secrets from them. Many broke down during these phases and said whatever the inquisitor's staff wished to hear. They were either offered a full pardon for doing so, if they could add a few accusations against others in the process, or they would be rewarded with strangling before burning, to save them the agony of the flames.

Obduracy was, however, met with a severer response. Fire was applied to the feet, the rack was used, but the most common methods employed by the Spanish Inquisition were the water torture and the hoist. In the latter the suspect's hands were tied behind his back and attached to a rope looped through a pulley. He was then lifted, arms painfully extended upwards behind him, and suddenly dropped in a series of jerks. Continued refusal to confess would see him pulled higher and higher, even to the ceiling, with weights attached to his legs, then dropped and jerked so violently that his arms and ribs were wrenched from their sockets, his spine damaged, the muscles of his torso, shoulders and back torn, and their blood vessels ruptured.

The water torture was a quieter proceeding. The suspect would be tied upside down on a ladder and a cloth stuffed into his throat. Then his mouth would be filled with water. If he tried to swallow the water he would choke on the cloth. As he was about to suffocate, the cloth would be pulled out and the kindly voice of the inquisitor would beg him, in gentle tones, to confess.

The penalties varied according to the readiness of confession and the severity of the original charge. Everyone found guilty had his property confiscated; penitents might be imprisoned for life or condemned to permanent surveillance, which included wearing the *sanbenito*, a shapeless dress coloured like the sulphur of hell, every Sunday and holy day. Impenitents and the seriously guilty were strangled or, more usually, burned at the stake. In a single year, 1488, in the city of Toledo, more than three thousand cases were handled. Torquemada received permission from the monarchs to build special prisons to hold these large numbers, for the ordinary gaols were overflowing.

Intelligent persecution knows that it will justify itself by the reaction it provokes. It did not take long for the *conversos* to grasp that Torquemada was intent on exterminating them. One group decided that, as the best form of defence was attack, they should assassinate the inquisitors before the inquisitors could kill them. Two were selected for death, and the assassins hid themselves in the church where the Dominicans came at midnight to pray. The assassins knew that 'God's hounds' (apparently not placing quite all their trust in God's protection) wore chain mail under their habits, and they were prepared for this. It happened that, on that fateful night, only one of the monks selected for death came to the church, but he chose to pray in a side chapel close to where the *conversos* were hidden. They could not resist the opportunity. His chain mail notwithstanding, he was stabbed to death and the assassins escaped. Shortly afterwards the other marked inquisitor was killed by poisoning.

The city of Toledo exploded into uproar. *Familiares* hunted for the conspirators; one committed suicide, several escaped to France, and the rest were caught. They had their hands cut off on the cathedral steps, were strung up on a gallows and, while still alive, were castrated and disembowelled. Finally their bodies were hacked into quarters for admonitory display.[19]

What played most directly into Torquemada's hands was the alleged discovery that certain *conversos* and Jews were trying to defend themselves not with arms, but with black magic which involved the ritual murder of a Christian child. One of the most celebrated cases of the Inquisition was that of a group of Jews, converted and unconverted, who allegedly had crucified a Christian boy on a Good Friday so that his heart could be used, along with a communion wafer, to perform some kind of ritual. The *conversos* and Jews arrested in this case were repeatedly tortured and spied on in their cells over a period of nine months before one of them – under the water torture – 'confessed' to everything, and Torquemada saw his chance. He consulted the professors of the University of Salamanca on the question of whether the Inquisition had jurisdiction not only over the *conversos* who had thus been found guilty, but also over the Jews who were implicated in the case with them. The learned professors said that the Inquisition indeed had that jurisdiction. Torquemada thus gained his carte blanche.

The so-called conspirators were burned on 16 November 1491. Those *conversos* who repented and professed their desire to die in the faith were repaid with strangling before the faggots were kindled. The Jews who adhered to their Judaism had their flesh torn by red-hot pincers before the fires were lit under them. But this was only the beginning of the end for Spain's Jews. Torquemada went to Isabella and told her that the case showed that no trust could be placed in the *conversos* as long as unconverted Jews dwelt among them. All unconverted Jews must be expelled. Briefly the monarchs hesitated, for the Jews were the crown's tax collectors, and the monarchs were at that moment involved in the expensive military endeavour of forcing Spain's Moors from the peninsula. But on 2 January 1492 Grenada fell, and the tax problem was suddenly alleviated. Torquemada renewed his persuasions, and within three months had secured a royal decree ordering all Jews to leave Spain, taking with them only what they could carry.

A famous incident followed. Leaders of the Jewish community appeared before the monarchs to insist on their loyalty, to remind them of their long history of service to the crown, and – well knowing where Ferdinand kept his sense of mercy – to offer the monarchs a handsome bribe of 30,000 ducats. Torquemada saw the monarchs glance at each other and pause. He strode forward. 'Judas sold Christ for thirty pieces of silver; you would sell him for thirty thousand,' he cried, throwing onto the table before him the crucifix he carried. 'Go on then! Sell him! But never say that I was party to the sale!'[20]

The decree stood. Jews exchanged their lands, their vineyards and plantations, their houses and warehouses, for a donkey, a bolt of cloth, a pair of shoes. One historian of these events imagined that from the decks of the ships leaving port to take Columbus to the Indies could be seen the crowded galleons taking expelled Jews into exile. The departing explorers and Jews left behind them a continuing process, for once the Jews were out of the way Torquemada turned his attention to the

Muslims who remained, and in due course – for Luther was alive, and history was on the march – it would be the turn of Protestants, and not just in Spain.

———

The atrocities of Torquemada are a salient part of the background against which the first protests in favour of religious liberty were raised – the first thought-out and articulated protests in modern times in favour of liberty as such. But they did not come straight away. Erasmus' moderate pleas in favour of leaving difficult questions to be resolved in the next world were made in the lull that followed the Spanish excesses, which people no doubt optimistically thought would be unlikely to occur elsewhere anyway. In the rest of Europe, apart from Savoy, the Inquisition was not so harsh in its methods, and not just because it lacked a Torquemada. And in fact not only was there a lull in Europe, as its educated classes, clergy included, fell under the spell of Erasmus, but the self-indulgent popes were concentrating their energies on matters other than (and often the opposite of) purity of faith.

The first two decades of the sixteenth century accordingly were the quiet before the storm, in which – dangerously for the Church, and for Europe – a considerable amount of thinking went on. There was Luther, for one, meditating upon the corruptions of the Church, and there were the men who, when the savagery unleashed by Reformation and Counter-Reformation eventually broke out, found that their minds had been made up for them by what had happened in Spain and elsewhere, and who could not tolerate intolerance and coercion.

There are three ways of viewing the Reformation initiated by Luther's act of protest against Church corruptions. One is to see it in this very light, as a chiefly religious event motivated by rejection of Roman practices and a desire for a more biblical Christianity. A second is to see it as a political event, in which a variety of temporal and clerical powers saw the upswelling of religious protest as an opportunity to escape the taxes and interference of the papacy, with its pretension to be the supreme authority in Christendom (considered as a theocracy with the pope as regent on earth).[21] A third is to see it as an intellectual revolution, aiming for liberty in the kingdom of the mind to free science and art from the proscriptions and censorship of dogmatic orthodoxy.

Unquestionably the Reformation was all three, and each of the three fed into the others in complex and reciprocal ways. Its underlying religious inspiration was however crucial, and in this sense it can be viewed as at the same time a liberation struggle. Luther aimed to set up a religious community free of Roman corruptions and closer to the biblical heart of the faith. That was one kind of freedom sought. But he also argued that an individual is his own priest before God; that is an even more fundamental freedom, for it concerns not the independence of one Church (his) from another (the Roman Church), but individual independence. Of course Luther found that he could not mean quite this when difficult practicalities obtruded, but it was a step in that direction, and perhaps unwittingly it was the same step mooted in the less fraught years just beforehand, when Erasmus said that scholars should be allowed to read and enquire into anything without interference.

To begin with Luther himself was strongly opposed to any form of persecution.[22] One of the propositions for which he was excommunicated was that burning heretics was contrary to the Holy Spirit's wishes. When he returned to Wittenberg after his exile in the Wartburg and began constructing what was to become the Lutheran Church, he maintained his opposition to any methods other than persuasion and education to correct the errors of those who did not join his congregation. Some of his followers had taken to committing violence against people who persisted with the Mass in Wittenberg, but Luther restrained them. Despite being profoundly upset by dissension in his own ranks, he stayed his hand even there, saying that all arguments and disagreements would work themselves out – and for the good – in the end.

The first Protestant persecutor was not, therefore, Luther but the prophet of Zurich, Ulrich Zwingli.[23] On the face of it Zwingli was an improbable candidate for persecutor; he was an Erasmian, a Renaissance man and, as a lover of the classics of antiquity, hospitable to the works and ideas of good pagans. But he took a different view from

Luther about a growing movement, inspired by the outbreak of reformatory ardour, which in 1521 was rejected by Luther himself: the Anabaptist movement.

The Anabaptists were so called because they did not accept infant baptism, arguing that people could only properly become Christian by mature choice and self-dedication, and that baptism therefore must take place in adulthood. In their view infant baptism was 'neither scriptural nor primitive, nor fulfilling the chief conditions of admission into a visible brotherhood of saints, namely, repentance, faith, spiritual illumination and free surrender of oneself to Christ.' An immediate implication of this is that the congregation of true believers is separate from society at large; it consists only of the regenerate, and is far from being an organisation of default membership. This further meant that the Church is not coterminous with the State, as orthodox views simply assumed, taking it that just as one is born a citizen, so one is baptised straight away into membership of the Church, therefore State and Church are the same body of people.[24]

Zwingli was not bothered by the re-baptism question itself, but he was very much bothered by the implications of the sharp distinction between Church and State entailed by the Anabaptist view. It constituted secularism, which in turn meant the effective de-Christianisation of the people, which in turn again meant – thought Zwingli – that the people were being abandoned to Satan. This was of course intolerable to Zwingli, and he was going to have none of it in Zurich. There was no canon law available in the new Protestant dispensation to cover the emergency, so Zwingli copied what contemporary temporal princes were doing, namely, reviving Roman law. (The princes had found this a useful means of overturning the feudal privileges of peasants.)[25] Zwingli likewise invoked an ancient Roman law dating from the Christian centuries of the empire, proscribing Donatism. The Donatists had held that only their baptism was valid, so if a Catholic joined them he had to be re-baptised into his new communion. As an anti-Donatist measure Christian Rome passed a law decreeing the death penalty for anyone who practised re-baptism. This law Zwingli now dusted off and applied vigorously to the emergency he faced. It availed nothing for Zurich's Anabaptists to say that since infant baptism was no true baptism, they were therefore not re-baptising; in 1525 they were rounded up and condemned to death, and the punishment was made to mock the crime itself – they were executed by drowning.

Luther disagreed with what Zwingli had done. 'It is not right, and I am deeply troubled that these poor people have been put to death so cruelly,' he wrote two years after the event. 'Let everyone believe what he will. If he is wrong he will have punishment enough in the fires of hell. Unless they are seditious one should contest such people with God's Word and the scriptures. You will accomplish nothing by executions.'

This sentiment is a clear statement of liberty of conscience, and a significant one. But in fact Luther's mind was in the process of changing on this score. Even as Zurich's Anabaptists were drowning in the waters of their lake, an event occurred which shook Luther's confidence in the prospects both of peaceful reform and the undesirability of persecution. This was the Peasants' War, in which one of his own former disciples took a leading role.[26]

The Peasants' War was a mass insurgency that broke out in the southern German states of Thuringia, Swabia and Franconia in 1524; some estimates say that as many as 300,000 people rose in revolt against their temporal princes and the Catholic clergy. Its sources were very complex, and it represented another instalment in violent expressions of economic and social discontent that had repeatedly broken out in the preceding two centuries in central Europe, as feudal arrangements disintegrated and were succeeded by oppressive and exploitative ad hoc measures implemented by the ruling elites of nobility and clergy. The upheaval caused by Luther's revolt against the Church emboldened the rebels, who believed that the repudiation of papal ways could be extended to a general overthrow of the existing order. Itinerant preachers of the reformed outlook carried Luther's message that each was to be his own priest before God; this made the peasants feel entitled to take into their own hands the remedying of the wrongs they suffered, and they believed that Luther would support them.

They were wrong. Luther was alarmed by the fact that his former disciple, Thomas Muntzer, from whom he had parted company over matters of doctrine (including infant baptism, which Luther believed in) and who had taken a leading position in the revolt in Thuringia, was threatening to take the process of reform in entirely the wrong direction. Moreover Luther desired the support of the ruling classes in establishing his reformed religion. As the revolt spread and news of atrocities committed by the peasant hordes – with whom many impoverished townsfolk and disaffected nobility had allied themselves – reached his ears, Luther became increasingly agitated. He picked up his pen and wrote a diatribe entitled 'Against the Murderous Thieving Hordes of Peasants', published in 1525, in which he urged the ruling classes in affected areas to be merciless in punishing the rebels. His opposition to the revolt was one cause of its collapse, although the main instruments of its defeat were the combined armies of the Princes of Saxony, Brunswick, Hesse and Mansfeld at the Battle of Frankenhausen, and the armies of the Swabian League at Sindelfingen. Before these decisive events the revolt had been dangerously successful; in the spring of 1525 it even seemed that the peasants and their allies would prevail. In the event, it has been estimated that more than 100,000 peasants died in battle and in the reprisals that followed.

This attempted revolution has echoed down the centuries. It was supported by noblemen such as the deposed Duke of Württemberg, Ulrich I, and Götz von Berlichingen, who thus entered literature;[27] and it was seen by Friedrich Engels in his classic book on the subject as proof of the materialist view of history. Historians of religion standardly view Thomas Muntzer as a fanatic who, before being beheaded after the defeat of his rebel army at Frankenhausen, recanted his Protestantism and attended a Mass. But socialists see the revolt as an epoch in their tradition, for the peasants' programme, the Twelve Articles, has a very interesting ring to later ears: it demanded that the people should be free to choose their own pastors, who were to preach only the pure Gospel, that they should be exempt from at least some of the taxes they were burdened with, and that they should have their rights of access to common land, grazing and fishing restored. They further demanded the abolition of serfdom, and the establishment of an impartial judicial system. By any lights these were reasonable demands, and poignantly implied the sufferings which had led to their being made.

The consequences of the Peasants' War were dramatic for Luther personally. Whereas previously he had been against persecution, he was now no longer so sure. He saw serious threats to Church, State, family and society from such upheavals and the anarchy they unleashed. He had been especially troubled by the atrocities committed by the peasant armies, such as the Massacre of Weinsberg. Now he began to think that revolutionaries like Muntzer should be suppressed before they could cause trouble. He clung for a while to his uncertainties; when the Diet of Speyer decided in 1529 that Anabaptists should be put to death everywhere in the Holy Roman Empire he said nothing, which meant that he did not condemn the decision. By 1531 he had concluded that the death penalty should be used to punish sedition and blasphemy, but he still maintained that it should not be applied to heresy, which he persisted in defining as merely 'incorrect opinion'. His attachment to this view is perhaps explainable by the fact that he was himself, in the eyes of Rome, a heretic – he had been excommunicated as such and did not wish to give hostages to fortune.

He maintained this view until the alarm of 1534 when a group of Anabaptists, invoking the name of the martyred Muntzer, rose in the Westphalian city of Münster and seized it. They did not hold it long, just long enough for their insurrection to cast a further and now final shadow of suspicion over Anabaptists everywhere. That was the last straw for Luther; he signed the memorandum penned by Melanchthon endorsing the resolution of the Diet of Speyer that all Anabaptists should be put to death. He substantiated this move not by changing his view on heresy (no doubt for the reason given), but by redefining blasphemy and sedition to cover what the Anabaptists threatened. The effect was the same.

The year of Melanchthon's Luther-signed memorandum, 1536, was also the year that Calvin published his *Institutes of the Christian Religion*. The timing is significant: it meant that Calvinism, a brand of Protestantism which was to prove far less concessive than Luther's, was launched when the first liberal phase of Protestantism was over.

*

Calvin went to Switzerland as a refugee from France, where Catholic-Protestant divisions were acute, and found in his new home equally acute divisions within the new Protestantism itself.[28] He was a young man, just twenty-six when he arrived in Basel, but he was already thinking differently about the starting point of faith. For Luther it was God's grace, which one cannot earn by works or supplication but merely accept if given through the mercy of Christ. For Calvin the starting point is the absolute supremacy of God, in comparison to whose eternal brilliance finite mortals are the merest and faintest of flickerings. 'The chief end of man is to enjoy the fellowship of God and the chief duty of man is to glorify God,' he wrote. Everything that does not conduce to either is a curse.

A major difference between the outlooks of Luther and Calvin concerned the *parousia*, the Second Coming. Luther, like the saints of the primitive Church, expected it imminently. Calvin, like St Augustine, did not. Instead he conceived of the unfolding of history as the field in which God's purposes for mankind would be realised, and he saw the faithful as the servants of this purpose. This is why his view of the nature of man's submission to God was not just a quietist or fatalistic one, for, he said, God's elect are here on earth to carry out God's work. The test to become one of the elect was passed if three conditions were satisfied: confession of faith, disciplined life, and taking of the Sacraments. Anyone who was confident of sincerity on all three counts could regard himself as one of the elect, and need worry no further. A century later the New England Calvinists reincorporated the requirement of a new birth – of being born again in the spirit – thereby reviving the terrible anxieties individuals felt over whether they really were one of the elect few, or one of the many damned, and damned from all eternity: there was nothing one could do to escape that preordained destiny.

This is not the place to tell the story of how Calvin, after taking up residence in Geneva at the invitation of William Farel – the man who had first converted the city to Protestantism – and then leaving and returning again, made Geneva his Church and the world centre of his adamantine brand of Christianity. In part he achieved this because those who could not agree with him left, and those from elsewhere who liked the sound of him came. These latter were numerous, fleeing persecution in the other lands of Europe, but any among them inclined to a habit of dissent – this being, perhaps, the reason they found themselves taking refuge in Geneva in the first place – soon discovered that they were not going to be given any latitude from the strict doctrines governing Calvin's congregation.

In particular, Calvin had no truck with squeamishness on the question of heresy. In his commentary on the infamous thirteenth chapter of Deuteronomy, enjoining the stoning of false prophets and 'dreamers of dreams', he wrote, 'This law might at first appear too severe. Why should anyone be punished thus for merely having spoken? But if anyone slanders a mortal man he is punished; shall we allow a blasphemer of the living God to go unpunished? If a mortal prince suffers injury, death scarcely seems sufficient revenge for it. Yet when the sovereign emperor God is reviled by a word, is nothing to be done? God's glory and our salvation are so intertwined that a traitor to God is also an enemy of humanity, and worse than a murderer because he leads poor souls to damnation. Some say that because the crime consists only of words there is no cause for such severe punishment. But we muzzle dogs; shall we leave men free to open their mouths and say what they please? . . . God makes it plain that the false prophet is to be stoned without mercy. We are to crush beneath our heels all natural affections when his honour is at stake. The father should not spare his child, nor one brother another, nor the husband his wife, nor the friend that friend who is dearer to him than life.'[29] And so on. Calvin concluded that if God was prepared to sacrifice even babies among the Amalekites (though 'we must rest assured that God would suffer only those infants to be destroyed whom he had already damned and destined to eternal death') then we must be unremitting in our pursuit and destruction of any who impugned his honour. There is no call upon man to be more compassionate than his inexorable deity, for the impugners are 'worse than brigands who cut the throat of a wayfarer'.

In light of Calvin's views it was inevitable that the first cause célèbre of religious liberty should be one whom he put to death for heresy in

Geneva. This was the Spaniard Michael Servetus, whose burning body was the first candle of the cause of liberty in the Reformation.[30]

Servetus was the product of the Erasmian moment in Spain. After the excesses of Torquemada, Spain had quietened its persecutions, a process that continued and deepened under the rule of Charles, grandson of Isabella and Ferdinand. He had been brought up in the Spanish Netherlands, speaking Flemish and educated by admirers of Erasmus, and when he mounted the Spanish throne he brought with him a Netherlandish entourage who spread Erasmus' influence in his new kingdom. It was this influence – its lack of dogmatism; its emphasis on reason; its admiration for the balance and good sense of pagan ethics; its refusal to grow heated over matters of theological controversy – that played a major part in muting the activities of the Inquisition there.

Charles's confessor was a Franciscan called Quintana, and on this man's staff was the young Michael Servetus. Quintana had been attracted for a while by Luther, but had decided after all not to quit his Church or his order. Servetus came from an even more orthodox background, having a brother who was an ordained priest and a mother who was a benefactor of the Church. Servetus' duties in Quintana's household were not onerous; he was able to pursue an interest in the mystical 'illuminist' movement in Spain mainly associated with the surviving and dedicated *conversos* community, and was given leave to study law at Toulouse University.

The main inspiration for what proved to be Servetus' life's work, however, was the problem of Judaism and Islam which his country had been at the forefront of addressing during Torquemada's time. How could it be, he wondered, that Jews and Moors refused to accept the truth of the Church's teaching, that God had revealed himself in Jesus Christ for the redemption of mankind? After much consideration he concluded that the problem lay in what Jews and Muslims had in common, namely, a commitment to belief in strict monotheism, and a concomitant rejection of the Christian message because one of its central planks is the mysterious doctrine of the Trinity, which states that God is one substance in three persons. Servetus knew that this seemed to Jews and Muslims to be plain tritheism – an impression surely strengthened by representations in art of the Father (an old man), the Son (the crucified Jesus) and the Holy Ghost (a dove or a beam of light) as three apparently separate beings.

At Toulouse University Servetus encountered young enthusiasts fervently studying scripture and commenting on the absence from it of central tenets of doctrine, among them the Trinity, of which there is not a single mention anywhere in the New Testament. Its three persons were mentioned, sure enough, but as three *separate* persons. Indeed, the Council of Nicaea long before, in the year 325, had decided that the nature of the deity required description in terminology not actually present in the scriptures, given the emergency being faced by the council (namely, the Arian heresy); and thus it was that the Father and the Son were said to be consubstantial, and that the Holy Spirit proceeded from them.[31]

These refinements did nothing for Servetus. He could not see why Jews and Moors should be excluded from God's grace on the basis of a doctrine that had no scriptural authority. He looked into the development of Trinitarian doctrine and found it wanting, from the analogical explanations provided by St Augustine and St Thomas Aquinas, to the attempted proofs offered by Richard of St Victor with his argument that God is love and love requires at least two persons, (the lover and the beloved) and to be perfect a third (so that jealousy is possible, but is not experienced) it follows that God must be three persons. There were others who argued that the Trinity is a mystery that cannot be explained or understood, only believed. None of this satisfied Servetus, understandably enough, so he rejected the doctrine of the Trinity, and thus set himself on course to be burned to death by Calvin.

He achieved this by developing a view of the relationship between God and Christ which controverted essential components of Christian doctrine. Apart from believing in the Trinity, the orthodox were also expected to believe that Christ was (thereby and of course) divine and not man, and that he existed eternally. Servetus argued that although the Word was eternal, it had been joined with the man Jesus to make the incarnate Christ, who was therefore separate from the Father, because unlike the Father he was not, by this fact, eternal. Not only did this deny the Trinity but it premised the participation of humanity in divinity. 'What is the mystery of the incarnation other than the mingling of man with God?' Servetus asked. 'Unless I believe this with regard to Christ's flesh I should have no hope, for we shall be made sharers in the divine substance even in the flesh as now in the spirit we are partners of the divine nature.'[32] Servetus thus implied the elevation of man, a characteristic Renaissance trope. Calvin took it to be a lowering of the status of God. Given his views about protecting the honour of God, his reaction to Servetus' views was wholly predictable.

Servetus published his views at Strasbourg in a book he called *De Trinitatis Erroribus* (*On the Errors of the Trinity*). He had left the service of Quintana when the Spanish court travelled to Bologna to attend the coronation of the new Holy Roman Emperor. The departure of the Erasmians from Spain brought their influence there to an end, and very soon there was a reaction to their legacy, prompted by increasing dismay among Catholics over the growing extent of the Reformation. The Holy Office in Spain placed Erasmus' works on the Index of Forbidden Books. No doubt the change in climate prompted Servetus to opt for the Protestant cities of Strasbourg, where Anabaptists were still welcome, and Basel, where Erasmus was buried and where a liberal climate still prevailed because of him, in hope of finding a welcome for his unorthodox views there.

Alas for Servetus, his views were too much even for these safe cities. He was told at both places that either he must accept that Christ is eternal and consubstantial with the Father, or he must leave. Whether out of naivety or hope, Servetus submitted his views to his former master Quintana, to the Bishop of Saragossa at home in Spain, to Melanchthon in Switzerland, and to the orthodox Catholic Jerome Aleander who had been Luther's adversary at the Diet of Worms. All denounced his views roundly, Aleander saying he was nauseated by them, Melanchthon saying they were unacceptable, Quintana saying he was shocked rigid by them, and the Bishop of Saragossa immediately denouncing Servetus to the Inquisition, who set about trying to get him back to Spain for trial, using his brother as a lure.

Servetus contemplated fleeing to America, but then decided that to do so would be to abandon his task, which was to bring an important truth to the world. He changed his name to Michael Villeneufve and went to France. There, at Lyon, he worked as a copy editor and proofreader, editing a new edition of the Bible and the geography of Ptolemy. He was a clever and widely read man, but not a wise or discreet one; he could not resist adding a preface to the Bible which said that the Old Testament prophets were not foretelling the future but preaching about their own time (calling into question prophecies about the coming of Christ in Isaiah and elsewhere). In his Ptolemy edition he quoted someone as saying that the promised land of Palestine was not a land of great promise – a witticism which came back to haunt him when he was standing trial, on the grounds that it challenged the veracity of Moses.

He then went to Paris to study medicine, and dissected corpses alongside the great Vesalius. His anatomical studies led him to discover the pulmonary circulation of blood, that is, the movement of blood from the heart to the lungs and back; it was another century before Harvey verified the total circulation. Once qualified Servetus returned to Lyon and there practised medicine for the next twelve years. And so his life might have run its course, anonymously and usefully, without further danger from his unorthodox Unitarianism. Alas, he could not leave theology alone. His contacts with other unorthodox views in Strasbourg and Basel had left their mark. He was interested in the prophecy of Revelation, which said that the *parousia* would occur 1260 years after a certain date, and he was convinced this was the date that Christianity had gone wrong, namely 325, the year in which the Council of Nicaea adopted Trinitarianism. Adding the two figures gave him 1585, a year not far ahead in his own lifetime. To this prognostication he excitedly joined the fruits of his dabblings in the mysticism of Renaissance Neoplatonism and the esoteric teachings of Hermes Trismegistus, which made him think that Christ is quite literally the light of the world, in that he informed (*in-formed*) all things, glowing in the heart of gemstones and glittering on the surface of water, illuminating the stars and planets from within and giving to all things their lustre and luminosity.

It was a serious mistake, therefore, for him to begin corresponding with Calvin, who, far from conceiving of Christ as in the world as its light, believed that he is utterly transcendent and beyond the world. But begin a correspondence Servetus did, drawn as a moth to a flame – literally, as it proved – by Calvin's fame and religious zeal, which latter he in his own way shared. No doubt he did this because he wanted to test his views against the mind of the most famous religious leader of the day, and perhaps he hoped that he might win over that icon of the faith. He did not even conceal his identity.

The differences between them quickly proved insuperable. Calvin sent Servetus a copy of his *Institutio* to put him right; Servetus wrote insulting comments in the margins and sent it back, and then sent a document of his own whose title, *Restitutio*, played on the Latin title of Calvin's book. Calvin sent Servetus' book back; in a letter to a friend he remarked that if Servetus ever came to Geneva he would not leave it alive.

This happened in 1546. The acerbic correspondence was at an end, but Servetus spent the next few years rewriting his *Restitutio*, and in 1553 he published it in secret at a small press near Lyon. It was an intemperate work, going so far as to compare the Trinity to Cerberus, the three-headed guard dog of hell. A Genevan Protestant read a copy of the book and wrote to a Catholic friend in Lyon to say that a monster was being nourished in the midst of that city. Because of Servetus' earlier presence in Switzerland and the similarity between the *Restitutio* and *On the Errors of the Trinity*, the Genevan divined who was the author, and from conversations with Calvin worked out that Servetus was masquerading as Michael Villeneufve in Lyon. All this he told his Lyon friend. And he did more; Servetus might be able to deny authorship of a book that bore only initials ('MSV' for Michael Servetus Villanovanus), but if the doctrines of the book were to be seen in actual letters written by Servetus, he could be caught. The Genevan had such letters – the very letters Servetus had written to Calvin.

In fact the Genevan had informed Calvin of the situation, and Calvin proceeded to do everything he could to have Servetus stopped, even collaborating with the Catholic Inquisition by handing over the letters and the copy of his *Institutio* with Servetus' manuscript annotations. Servetus was duly arrested and questioned, but daringly escaped from the prison in which he was held. In his absence he was found guilty and his effigy was first strangled and then burned. Every available copy of his *Restitutio* was burned too; only three are known to be extant today.

Amazingly, when Servetus fled from Lyon he went to Geneva. Some visitors from Lyon recognised him in a Genevan church one Sunday morning, and reported the fact to Calvin. One theory as to why Servetus went to a city where he assuredly knew he would be in great danger is that he was in league with a group of Calvin's opponents intent on a coup. As it happens, at that very moment Calvin was rather precariously wrestling with these opponents, one of whom he had lately excommunicated, so the theory has some plausibility. On the other hand, independently of Calvin, the city fathers of Geneva were exceedingly unfriendly towards heresy, and it was with them that Calvin had laid his information against Servetus; so whether or not a coup against Calvin had succeeded, Servetus would still have been in mortal danger.

In any case when Servetus was arrested, as he straight away was, he claimed he had arrived only the day before, and had bespoken a hire boat to take him onwards towards Zurich the very next day. He claimed that he was planning to move to Italy to practise medicine there. The Genevans might have let him do as he planned, for it amounted to banishment from the city, but Calvin had other and better ideas. He designed to stamp out the heresy of Servetus' views, vile as he conceived it to be, and no doubt there was more than a tincture of revenge for the insults Servetus had heaped on him and his book in the course of their correspondence.

At his trial Servetus was spared none of his crimes, from the small to the great, from the joke about Palestine to the dreadful heresy of his attack on the Trinity and his claims about the relation of God and man. This last was the most serious point at issue between Servetus and

Calvin. Servetus said that Calvin's emphasis on original sin and predestination made man a mere stone, without freedom and agency, while Calvin said that Servetus' doctrine of humanity's participation in the divine was an insult to God because it made him party to the failings of the flesh. In this sense the battle of views between them reprised the contrast between the Renaissance and the Reformation, making the latter seem, in these respects, a Counter-Renaissance.

Servetus behaved badly during his trial, vituperating Calvin and demanding that the judges should put Calvin on trial in his place and give Servetus his goods in compensation. The court denied him a defence counsel. He was alone, frightened, soon in rags, and eaten by lice. When a request came from the Inquisition in France that he be handed over to them he begged the Genevan court not to remit him, but to finish with him there. This they did, after consulting the other Protestant cities of Switzerland, which counselled severity but not the death penalty. The Genevan city fathers condemned Servetus to death anyway, for denying the Trinity and rejecting infant baptism. 'We syndics, judges of criminal cases in this city, having witnessed the trial conducted before us at the instance of our lieutenant against you, Michel Servet de Villeneufve of Aragon in Spain, and having witnessed your confessions and writings, judge that you, Servetus, have for long promulgated false and thoroughly heretical doctrines, despising all remonstrance and correction, and have with malice, perversity and obstinacy spread even in printed books opinions against God the Father, the Son, and the Holy Ghost, in a word against the fundamentals of the Christian religion, and that you have tried to make schism and trouble in the Church of God by which many souls might have been ruined and lost, a thing horrible, shocking, scandalous and infectious. And you have had neither shame nor horror of setting yourself against the Divine Majesty and Holy Trinity, and have obstinately tried to infect the world with your stinking heretical poison . . . we sentence and condemn you, Michael Servetus, to be bound and taken to Champel and there attached to a stake and burned with your books to ashes.'[33]

Evidently Servetus had not been expecting the death penalty. He cried out for pity, and back in his cell he sent for Calvin and begged his forgiveness. Calvin coldly said he should try to seek it from God. When he was taken to the stake he was accompanied by William Farel, the man who had brought Calvin to Geneva in the first place. Farel tried to persuade him to renounce his errors, but Servetus remained silent. His book was tied to him, and the flames were lit. He was heard to pray, 'Have pity on me Jesus thou son of the eternal God.' Farel remarked that if he had moved the adjective – 'Have pity on me Jesus thou eternal son of God' – he might have been saved.

Many had been burned for heresy before Servetus; he was not the noblest or most striking of those who thought differently from one or another orthodoxy, or from all, yet his execution was a turning point because it at last prompted the sixteenth century to engage in a full debate on the question of religious liberty.

Servetus' death prodded the conscience of Sebastian Castellio, whose attack on the prosecution and execution of Servetus became the rallying cry for liberty in matters of belief.[34] He was a native of Lyon, where he had distinguished himself as a student of the classical languages to such an extent that his fellow students changed his surname of Chateillon to Castalio, in tribute to Castalia, the nymph of the fountain which sprang at the foot of Mount Parnassus. Like many who grew up during the first two decades of the Reformation, Castellio had pondered and watched; but in 1540, when he was twenty-five, three Lutherans were burned at the stake in Lyon by the Cardinal de Tournon, and the shock of the event made up Castellio's mind. He left Lyon for the Protestant city of Strasbourg, famous for its hospitality to dissent and home at that moment to Calvin, in temporary exile from Geneva. Castellio arrived there ten years after Servetus' own short stay in the city.

Castellio lodged with Calvin, and they immediately found themselves in accord on the important question of educating Protestant boys in the classical tongues but without the associated pagan literature. Calvin wished to see Protestant youths reading the Bible in the excellent Latin of Cicero, rather than having to exercise their minds on the obscenities of Ovid or Terence. Castellio therefore undertook the labour of rendering biblical stories into parallel Latin and French texts, setting them alongside each other on the page. The resulting *Sacred Texts* was a bestseller, and remained one through scores of editions until well into the eighteenth century.

In essence the *Sacred Texts* was a book for children, whose express purpose was to inculcate good Latin. But it demonstrated an innocuous-seeming bias in Castellio's outlook which was to have major consequences later; for Castellio appeared to favour those tales in the Bible which manifested kindness, gentleness and hospitality, and was upset by the cruelty reported in others. Thus for example his rendition commended Abraham's welcome of the angels, and roundly condemned Joseph's brothers for first plotting to murder him and then selling him into slavery.

At one point Castellio was offered a ministry to supplement his schoolmaster's wages when these, upon his marriage, proved inadequate to his needs. But he could not agree with the Calvinist Church on certain points of doctrine: he did not think the Song of Solomon an allegory, but a lascivious poem, and he thought Calvin wrong to suggest that the story of Christ's descent into hell was likewise an allegory. He therefore took his new family to Basel where he survived by doing various odd jobs, including editorial work for the famous publishing house Oporinus. He had parted on good terms with Calvin who, though disagreeing with him on the aforementioned points of doctrine, nevertheless wished him well and wrote him a copious and complimentary reference.

But all Castellio's energies in his spare time were devoted to producing new translations of the Bible into Latin and French, in the first continuing the endeavour to make good Latin of Ciceronian standard the vehicle of the divine truths, and in the second trying to make the vernacular immediate and accessible to the common man. The most notable aspect of this work is the preface to the Latin version, which Castellio addressed to the youthful Edward VI of England, the son for whose begetting Henry VIII had severed the Church of England from Rome. The preface was a plea for religious tolerance and liberty. At first blush it might have seemed that there was something conventional or reflex about this dedicatory gesture; Calvin himself, in dedicating his *Institutio* to Francis I of France, had used the occasion to petition him to show clemency in all matters of religion. But in Calvin's case the plea was designed to protect his own views – and his followers – from persecution, not to urge a general tolerance of differences in faith. After all, Calvinism was the right view, which meant the others (the Roman one, for a prime example) were wrong.

But Castellio had a much more general aim in mind: true liberty of conscience and observance. He knew from his labours as a translator of the Bible that 'the scriptures are full of enigmas and inscrutable questions which have been disputed for over a thousand years without agreement, nor can they be resolved without love, which appeases all controversies. Yet on account of these enigmas the earth is filled with innocent blood. We certainly ought to fear lest in crucifying thieves we crucify Christ unjustly. If we suffer Turks and Jews to live among us, the former of whom scarcely love Christ and the latter dearly hate him, if we suffer detractors, the proud, envious, avaricious, indecent, drunkards and like plagues, if we live with them, eat with them, and make merry with them, we ought at least to concede the right to breathe common air to those who confess with us the name of Christ and harm no one, who are indeed of such a temper that they would rather die than say or do anything other than that which they think they ought to say and do. Of all men this sort is the least to be feared because he who would rather die than say what he does not feel is not open to bribery and corruption. I venture to say that none are more obedient to princes and magistrates than those who fear God in simplicity and obey him to the extent of their knowledge.'[35] And then Castellio sounded an Erasmian note, arguing that decisions over matters of controversy could be left for the time when all things will be made clear: 'On controversial points we would do better to defer judgement, even as God, who knows us to be guilty, yet postpones judgement and waits for us to amend our lives.'

In August 1553 Castellio was made a Master of Arts of the University of Basel and given a teaching appointment there. His circumstances at last looked set; he had acquired a European reputation as a scholar and translator, had a prestigious appointment, and had found an agreeable place to live and work. He might have looked forward to a quiet professorial life for the remainder of his days. But two months later Servetus was burned at the stake in Geneva, and Castellio's indignation and opposition were vividly roused. He immediately set to work on his *Concerning Heretics, Whether they are to be Persecuted.*

For reasons of caution Castellio did not publish the book under his own name, but issued it as if it were an anthology of opinions by liberal-minded authors under the editorship of a supposed Martin Bellius, Castellio's pseudonym, although his authorship was early guessed. As a result of this device religious liberalism was thereafter called Bellianism. He even used a spurious place of publication, citing it as Magdeburg, though in fact it had been printed by the house of Oporinus in Basel.

The result was a tumult of controversy. Calvin replied in a tract entitled *A Defence of the Orthodox Faith Against the Errors of Michael Servetus,* and Theodore Beza essayed a refutation of Castellio under the same title, *Concerning Heretics.* Castellio wrote replies to both, and in addition a set of dialogues on the question, but none of these were published in his lifetime, for he did not have long to live; indeed by the time the Genevan consistory had persuaded the reluctant authorities in Basel to begin proceedings to put him on trial, he was already dead.

The key to Castellio's case in his *Concerning Heretics* was the distinction to be made between what is essential to the Christian faith, and what is inessential. As it happens the distinction marks the birth of fundamentalism, strictly so called, because it implies that there are fundamentals of the faith to which any Christian must subscribe in order to be such, but that everything else doubtful or controversial can be believed or not at the individual's own discretion, for these questions are not fundamental. However, Castellio's list of inessentials was scarcely likely to placate the Calvinists or many others: they included predestination, the Trinity, and the nature of heaven and hell.

Key to this key issue, moreover, was the point on which the theologies of the Reformation collided and split, and that is the question of salvation. If asked what are the essentials of the faith, the answer had to be: whatever is necessary to ensure salvation. Castellio was enough of an Erasmian to see the inexorable logic of the argument that only those things can be essential for salvation which can be known with certainty, therefore those things which cannot be certainly known – those many points of controversy and dispute – cannot be essential for salvation. The point is sometimes put in terms of what the Penitent Thief was able to grasp as he hung on the cross, and which prompted Christ to take him 'this day to paradise'. If the Penitent Thief – if the simple fishermen and tax collectors who were the Apostles – could grasp the essence and be saved, ignorant of the complex theological disputes which in the centuries since had supervened at such cost and with such bloodshed, how could any of these latter be insisted upon?

In their replies to Castellio both Calvin and Beza labelled him a sceptic on the grounds that he was effectively rendering almost all of Christian doctrine suppositious. In his response Castellio appealed to the distinction, made familiar by the philosophers of antiquity, between faith and knowledge. He cited Aquinas in support of the mutual exclusivity of knowledge and faith; the Learned Doctor had said that what is known is not believed because belief is a lesser epistemic state than knowledge, and by the same token what is believed is not known.

The point was an exceedingly important one, for Calvin took the exact opposite view: that faith is one with conviction, certainty, assurance and knowledge, and that is why anyone who promotes error has to be stopped for they will mislead people into eternal damnation. Indeed it was an urgent duty to stop them. To allow liberty of thought on matters of doctrine was therefore, as Beza put it, 'a most diabolical dogma'. Castellio's response to this was emphatic. Scripture is replete with enigmas. All sects are certain of the truth of their own interpretation, so who is to say who is right? 'Calvin says that he is certain, and they say they are; Calvin says that they are wrong and wishes to judge them, and so do they. Who shall be judge? Who made Calvin the arbiter of all the sects, that he alone should kill? He has the Word of God and so have they. If the matter is certain, to whom is it so?

To Calvin? But then why does he write so many books about manifest truth? . . . In view of all the uncertainty we must define the heretic simply as one with whom we disagree. And if then we are going to kill heretics, the logical outcome will be a war of extermination, since each is sure of himself. Calvin would have to invade France and all other nations, wipe out cities, put all the inhabitants to the sword, sparing neither sex nor age, not even babies and the beasts. All would have to be burned save Calvinists, Jews and Turks, whom he excepts.'[36]

The unimpeachable logic of this assault, and its merciless exposure of the absurdities of Calvin's position, must have stung. But Castellio's central point was even more telling: that the questions of doctrine that were most controversial were the ones for which people like Servetus were being made to suffer the death penalty. How, Castellio demanded, could this be justified? 'No one doubts that there is a God, whether he is good and just, whether he should be loved and worshipped, whether vice should be avoided and virtue followed. Why? Because these points are clear. But concerning baptism, the Lord's Supper, justification, predestination, and many other questions, there are capital dissensions. Why? Because these points are not cleared up in Scripture.' The solution was to leave the controversial points to the indefinite future; now we see as through a glass, darkly, then all things will be clear.

What is perhaps most interesting about Castellio's case for liberty of conscience is its basis, which is an appeal to reason. In this he anticipates what, within a generation of his own day, came to be the irresistible ground of progress: the revived free application of human reason to the great questions of man and the world, giving birth to science and a new age. 'Revived' is the apt word, for the application of untrammelled reason was the intellectual spirit of ancient Greece, the birthplace of philosophy. That is why, much earlier, Petrarch and others had themselves chosen the term 'Renaissance' to describe their own age, a different kind of 'born again' era, not of faith but of scepticism, enquiry, open-mindedness, and receptivity.

The central place given to reason by Castellio in his argument concerned the fact that neither empirical evidence nor revelation is an infallible guide, and each therefore requires correction. The instrument of correction is reason. Reason is, he wrote, 'the daughter of God. She was before letters and ceremonies, before the world was, and she is after letters and ceremonies, and after the world is changed and renewed she will endure and can no more be abolished than God himself. Reason, I say, is a sort of eternal Word of God. According to reason Jesus Christ himself, the Son of the living God, lived and taught. In the Greek he is called Logos, which means 'reason' or 'word'. They are the same, for reason is a kind of superior and eternal word of truth always speaking.'[37]

And to reason Castellio conjoined ethics, by which he meant manner of life, deeds and works. In this he repudiated the key Reformation doctrine that justification comes by faith alone, and that works avail nothing. He applied the idea that 'by their fruits ye shall know them', remarking that just as one could judge the merits of different medical theories by seeing whether they worked in practice, so one could judge the value of different theologies by what their effects were in the lives of their votaries. For Castellio it mattered that these effects should be an internal soundness of moral outlook, from which good practice would automatically flow. He was disparaging about the Calvinist attitude to morality, which appeared to insist exclusively on outward show; the Genevan consistory stated that a minister should be dismissed if found guilty of 'heresy, card-playing and dancing', but merely admonished for 'scurrility, obscenity and avarice'. Thus what was inward was of far less moment than outward conformity, just as it had been with the Philistines, the whited sepulchres accused by Christ.

This inward–outward distinction led Castellio also to distinguish sharply between matters of the spirit and matters of the flesh. Religion was entirely of the former, so punishing the latter was pointless. 'Religion resides in the heart and not in the body, which is why the swords of kings and princes cannot reach it. The church can no more be built by persecution and violence than a wall can be built by cannon blasts. Therefore to kill a man is not to defend a doctrine but simply to kill a man.'[38]

The implication of Castellio's view that faith and morality are inward matters, consisting in loyalty to personal conscience, is that neither is possible without liberty. Indeed the sum of his view is that reason and the ethical life can be premised on nothing other than liberty. For him the point was individual responsibility, based on the fact that each man has to be saved by his own faith, not by the faith of another. Conscience therefore should not be coerced, for the good reason that it cannot be coerced without destroying the man who is thus forced, and with him his soul too. And when a man was burned for refusing to act against his conscience, it was not those carrying out the auto-da-fé who were asserting loyalty to their faith, but the condemned man himself.

Although the destruction of a man and his soul was the worst outcome of persecution, it had other bad consequences too, Castellio observed. One was that it advertised the supposed heresy it was designed to punish, spreading its tenets among the populace who would then discuss why the heretic had been condemned. Another was that it would foster sedition, for all forms of coercion and tyranny rouse opposition, and people afraid of persecution rise up in rebellion to defend themselves by attacking first.

Although Castellio's replies to Calvin and Beza were not published until after his death – some of his writings remained unpublished until well into the twentieth century – his *Concerning Heretics* was a powerful blow on behalf of the case for liberty of conscience, and it rang through the century all the more loudly as the wars of religion and the violence of religious faction grew. From the present perspective Castellio reads as a true modern, and in him one sees the spirit of the Renaissance forging its way towards the spirit of the Enlightenment in which his views, dangerous and controversial in his own day, became the commonplaces of educated opinion.

As later chapters show, this was far from the end of the quarrel between religion and freedom of thought. But it was the emphatic beginning, and once people began to think in terms similar to Castellio's it became increasingly difficult for the Church, and soon too for temporal authorities, to resist the multiplication of voices – and their questions, and their answers – that began to be heard on the subject of liberty. One of the first consequences outside the domain of religion itself was felt in philosophy and science, as the seventeeth century dramatically demonstrated.

3

Freeing the Mind

THERE CANNOT BE a clearer mark of the progress of liberty of thought than the contrast between the world views of science and religion, nor of the hard-won nature of that progress than the struggle to liberate the former from the latter. Liberty of thought is the essence of enquiry, and free enquiry produces a conception of the universe totally different from any that thinks the world was created as a theatre for the moral and spiritual destiny of humankind by anthropocentric gods. The story of the rise of science is also the story of the struggle by religious orthodoxy to retain control over how the universe is to be seen, and where the limits of legitimate enquiry lie. To make science possible, religion's claim to hegemony over the mind had to be broken.[1]

It is important to be clear about the purport of the preceding chapter. Sebastian Castellio gave eloquent voice to an attitude that has become virtually reflex in the modern Western world, and he voiced it because he was among the more courageous and clear-minded of those who, rejecting the example of the Inquisition (especially in Torquemada's Spain), were shocked anew that a Reformed Church should reprise that infamy in its execution of alleged heretics. The type of attitude he represented prevailed specifically in connection with religious liberty, but he expressed it in a complex and turbulent time, so much so as to make it seem as if the sixteenth century itself was – after its first two decades of Erasmian tranquillity – the very opposite of a liberalising century. The chief figures of the Reformation were, as the preceding chapter shows, hardly models of liberality themselves, and the Counter-Reformation that began in the 1540s was the Roman Church's campaign to re-establish its authority, plunging Europe into wars that lasted on and off – and more on than off – for the next hundred years, with an unprecedented loss of life: it was the worst period of conflict in Europe's history to that date, and the dead numbered in millions.[2]

But the point is that ideas and attitudes, once they penetrate into the minds of more than a coterie, acquire a life of their own, a life too vigorous for their immediate circumstances to quash. And indeed some of the fruits of the argument for liberty appeared surprisingly quickly. Zwinglism achieved a measure of toleration in its own areas as early as 1531 as a consequence of the Peace of Kappel. Protestantism in general was effectively secured by the Peace of Augsburg in 1555, which established the principle *cuius regio, eius religio*, the religion of the local prince is the religion of his people. It was a recognition that Protestantism had become too strong for the Catholic power of the Holy Roman Emperor to overthrow it, at least at that point; it was a temporary recognition only, for in 1618 a different Emperor, Ferdinand II, tried again to reconquer Protestant Europe for Catholicism, and it was not until the Treaty of Westphalia in 1648 that the endeavour was at last given up entirely. But Augsburg brought to a temporary end a generation of wars between princes of different religious persuasions and the Catholic Empire, although the forces even then being unleashed by the Counter-Reformation and Calvinism, representing more extreme views than had been opposed hitherto, did not allow Augsburg's peace to last very long.[3]

Even as the Council of Trent (1542–1563) reaffirmed the Catholic doctrines that Luther had challenged, and drew sharper and clearer lines in its view of the difference between orthodoxy and heresy, so on the other side Calvinism was making gains: first in the Netherlands, where the Pacification of Ghent in 1576 established its claim, and in 1598 in France where, by the Edict of Nantes, Henri IV granted toleration to the Huguenots. It was highly appropriate that Henry IV did this; he had himself been a Huguenot before converting to Catholicism to ensure his throne ('Paris is worth a mass,' he had laconically remarked). The Edict did not bring the shedding of French blood between Catholic and Protestant to an end – within decades some of the horrors of the St Bartholomew Day's Massacre were repeated at La Rochelle – but it damped down the immediate strife in what are known as the Wars of Religion. Until the Huguenots fled France after the Revocation of the Edict of Nantes in 1685 there was always a danger, and occasionally the reality, of renewed internecine murder.[4]

Elizabeth I made Anglicanism secure in England after the burnings at the stake encouraged by Queen Mary ('Bloody Mary'), who in her short reign tried by force and fire to re-establish Catholicism. The milder and more reluctant persecution of Catholics by Elizabeth in her far longer reign is commemorated by a convent to the martyrs of Tyburn in what is now Marble Arch in London.

Thus four main brands of Protestantism were rooting themselves in Europe during the sixteenth century, within decades of Luther's nailing his theses to Wittenberg's church door. The process was attended by violence, persecution, suffering, struggle and sorrow, and although its bloodier periods were largely over by the middle of the following century, its consequences continued to be felt for centuries beyond. Only think: it was not until 1828 in England that the Test and Corporation Acts were repealed, removing disabilities from Dissenters and Catholics which had kept them from the universities, Parliament and other aspects of mainstream British life because they would not subscribe to the Thirty-Nine Articles of the Church of England. In my own living memory as a child after the Second World War, Catholics in Britain, apart from the recusant aristocratic families, were regarded as second-class, ignorant and peasant-like – largely because of the example of the impoverished priest-ridden (as they then were) Irish who suffered from having too many children in each family.

By the beginning of the seventeenth century Protestantism had already begun to spread to the New World as the quest for freedom to believe and practise gathered momentum. It had been predicted by opponents of reform that the fragmentation of the Church would not end with a single split, or a split into three or four. Sectarianism breeds sectarianism, and breakaway groups were soon forming, invariably beginning with dissent from the founding Dissenter group. The example of the peculiarly feverish divisions in the Church in Scotland – first into the Free Church, part of which broke off into the 'Wee Frees', part of which broke off again into the 'Wee Wee Frees' – is a classic case. In England dissent was coeval with the securing of Anglicanism, and was a main factor in the revolution and civil war that wracked the country in the middle decades of the seventeenth century.[5]

As this tumultuous history shows, the urge for religious liberty worked like dynamite in the system of Europe, but its imperfect realisation and its productivity of conflict showed that there was a problem still to be resolved in what it meant. For the religious liberty sought in the sixteenth century had a twofold character: liberty of a dissenting group from the authority of Rome, and liberty of the individual to think and believe as he chose. The examples of Luther, Zwingli and Calvin show that as leaders of reform movements they were interested only in the former, though in his early phase Luther thought – for personal as well as theoretical reasons – that the two were the same thing. Realities forced upon him a change of mind, as they too often do upon leaders of real people in the real world.[6]

Even as the seventeenth-century struggles of religion continued in their different forms across Europe, from the civil strife in the British Isles on its western margin to the war-ravaged central German states, the case for liberty – and now more especially liberty of thought, a more general and inclusive notion than liberty just of religious conscience – continued to be argued, and with increasing confidence as application by both temporal and ecclesiastical authorities of the death penalty and other harsh forms of punishment decreased in matters of religious difference. True, Giordano Bruno was burned in Rome in 1600 and Cesare Vanini died at the stake in Toulouse in 1619, the first for heresy and the second for atheism, and they were far from alone among victims of religious persecution; but although wars were fought with religion as a motive, the seventeenth century was not fifteenth-century Spain, and the difference in climate allowed more direct discussion of the entitlements of individual conscience.[7] Moreover, the liberties thus argued for ceased to be specifically and wholly a confessional matter, but were a development into the more general claim of liberty as such.

Two champions of liberty stand out in the literature of the debate in this period: John Milton and John Locke. The former is an especially interesting figure, for he did not represent a party or a movement, nor did he campaign at times of crucial significance for the cause of freedom, but instead was motivated largely by his personal experience of unfreedoms, and gave eloquent voice to arguments that would, if accepted, widen the boundaries of individual discretion and – very importantly – freedom of expression.[8]

Milton's first campaign for liberty was however provoked by a matter of religion as such. He was a Puritan, and he objected to the crown's determination to impose uniformity of religious observance – though not of belief; the distinction is important – on England. To say that Milton was a Puritan is to invite a distorting stereotype of what that term implies. There were indeed Puritans who campaigned to close theatres, ban dancing, and impose day-long silent devotion to prayer and Bible reading on Sundays, but Milton was not of them. In Rome as a young man, during his Italian tour, he fell under the spell of the alluringly bright-eyed opera singer Leonora Baroni, and his descriptions – written as a much older man – of Adam and Eve enjoying affectionate tenderness in the premalic bliss of Eden reveal a distinctly permissive side to the moral philosopher in him.[9] For one so devoted to the cause of liberty that is as it should be. And it followed from the fact of his being a man of the Renaissance, a lover of beauty as well as a classicist and scholar. At the same time he loathed Roman Catholicism; Rome was the 'whore of the Apocalypse', and his attachment to toleration did not extend to Catholics in England. But neither could he agree with his more austere co-religionists about the theatre – he had written a masque for performance; perhaps the vision of one such as Leonora hovered before his inward gaze even then – and this saved him from the thoroughgoing intolerance of those who demanded tolerance from the Establishment for their own existence.[10]

What he did not approve, however, was the Stuart determination to have religious uniformity of practice as the price of latitudinarianism in belief. The argument for this turned on a version of the distinction between essentials and inessentials for salvation. Anglicans could challenge Dissenters to say why, if certain matters are inessential to salvation, they could not go along with them in church services in order to promote social cohesion. The answer was not to come until John Locke gave it towards the end of the century, but anyway the Dissenters would not agree; and Milton was among them.

On mounting the English throne James I had said, 'No religion or heresy was ever extirpated by violence or the sword, nor have I ever judged it a way of planting truth.' He made the point partly because his mother was a Catholic – he was not – and England wanted no hint of Catholicism near the throne, and partly because he sincerely believed it. Nor did he propose importing Presbyterianism from Scotland to England; he was only too glad to be shot of the dour Presbyterians of his northern kingdom when he travelled to the warmer south to be crowned. But he believed in the cohesion to be gained from a national worship, and approved of the Church of England's episcopal structure, which gave him (as head of the Church) a large measure of useful control. And so he and his son, Charles I, sought to promote uniformity of practice while tolerating latitude of belief.[11]

Milton leaped to the defence of the anti-uniformity cause, beginning with a tract against the imposition of prescribed prayers as in the Book of Common Prayer, the very name of which was a provocation to him. It smelled of popery and the mass, because it controverted the essential Protestant principle that each is his own priest before God by interposing artificial forms and other men's words between individuals and God. It was a short step from there to an attack on the bishops and the episcopal system itself, which England had retained from its Catholic days as a check on the over-proliferation of sects and dissenting coteries, feared – not without good reason, as the pitiful spectacle of the rest of Europe demonstrated – as a source of fragmentation and internecine conflict. Milton was scathing: let us praise bleak and fruitless winter for keeping down weeds and tares, he wrote, if all that matters is that there should be none of these. But 'bondage' to winter would be better than 'frozen captivity [in the] bondage of prelates'. In any case, he continued, it is good that there should be tares among the wheat: 'Sects and errors it seems God suffers to be for the glory of good men, that the world may know and reverence their true fortitude and undaunted constancy in truth.'[12]

Milton thought he was defending the Presbyterian cause with these arguments, but he was mistaken. One reason was that the Presbyterians objected to prelacy not on the grounds that it represented conformity and the suppression of dissent (which they were just as keen to suppress as King Charles I and his bishops) but because it was not in the Bible, and thus not ordained by God. The prelates of the Church of England wished to impose uniformity of observance and Church structure on Scotland; the Presbyterians wished to impose their alternative on England. The result was war between the two kingdoms, and – for other reasons besides – war within England itself. The king and his bishops lost.[13]

One result was that the victorious regime was more austere than the old, not least in the censorship and licensing of books, and this was both an immediate inconvenience and another provocation to Milton, who had just had a bad experience and wanted to write in favour of an important reform relating to it. He had married a girl of seventeen, half his age, and after just one month of the opposite of connubial bliss in Milton's London home she had hastened back to her father's country house. It seems that he had expected an Eve to tend quietly to his household as he spent long days over his books, and then to tend quietly to his needs when he came weary to the fireside at the day's end. She, perhaps, had married him to escape the countryside, dreaming of city lights. But both were bitterly disappointed. Milton set to work on a series of pamphlets advocating divorce on grounds other than adultery, which was then the only possible escape.[14]

Presbyterian licensers were not inclined to look with any favour on tracts advocating divorce. So in addition to arguing for divorce, Milton had an additional case to make for freedom of speech, in order that he could argue for divorce; and because freedom of speech is fundamental to individual liberty in any respect, this move was of the first significance.

The traditional Catholic view of marriage has always been that it is for the procreation of children and a second-best protection against sin (second best, that is, to chastity). This latter – 'better to marry than to burn' – was a Lutheran consideration too. The first element is an ancient one derived from the earliest Judaic morality, which was a morality of herdsmen eager to increase their livestock; for them any wastage of sperm not directed at the possibility of conception was a grave dereliction. That is why Onan was struck dead by God for spilling his seed on the ground, and why the Catholic Church regarded rape as less serious than masturbation because the former might at least result in conception.

The view emerging in Milton's day, and for which he argued passionately in his pro-divorce tracts, was that marriage was not instituted of God for procreation or as a remedy against sin, but for the reason given earliest in the Bible: that it is not good for man to be alone. This premise of companionship entailed that marriage should be an accordance of hearts and minds. 'In God's intention,' Milton wrote, 'a meet and happy conversation is the chiefest and noblest end of marriage . . . The chief society thereof is in the soul rather than in the body, and the greatest breach thereof is unfitness of mind rather than defect of body . . . Since we know it is not the joining of another body will remove loneliness, but the uniting of another compliable mind; and that it is no blessing but a torment, nay a base and brutish condition to be one flesh, unless . . . nature can in some measure fix and unite the disposition.'[15]

No one now could disagree with this, and it is a lucid first statement of what was, by Victorian times at the latest (except within the dynastically minded aristocracy) a complete change in attitude to the nature of marriage. From being a domestic contract often involving people very different in age and educational attainment, it became a companionate marriage of people similar in age, station and eventually educational level, as it is today. But in the mid-seventeenth century this was social heresy, to say nothing of seeming to invoke Scripture to nefarious ends. Milton had to avoid the censors in order to publish the pamphlets, and it was this that led him to write his famous defence of free speech. In the first of his divorce tracts he had in the preface signalled the need for such a case by pleading that 'the womb of teeming truth' not be closed by censorship. Now, in 1644, in his *Areopagitica* – named for the Areopagus, the Hill of Mars in Athens where in ancient times citizens met to debate freely – he mounted a magnificent defence of the principle of free speech.[16]

Milton defended books as distillations of the best endeavours of their authors, indeed the seasoned life of their authors stored and preserved in print, to destroy which would be to destroy not merely a life but 'the precious lifeblood of a master spirit, embalmed and treasured up to a life beyond life'. For the risk is that truth will be rejected in the process, 'and revolutions of ages do not oft recover the loss of a rejected truth, for the want of which whole nations fare the worse'. He then turned his attention to truth itself, as something which is the object of a continuing search by mankind rather than the locked-up possession of a church. Mankind will reach the truth if left free to do so; the danger to the quest is not in the multitude seeking it – this indeed is a guarantee that it will eventually be uncovered – but that 'the fearfulness or the presumptuous rashness of a perfunctory licenser' should stand as gatekeeper in its path. Great minds, great truths might be lost by this, and it is a calumny on the people that they are to be protected from thinking for themselves: 'What is it but servitude like that imposed by the Philistines, not to be allowed the sharpening of our own axes and coulters, but we must repair from all quarters to twenty licensing forges.'

There is not only a case for free speech here, but the germs of a case for democracy besides. The people can be trusted to arrive at truth and flush out error better than a few appointed officials whose timidity or arrogance might make them silence truth to the detriment of all. Is it, Milton asked, that we dare not trust the people with a pamphlet? Do we think them such a 'giddy, vicious and ungrounded' people?

Then he adds, 'Let truth and falsehood grapple . . . Truth is strong.' The grappling is important, for truth emerges from contests with error, needing exercise just as virtue does: 'I cannot praise a fugitive and cloistered virtue unexercised and unbreathed, that never sallies out and sees her adversary'; just so with truth. And then Milton says a most significant thing: 'A man may be a heretic in the truth; and if he believe things only because his pastor says so, or an assembly so determines, without knowing other reason, though his belief be true, yet the very truth he holds becomes his heresy.' The intellectual responsibility to seek, to find, to engage with truth, to make it one's own, to understand its grounds, to acknowledge it when one meets it and defer to it as truth: this is an individual responsibility, an epistemic obligation that each must shoulder.[17]

The other side of the equation in this point is the objectivity and obduracy of truth: it is independent of our wishes, preferences and hopes; therefore to encounter it is to acknowledge its authority. The implication of this crucial commitment is found at its fullest and richest in the scientific revolution that was occurring even as Milton wrote. Of course this meant that Scripture and tradition were exposed to the unblinking eye of the truth-seeker, no longer protected by the thick damasks of Church authority and threats of heresy.

Milton put the next point in the form of a question: '[I]s it not possible that [truth] may have more shapes than one? What else is all that rank of things indifferent, wherein truth may be on this side or on the other without being unlike herself?' This is not early relativism, in the sense of a claim that there are as many truths as there are seekers after truth, but a challenge to consider that one and the same truth might be approachable from different directions. It is a point that changed the landscape from one in which truth is owned by ecclesiastical authority to one where truth is an independent and complex thing that each individual not only may but *must* seek on his own account. It is not, to repeat, that Milton expected each to arrive at subjective truth, but at objective truth by his own means and on his own responsibility.

Three different and equally important consequences flow from accepting this point. It fortifies the claim that each must be free to think for himself: that touches the freedom of the enquirer. It licenses the idea of the unrestrained pursuit of truth: that touches the freedom of enquiry. It also thereby undermines further the idea of imposing uniformity of liturgy and worship. In support of this latter consequence Milton cited St Paul's attack on outward shows of behaviour and ritual, so important to the Philistines, replacing it instead with a requirement for inner sincerity.

As a paragraph in the history of Christianity this last matter is worth pausing over. In its medieval heyday, when the Church was in effect a Europe-wide monarchy and 'Christendom' was more than a geographical category, the idea of anything that would fragment the unity of the faith and its organisation was anathema. But the Reformation had done just this, and the continuing divisions into more and more sects had permanently killed the idea of a single, united Christian empire once and for all. Before long the opposites of unity – that is, diversity and variety among Christian communities – were being hailed as virtues, not least by groups such as Remonstrants and Baptists in the Netherlands and England respectively, who most stood to gain from it. Rome has never ceased to mourn its passing – the 'rending of the seamless robe of Christ' – as it has never ceased to mourn the much earlier split between itself and Eastern Orthodoxy.

Neither the Cromwellian period, ending as it did in martial law, nor the Restoration, with its limited punishment of the regicides and general amnesty otherwise, gave Milton any comfort, although in his retirement and blindness he could turn at last to the work on which his enduring fame rests, beginning with *Paradise Lost.* Cromwell had found that the realities of governing an unsettled people had forced him to make hard choices between opposing principles, and that whatever he did was sure to anger at least one half of the country.[18] The Restoration brought back with it not only most of what the Revolution had fought to displace, but it also introduced the riotous manners of an irresponsible aristocracy – the Earl of Rochester and his libertine friends in the vanguard – whose libertinism seemed to mock the liberty that Milton had championed, for the licence of an unrestrained clique is almost always enjoyed at the expense of the genuine liberty of others.[19]

The swaggering Cavalier epoch was relatively brief, and ended with a genuinely brief but salutary reminder of what the previous century and a half of reformatory struggles had been about. The lesson lay in the danger, as those unfriendly to Roman Catholicism in England saw it, posed by James II, a Catholic whose actions on coming to the throne manifested an intention to increase indulgence for Catholics and to insert them into office. It has been surmised on strong grounds that in this he was only continuing what Charles II, though officially an Anglican, had been meditating anyway: remodelling England on French lines as a Catholic absolute monarchy. This was not a contradiction in terms any more than it was in France itself, where the Church's independence from Rome was effectively complete, giving Louis XIV irresistible authority in all estates of his empire. Unlike Louis XIV, England's Charles II had no intention of restoring intolerance: 'I am in my nature an enemy to all severity for religion and conscience, howsoever mistaken it be, when it extends to capital and sanguinary punishments', he said – an interesting remark, because it did not rule out other tough punishments. And indeed these came during his reign, but it was not Charles himself who inspired them. He realised soon enough that his hopes for a Catholic restoration were impracticable, and that if he was going to recover royal powers lost with his father's head it would have to be as a Protestant.[20]

So Charles II did nothing (unlike his openly Catholic brother James later) to inflame anxieties, but they were inflamed anyway, for a king with Catholics for a mother and brother who wished to show indulgence to denominations other than the established Anglican Church raised suspicion enough just by those facts. He had to accept the Test Act of 1673 excluding anyone from public office who would not disclaim belief in transubstantiation. It seems incredible now that an Act of Parliament, and such an illiberal one, could turn on a question about such a matter; but so it was.

Anxiety about nonconformity to the Established Church was not only directed at Roman Catholicism, however. Cromwell's banning of the Book of Common Prayer, among other turpitudes as the Restoration saw them, showed the dominating Church of England party that the dissenting sects could not be trusted either. A number of disabilities were enacted against the Dissenters to punish them for their disloyalty, and to settle some painful old scores from the Commonwealth period: the Conventicle Act banned meetings of more than five persons at a time, and the Five Mile Act forbade any nonconformist minister to come within five miles of any city. The Act of Uniformity required that all clergy should use the newly revised (in 1662) Book of Common Prayer, should forswear any allegiances of the Commonwealth period, and promise never to take arms against the Crown. The clergy were given a period of grace to comply with the terms of the Act, after which any who did not were to be removed from their livings. In the event nearly two thousand refused to comply, and were ousted from the Church.[21]

The risk of penury seems in the end not to have been the fate of too many of these 'Bartholomeans' (the grace period extended to St Bartholomew's Day in the year of enactment), most of whom found other employment, as ministers, in schoolmastering, in secretaryships, or wherever their education would serve them. Harsher penalties awaited those who were already Dissenters and who were caught by the Conventicle and Five Mile Acts. One was John Bunyan, who languished in Bedford gaol for eight years as a result.[22]

But these punishments hardly approximated the Spanish Inquisition in punitive scale, and if anything they demonstrate how moderate the attitude towards difference of views had become. For although there were indeed disputes over doctrinal matters in the offing – they were after all what had originally divided the sects from one another and all of them from the Established Church, even on matters of Church structure – the principal motivation for the disabilities was not a theological, but a political and social one: on theology the Church of England was thoroughly latitudinarian.

Two events looked set to upset matters properly in 1685, however. One was James II's accession to the throne, attended by the failed attempt by the Duke of Monmouth to prevent him from taking it. The other was Louis XIV's revocation of the Edict of Nantes, issued by Henry IV nearly a century before to protect the Huguenots. For years Louis had been making life difficult for the Huguenots, and observers had long been expecting him to move against them definitively. Many Huguenots fled to England, and their presence was a vivid reminder to the English of the danger that Catholicism still posed to Protestantism. So the appearance on the English throne of an avowedly devoted Catholic was not, in these circumstances, a calming event, any more than Monmouth's failure to prevent him from taking it. And news from further afield in that same year heightened the anxieties of those concerned about James II's intentions: in Savoy toleration was revoked for the Waldenses, and the Rhine Palatinate, long a Protestant princedom, had just passed into Catholic hands.

In 1687 James issued his Declaration of Indulgence, using his own royal authority to circumvent Parliament to do so. This was seen as a provocative act on its own account, but, worse, it was also seen as a first step in the restoration of Catholicism. A number of bishops refused to read the declaration in their cathedrals and were arrested and imprisoned in the Tower of London. That was the moment when the conspiracy that had been forming against James saw its chance. Within a year he had effectively been deposed, and the thoroughly Protestant and highly able William of Orange was on the throne as co-monarch along with Mary Stuart, Charles II's Protestant daughter.[23]

In the ship that brought Mary from Holland to ascend the throne with her husband was the philosopher John Locke, who had been living in exile for the preceding five years as a refugee from the attentions of Charles II and James II; he had been a close associate of the late Earl of Shaftesbury, one of those involved in trying to prevent James II's Catholic succession. When he returned to England to witness the success of the Glorious Revolution, Locke had with him the manuscripts of three works that were to establish his permanent fame – he was already in his fifties and had not yet published anything, an indication more of his caution than a lack of authorial intent. The works were the first *Letter Concerning Toleration* and the first of his *Two Treatises of Government*, and his major philosophical treatise *An Essay Concerning Human Understanding*. The *Letter Concerning Toleration* and the *Treatise of Government* proved to be vital contributions to establishing the trend of liberty, and the second of them was quoted in the documents of the American and French Revolutions of the next century. Locke's writings were thus a major formative influence on the eighteenth-century Enlightenment, along with the equally great influence of Newton and Spinoza.[24]

What Locke had to say in the *Letter Concerning Toleration* was not original, nor was it what had helped prompt the Glorious Revolution. Rather it provided justifications, explanations, and post-facto rationalisations (in the literal, non-pejorative sense of this last term) of the ideas informing that event, and of the only partially successful attempt of the new King William III to legislate for toleration by making the Established Church as comprehensive as possible, allowing dissenters of various stamps to dispense with the obligation to affirm whichever article of the Thirty-Nine was not acceptable to them. The effort was only partially successful because the Church of England was still intent on encouraging conformity in practice – let actual belief fall where it may – in the interests of cohesion, and in consequence it would accept limited exemptions only.

It will be remembered that the Anglican view was that, since sectarian differences turned on non-essentials, there was no reason why votaries of the sects could not go along with Church of England forms of worship for the sake of unity. Locke argued that even the non-essentials matter to the believer, and it is unfair to expect him to temporise for form's sake over something that deeply engages his conscience. Moreover if worshippers are in church under protest, and secretly feel at odds because their relationship with God is being conducted in ways they do not approve, there will not be unity anyway. 'Open dissenters are better than secret malcontents,' he wrote. 'If all the dissenters were forced into the church we should then have only an exasperated enemy within.'[25] For Locke a church was a voluntary organisation, not one to which people belonged automatically by birth

– just the point that Zwingli had rejected in his opposition to the Anabaptists. And here the note of freedom is sounded with complete clarity, showing how the tendency of thought about liberty of conscience had been evolving since the Reformation began: 'A Church, then, I take to be a voluntary society of men, joining themselves together of their own accord, in order for the public worshipping of God, in such a manner as they judge acceptable to him, and effectual to the salvation of their souls. I say it is a free and voluntary society. Nobody is born a member of any Church; otherwise the religion of the parents would descend unto the children, by the same right of inheritance as their temporal estates, and everyone would hold his faith by the same tenure as he holds his lands; than which nothing can be imagined more absurd.'[26]

Absurd it may be; but here Locke is far from thinking of the tyranny of religious succession exercised over children by devotee parents intent on inculcating religious beliefs in them long before they can judge the merits of what they are being told to believe. He is certainly not thinking of Judaism or Islam, individual members of which faiths would not at all think it absurd that they inherit their religion from their parents. 'No man by nature is bound under any particular Church or sect,' Locke continued, 'but everyone joins himself voluntarily to that society in which he believes he has found that profession and worship which is truly acceptable to God . . . if afterwards he discovers anything erroneous . . . why should it not be as free for him to go out as to enter?'[27]

Why not indeed? In stricter versions of Islam a person might be killed for apostasy – abandonment of the faith – as apostate Jews were in Old Testament times, and as Christian apostates and heretics were not long before Locke's own time. But here Locke was asserting the liberty of the individual – of the individual, note – to make choices about a matter which had formerly been thought far too important to be left to individual determination. From today's perspective Locke's use of the term 'free' in this context does not seem as bold and fresh as it must have seemed when he wrote it down.

True, it was no longer dangerous to say what he did, as it had been for Servetus and Castellio; that was the gain seen by the hundred years since their time. But the use of 'free' was radical enough, because its implications were far reaching. Indeed it strictly implied that a man should be as free to be a Catholic as a Quaker, and that was not a degree of toleration that quite all of Locke's contemporaries had in mind. Neither, as it happens, was Locke himself prepared to go as far as complete toleration for Catholics, on the ground of their undesirable allegiance to a foreign power – the pope – a point always sensitive in Protestant countries which had experienced the negative effects of a division of loyalties. One of these – the religious loyalty – is deep enough to trump all others, and in certain circumstances makes a man turn traitor, or become a terrorist on behalf of his religion against his own people, as Guy Fawkes did; and he is not the last who proposed to blow up his fellow countrymen on such a ground.[28]

But the only people from whom Locke would entirely withhold toleration were atheists, for in his view 'without God all is dissolved'. He meant morally; he seems not to have understood what would constrain atheists from committing atrocities, which makes one wonder how he thought Socrates and Aristotle managed so far back in classical antiquity without a punishing and rewarding deity to keep them in check. For everyone else he wished to see differences in point of view tolerated, and correlatively he wished to see the Church of England made comprehensive enough in its doctrine and practice for there to be little need of nonconformism anyway.

The root of Locke's attitude to toleration, and therefore to the need for acceptance of individual liberty of conscience, was epistemological. He had shown in detail in his *Essay Concerning Human Understanding* what are the limits of knowledge for finite human capacities, and on that basis did not think it right that anyone or any Church should 'peremptorily require demonstration and demand certainty where probability only is to be had', meaning by 'demonstration' logical proof, and by 'probability' conjecture or belief.[29] This then led to the practical point that it is wrong to persecute people in order to force them to accept one or another way of believing, for at best the result can only be to create hypocrites who assent in order to save their skins.

Belief is only properly formed and sincerely held, said Locke, when the evidence available to a person, and his application of reason to it, give him his warrant for holding that belief. No one else is warranted to dictate that he should believe it.

A crucial factor in the development of Locke's thinking about liberty was his five-year exile in the Netherlands. Even after his proscription was raised he remained there, ostensibly on the ground that to accept a pardon from the British government (the pardon had been arranged by William Penn) would be an admission that he had indeed been party to one of the plots to prevent the Catholic succession, something he always denied. But another reason assuredly was that the Netherlands was then the safest refuge in a Europe which, misleadingly as it turned out, seemed on the brink of a reversion to Catholicism and its hostile attitude to Protestantism. Locke and others believed the events described above, in France, Savoy and England itself, to be portents of this. But in the Netherlands different sects lived side by side in mutual toleration, or at least accommodation.[30]

Here Locke met Labadists, Mennonites, Quakers and Remonstrants. He lived for a time with a Quaker, Benjamin Furley, and with refugees from France such as Pierre Bayle, the rationalist author of the *Philosophical Dictionary*, and Jean le Clerc, editor of the works of Erasmus. And perhaps most significantly for his own views he met Philip van Limborch, the Remonstrants' leader, a man who was intellectually in the direct line of descent from Castellio.

Bayle's ironies were a potent force for making people think afresh about problems. He pointed out that if a person is convinced that it is right to save others' souls by force if necessary, and necessity beckons, then he is justified in using force – even if he is objectively speaking in error. This is of course a *reductio ad absurdum* of any position that bases itself on subjective certainty. Worse, it points up the dilemma facing the public official confronted by individuals standing on their individual consciences in opposition to the public good. In Bayle's view, each must stick to his obligations, and therefore the official must punish the individual; thus a mad inevitability enters the picture, in which each recognises the inexorability of the other's position but is helpless to do otherwise.[31]

Locke could see no way out of this problem either, unless it were by accepting the lesson of his epistemological enquiries, that neither the official nor the dissenter was entitled to expect the other to conform to his own view in what was a matter not of demonstration or evidence but 'probability', and both must therefore seek to refrain from the conflict that would arise from dogmatic insistence. But this obviously does not address the question of sincerity of conviction and the duties it imposes, unless a further step is taken: that of persuading people that sincerity of conviction does not impose a duty to oblige others to believe likewise.

It is a striking fact that the only two thinkers in the sixteenth and seventeenth centuries who wrote about both liberty and epistemology – and invoked their views about the latter in support of their views about the former – were Locke and Castellio. After Locke had published his *Essay Concerning Human Understanding* he and van Limborch, his friend from his days of exile, corresponded on whether to publish a complete edition of Castellio's works; Locke was sure that they would be warmly welcomed in England.

Locke's own writings on toleration breathed the Castellian and Erasmian spirit which already quickened the sense of liberty in the Netherlands. 'I appeal to the conscience of those that persecute, torment, destroy and kill other men upon the pretence of religion,' he wrote, 'whether they do it out of friendship and kindness toward them, or no; and I shall then indeed, and not till then, believe they do so, when I shall see those fiery zealots correcting, in the same manner, their friends and familiar acquaintances, for the manifest sins they commit against the precepts of the Gospel; when I shall see them prosecute with fire and sword the members of their own communion that are tainted with enormous vices, and without amendment are in danger of eternal perdition; and when I shall see them thus express their love and desire of the salvation of their souls, by the infliction of torments, and exercise all manner of cruelties . . . why then, does this burning zeal for God, for the Church, and for the salvation of souls – burning, I say literally, with fire and faggot – pass by these moral vices and wickednesses, without any chastisement, which are acknowledged by all men to be diametrically opposite to the profession of Christianity; and bend all nerves either to the introducing of ceremonies or to the establishment of opinions, which for the most part are about nice and intricate matters that exceed the capacity of ordinary understandings?'[32]

In effect these questions, scoring palpable hits on any who would justify coercion to induce conformity – whether in belief, as in Castellio's time, or observance for the sake of public order, as in Locke's time – amounted to an abolition of the very concept of heresy. For every argument against burning at the stake was an argument against civil disabilities. That is why Locke was not happy that King William's Act of Toleration had been so watered down by the Church; he wrote to van Limborch, 'It is not what you would wish, but it is something.'

Locke's *Letters Concerning Toleration* were controversial when published, and stimulated a vigorous, sometimes acerbic, debate; but when Voltaire visited England in the 1730s he found a practical settlement of religious affairs to applaud. Had he known more of the disabilities under which dissent laboured he might have thought that the English type of compromise, which always involves some turnings of blind eyes to injustice, was not as satisfactory as it appeared. His own attacks on clericalism in France were intended to bring about what he saw as the laissez-faire of England, rather than as a harbinger of French Revolution attitudes to religion, but in practical terms Voltaire's writings encouraged the latter, from which the Church in France has never since recovered.[33]

It is not too much to claim that by the time Locke published his *Letters* the intellectual argument for religious liberty had been won, and now it was only a matter of time – more than a century in England, just under a century in America and France – for it to take final concrete form in an effective secularism which demoted religion to the private sphere as regards matters of belief, and the churches to each counting for one among competing interest groups in civil society along with political parties, trades unions and the like. As an Established Church the Church of England retains the anomaly of twenty-six seats for bishops in the House of Lords at a time (the time of writing) when its active constituency of churchgoers in the country is about 3 per cent of the population and declining. But Establishment is an anachronism whose life is drawing to a close.

———————

Such was the course and fate of the struggle for *religious* liberty, with its first additional fruits in liberty of expression, demanded by Milton and applied – in effect, assumed – by Locke. Grant Lord Acton his claim that religious liberty is the source of all modern liberty, but note – to repeat – that liberty of religious conscience was also, and in the end more importantly, a stalking horse for the liberties that people who cared about them really desired: a general liberty of thought and enquiry, and political liberty. And indeed a different, powerful, and in many ways more consequential fruit of the quest for liberty had also quickly ripened in the struggles of the sixteenth and seventeenth centuries: the liberty of enquiry that produced the scientific revolution. To see just how revolutionary this revolution was, one has only to contrast the world views existing at its beginning and end.

What most leaders of Christian denominations, and certainly of the Roman Catholic Church, regarded as an acceptable view of the nature of the universe – acceptable because conformable to Scripture, and authorised by the holy doctors of the faith, especially St Thomas Aquinas – consisted in a combination of Christian theology and Aristotelian philosophy. The synthesis of the two had been magnificently effected by Aquinas, who harmonised Aristotle's science, the astronomy of Ptolemy, and the medical theories of Galen with their picture of the material side of man's being, into a unified philosophy fit to serve as the handmaid of theology.[34] This elaborate and masterly synthesis is known as Thomism, and it provided a framework for thinking about the world even for Protestant thinkers in the sixteenth century, as well as parameters for what could be considered theologically acceptable in scientific and metaphysical enquiry. It did this even though there were plenty of disputes among the 'Schoolmen' – the philosophers of the medieval schools (universities) – over matters of detail. In overarching design the theologically acceptable lineaments of a world view were familiar.

The label 'natural theology' means the study of questions about the existence and nature of God independently of revelation, and was regarded as legitimate as an exercise of the reason God had given to humankind, so long as humankind did not use it to stray over doctrinal boundaries into heresy or blasphemy. Various arguments were advanced to prove the existence of a deity and to make sense of its omnipotence, omniscience, infinity, and other divine attributes, the two sets of considerations being linked. For a prime example: if God is a necessary being, that is, one that cannot fail to exist, then that very fact establishes his existence. This proof rests on logic alone, demonstrating his existence from his essence. Another and more famous proof by logic alone is the Ontological Argument, which states: something in the universe is the most perfect thing it contains; a perfect thing that actually exists is more perfect than one that does not exist; therefore, the most perfect thing exists, and that is God.

Other arguments rested on empirical premises, such as the Cosmological Argument, which states that because everything in the universe has a cause, so the universe itself must have a cause, which implies the existence of a self-caused cause of everything, which is God. An argument many found compelling later, in the eighteenth century and afterwards, rests on the appearance of design in nature: this is called the Teleological Argument. Since the wonders of nature are so intricate and seem to answer elaborate purposes, they cannot have happened by chance, but must have a designer; the designer of the universe and all its complex and remarkable contents is God.

It comes as a surprise to find that two of these arguments, all of them easily refutable, retain a hold over some; the Ontological Argument has one or two champions among those who claim that the technicalities of modal logic show it to be valid, while the Teleological Argument has a substantial following among those who reject evolutionary biology as a description of how living organisms developed on the planet.

These arguments fail. It is an instructive exercise to look at the reasons why, but that is a task for another place.[35] There is little disagreement among philosophers and scientists about those reasons, and they are joined by some votaries of faith who point out that it is anyway a greater merit to believe in religious propositions independently of evidence and proof, and that these arguments are therefore pointless. Yet others again, while not disagreeing with this line, add that the nature of deity is so inscrutable that attempted proofs must of course fail, because they cannot hope to premise a secure enough understanding of what they purport to prove the existence of in order to be successful.

In the sixteenth century and before, of course, the principal source for understanding God, God's purposes for mankind, and the nature of the universe, was revelation. The Roman Church had long since added its own authority as a source of understanding too, and this is what the Reformation denied in connection with theology and morality. But Rome and Reformation were tacitly agreed in regarding revelation as the last court of appeal on matters of science. In this connection all was clear: Scripture said that God had created heaven and earth, and had populated them with uncountable creatures – 'creatures' literally meaning 'created beings' – among them a vast angelic host, of whom one third had rebelled (so said some authorities) and followed Satan into hell, from there to labour at thwarting God's plan for mankind. God's first human creatures, Adam and Eve, were tempted from their obedience to God by Satan, which meant that the whole human race suffers the fallen nature of its first parents. The swarms of rebel angels, now demons, roam the world in search of immortal souls to capture for damnation by encouraging wickedness such as fornication and heresy.

In his attempt to rescue mankind God tried various expedients: massacring all but a handful of them in order to start over; sending prophets and teachers, many of whom were ignored, driven away, or even killed; and finally and perfectly by taking human form and sacrificing himself. How men measure against that sacrifice will be judged on the Last Day, an event expected with great confidence by almost every generation of the faithful since.

These beliefs, leaving aside the fine details which nevertheless sent so many to the stake for disagreeing over them, were established by theologians some centuries after the death of Christ. But theories of the natural world were much older, and in the sixteenth century were still in essence Aristotelian. In this view the physical world consists of combinations of earth, air, fire and water. These four elements can manifest any two of the properties *hot, cold, wet* and *dry*, combining them to give the characteristic nature of physical entities: for example, earth is cold and dry, water is cold and wet; fire is hot and dry, air is hot and wet. Each of the four elements has its natural place; earth, being heavy (and morally base) tends towards the universe's centre. Water is heavy too, but not as heavy as earth, so it lies on top of the earth. Air naturally inhabits what would otherwise be the emptiness between water and fire, which latter is the lightest element, at home high above the earth, where it can be seen winking and twinkling at night.

We never meet the elements in their pure form; they come only and always as admixtures. This is easily proved by experiments in chemistry in which the elements are separated or purified, for example by the application of heat. This insight prompted alchemy; if everything is an admixture of the same elements, and if these admixtures can be separated out and recombined, then precious metals can be formed from base metals, and it must be possible to find the substance that would guarantee longevity. For example: gold is the most desirable metal because it is the best and most beautiful stuff in the world. Its being so implies that it must be a perfectly proportioned blend of the four elements. Accordingly baser metals need only to be rearranged into those perfect proportions in order to become gold.

Alchemists also thought that because gold is a perfect compound, it must be a perfect medicine too. Belief in its universal efficacy led to it being taken in liquid form. It has never proved itself any better as medicine for the body than as medicine for morals.

Aristotle taught that in addition to the 'natural motion' of earth and water downwards, and air and fire upwards, things would only move if something else applied an impulsive force to them, just as a ball is moved by kicking it. If the pushing force stopped, so would the objects in question. As this shows, there was no concept of inertia in Aristotelian science. This was the principal reason why a God had to exist, first to get things going, and then to keep them going. As our earliest forebears had doubtless believed, this was additionally necessary given that it is quite obvious that no other identifiable agency is impelling the moon across the sky, causing the wind to blow, or the tides to rise and fall.

The astronomy of antiquity was likewise accepted almost wholesale by Christian orthodoxy. Stars and planets were thought of as orbiting a stationary Earth at its centre, carried along in crystalline spheres that had been set moving by God and which were kept moving, according to some authorities, by superior angels called 'Intelligences' whose particular duty was to preserve the heavenly bodies in their correct orbits. The Moon is the lowest and closest of the heavenly bodies, and the basest; its sphere revolves around the Earth fastest. The next spheres, in ascending order, are Mercury, Venus, the Sun, Mars, Jupiter and Saturn, each turning more slowly than the one below it. These bodies are composed of a fifth element – the 'quintessence' – and travel in perfect circles round the Earth. They are unchanging and perfect. As they eternally rotate they pour divine music into the universe, inaudible to humans because of their base bodies. Those who get to heaven will hear the music of the spheres there.

And the theory does not stop there: from the medico-psychological theory of bodily humours to astrological theories of character and destiny, and thence to the theory that the world of men is divinely ordered, it provides an account of mankind's hierarchy from the lowliest peasant to the emperor on his throne. This is the theory of 'degree', and the order of things is even more inclusive than the social hierarchy just mentioned; indeed it runs all the way from the deity to the worm, with man as the link between angels and beasts – having something of the nature of each – and thus also the bridge between heaven and earth. This theory had its nuances: angels might know more than men do, but men are better than angels at learning; men are more intelligent than beasts, but beasts are stronger, and so on.[36]

Such was the world view that for centuries had constituted the outlook of the educated, right until the beginning of the seventeenth century. It is hard now to imagine what it was like to hold these essentially comfortable beliefs – for man and his world were the centrepiece of creation, and in worldly terms its lords – and then to be presented with radically different and unnerving new theories such as the idea that the Earth is not at the centre of the universe, and indeed moves through space in a universe unimaginably larger and emptier – and far less human-orientated, if human-orientated at all – than they could comprehend.

Moreover these new theories straightforwardly controverted the Scriptures. The suggestion that the Earth swings through space around the Sun had to be a lie, and an act of temerity too, for does not the fifth verse of Psalm 104 say that God had 'laid the foundations of the Earth, that it should not be moved for ever'? Had he not made the Sun stand still as a sign for Joshua, and did this not conclusively entail that the Sun moved?

Much was at stake in the confrontation between science – the new science, premised on the view that the authorities governing it were observation and reason, free from the need to conform to antecedent pieties – and scriptural and ecclesiastical authority, asserting the established teachings just described. It is instructive to notice how the Counter-Reformation's new vanguard, the Jesuit order, with its focus on education as a prime weapon in the war for the recovery of Christendom's lost souls, described its curriculum in its *Ratio Studiorum* (schedule of study). It baldly states, 'In logic, natural philosophy, ethics and metaphysics, Aristotle's doctrine is to be followed.' This was the instruction issued by Francesco Borgia, general of the Jesuit order, in a memorandum which further laid down that no one must 'defend or teach anything opposed, detracting, or unfavourable to the faith, either in philosophy or theology. Let no one defend anything against the axioms received by the philosophers, such as: there are only four causes, there are only four elements, there are only three principles of natural things, fire is hot and dry, air is humid and hot. Let no one defend such propositions as that natural agents act at a distance without a medium, contrary to the most common opinion of the philosophers and theologians . . . This is not just an admonition, but a teaching that we impose.'[37]

In light of such attitudes it is hardly surprising that new and astonishing theories about the world were greeted with strident opposition and sometimes the harshest measures of persecution. And indeed the first mooters of revolutionary theories did not even try to offer them as an alternative truth; the preface to Copernicus' classic work said only that hypothesising a heliocentric arrangement of the heavens made the mathematics of astronomy easier to do, so readers must take it that it was a device, an heuristic, and not a claim that he was suggesting should be taken literally.[38]

Today's orthodoxy – and here is the contrast with how matters stood at the beginning of the seventeenth century – is that science is an impersonal, objective endeavour which strives to be as exact as possible in its use of measurement and quantification when formulating and testing hypotheses. It seeks to exclude bias, and to proceed in publicly scrutinisable ways, with its results being open to the challenge of independent verification and replication of results. Observation, strict reasoning, careful protocols governing experiments, and constant exposure to review, are the norms that constitute the least of what is expected of scientific procedure. The objective or at least convergent results of scientific enquiry are massively endorsed by outcome, good and ill: it is easy to argue that the good outweighs the ill, despite some of the horrors (nuclear weaponry for example) constituting the latter. But the applications of scientific discovery to the world via technology are powerful testimonies to its success and – arguably – its advance towards truths about the world.[39]

The universe revealed by science is very different from Christianity's universe. The latter is a small man-centred creation existing specifically for the moral testing of human beings. In this picture the small and the large lie within the range of man's imagination; in the new picture the small and the large can only be understood through the lens of mathematics, a conceptual instrument of immensely greater penetration and accuracy than human imaginings. From Galileo and Newton to relativity theory and quantum mechanics – to say nothing of the advances in chemistry, the biological sciences and technology – the rich, deep, powerful theories of modern science make theology and the metaphysics of the past look extremely limited and naive as accounts of the universe.

In the picture which has transcended these armchair speculations, both the small and the large come into focus as aspects of a careful account of the structure and properties of matter, and the structure and properties of the universe constituted by it. Matter is theorised as consisting of quarks and leptons, the former constituting the nuclear particles of protons and neutrons, the latter the electrons constituting the atomic shell and neutrinos. The forces binding atoms together are the strong and weak nuclear forces and the electromagnetic force, the two latter now combined in theory into the electroweak force; unification of all the atomic forces, and of them with gravity, constitutes a grail of theory. The atomic forces are carried by gauge bosons. Quarks have a variety of properties that determine their interactions; subatomic physics has given them such entertaining names as 'charm' and 'colour', and some are 'up-quarks', some are 'down-quarks'. The effects and interactions of 'colour' properties are described in quantum chromo-dynamics. But these understandings of the microstructure of matter suggest deeper levels of structure still, with various hypotheses under discussion to conceptualise them, such as string theory.[40]

At the other end of the scale the universe is described by contemporary astronomy to be billions of times larger than the little set of spheres imagined by sixteenth-century theologians. Their universe was at very most about the size of the inner area of the solar system as it is now understood. Today the most distant detectable objects in the universe are calculated to be about thirteen billion light years away, a light year being the distance that light, moving at 186,000 miles per second, travels in a year. In the Aristotelian and theological universe stars were thought to consist of a crystal sphere through holes in which the ethereal fire could be seen, a decorative outer layer provided by God to separate the material world from heaven. Modern astronomy says that the trillions of stars in each of the huge numbers of galaxies dispersed throughout space are suns, some like our own sun and others of a variety of types depending on their age, each going through an evolutionary cycle ending in collapse.[41]

Some forms of later theology have learned to live with atoms and galaxies, revising themselves enough to domesticate them as further proof of the majesty of God and his power. Less happy has been the relation of theology to biology, for the latter has shown that life on Earth evolved from less complex forms by processes of response to environmental pressures, which selected mutations in succeeding generations that best helped the organism to survive until reproductive age in the given environmental conditions. Planet Earth is about four and a half billion years old; life has existed for about four billion years, for a long time in microbial form. The variety of living things that historically and in the present descend from these earliest forms have taken hundreds of millions of years to diversify and develop, with the great majority of life forms that have ever existed now being long extinct.

The discovery that human beings belong in the same biological family as the other great apes, with chimpanzees as our closest relatives, and that chimpanzees, humans and gorillas shared a common ancestor in the very recent biological past – about five million years ago – puts the cap on matters so far as literalist readers of the Bible are concerned: they simply cannot and do not accept it. The simpler, safer, and more humanly satisfying (because more humanly flattering) story of Genesis and all that follows stands in such contrast to these impersonal immensities that for anyone taught the Bible story from childhood, these scientific views must seem positively insulting.[42]

This sketch, in these quick broad strokes, illustrates the contrast between the theology-shaped science of the sixteenth century and what has since developed in the course of humankind's greatest ever achievement, the development of genuine science in modern times.

Central characteristics of the scientific attitude are scepticism and a preparedness to revise one's views when they are shown to be mistaken. Science requires liberty; it cannot march to a non-scientific agenda, whether political or theological, without soon going wrong. If sixteenth-century theology-shaped science is not example enough, excellent other examples are provided by 'Soviet biology'[43] and by the elaborate agricultural miracles of rice production in China, in which yields were increased tenfold and more by Chinese scientists – in fact of course by the deception of filling paddies with harvested rice from other farms, so that when senior Party officials passed by they could see the superabundance of grain that Marxist–Leninist–Mao Zedong agricultural science had made possible.

This last is somewhat analogous to the atmosphere that prevailed in the late sixteenth century, when Church leaders required of scientific enquiry, then poised at the beginning of its great revolution, that it should at no point controvert theological orthodoxy. And leaders of faiths were prepared to persecute to ensure as much, if necessary. The key story, familiarly, is that of Galileo Galilei, and in the annals of liberty – here of liberty of thought and enquiry – it is central.[44]

Galileo's story is important because it marks the last major effort by the Church to stem the onset of the scientific revolution. It begins in 1543 with the publication of Copernicus' *De Revolutionibus Orbium Coelestium*, which sets out a heliocentric (Sun-centred) model of the universe, with the intention of providing an easier way to describe the pattern of movements of the heavenly bodies than that provided by Ptolemy's geocentric (Earth-centred) model. Ptolemy's model, devised in the second century AD on the basis of centuries of preceding astronomical observation and speculation, premised the idea that the heavenly bodies – the stars, Sun, Moon, and five then known planets – move in perfect circles round the Earth, because circles are the most perfect of the geometric figures. Because observations of planetary movements did not accord with this premise, a modification had to be made: Ptolemy proposed that the planets move in a perfect circle around a point which itself describes a perfect circle around the earth. This little rotation within the larger rotation is called an 'epicycle'. The points themselves sit in the plane of a crystal sphere which perfectly circles, well, not the Earth exactly, but a set of points (the 'equant' points) situated just a little way off-centre from the Earth, one for each of the heavenly bodies. This adjustment was required to account for further observed anomalies of the stellar and planetary configurations.

Obviously these ad hoc refinements suggest that the model is not satisfactory; it is like the extra rice imported to the paddy field, because it is an effort to make the observations – altogether too stubbornly independent for the task – conform to a presupposed belief. The much older idea, dating to Aristarchus in the third century BC, five hundred years before Ptolemy, that the Sun is at the centre of the universe and that the Earth and other bodies orbit it, recommended itself to Copernicus as a simplification, and when he tried it out he found it worked.

Copernicus was a Pole from Torun on the Vistula. His father was wealthy and paid for him to study in Italy where, in the early years of the sixteenth century, he imbibed humanist culture and published translations from Greek texts into Latin – a characteristic hobby of Renaissance humanists – while studying law and medicine. Back in his native Poland, appointment to a sinecure as a canon of Frombork Cathedral allowed him to devote his life to study.[45]

His innovative thinking in astronomy was inspired while he was still in Italy by reading a summary of Ptolemy, published together with additional observations and questions by a German scholar called Regiomontanus (Johannes Mueller; his choice of Latin name reflects his place of birth, Konigsberg).[46] In this work Regiomontanus discussed a problem with Ptolemy's model that had long been recognised, namely, the fact that it does not square with observations of the Moon, whose apparent size does not fluctuate as it should – regularly getting larger and smaller in appearance as it approached and then withdrew from Earth – if it were moving in a perfect circle round its own equant point. Copernicus solved the problem by hypothesising that the Moon orbits the Earth, and the Earth, the other planets and the crystal sphere of the stars orbit the Sun. This gave the satisfying result that the universe has a single centre (and not a rash of equants in the region of the Earth) but it introduced other problems of its own. For one thing, if the Earth is flying round the Sun, why is there not a wind of passage blowing steadily in our faces? Why are the seas relatively placid, and not rising and rushing over the land as the water in a bucket spills over the edges when the bucket is swung? If the Sun is at the centre of everything, how come the Earth and planets do not fall into it? And if the crystal sphere of stars goes round the Sun too, it must be at a vast distance from the planets, making for a huge and inexplicable gap between them and the solar system. Why would God create the universe in such an odd shape?

There was nothing available in sixteenth-century knowledge to suggest answers to these puzzling questions. But there were other aspects of the Copernican model that gave it a compelling ring. For one thing it enabled Copernicus to answer a different puzzling question, namely, why Venus and Mercury are only visible at dawn and dusk whereas Mars, Jupiter and Saturn can be seen at any time. Ptolemy had said that the first two keep the Sun company on its voyage round the Earth, but Copernicus saw that the difference must imply that Mercury and Venus have orbits inside Earth's, meaning that they are closer to the Sun, while the orbits of the other three lie outside the Earth's orbit. He was able to put the planets in their right order by inference from the pattern of their orbits relative to the Earth and Sun: moving outwards the order is Mercury, Venus, Earth, Mars, Jupiter, Saturn.

Although he arrived at these ideas early Copernicus did not publish them until the last year of his life. The story is told that a finished copy of his book reached him from the publisher as he lay on his deathbed; dramatic, but probably apocryphal. He was persuaded to publish at last by his friend Georg von Lauchen, also known as Rheticus, who was the mathematics professor at Wittenberg University. As an interim measure Rheticus published in 1540 an epitome of Copernicus' system. A Lutheran minister called Andreas Osiander was employed to make Copernicus' own manuscript ready for the press, a task he had to take full responsibility for when Copernicus became fatally ill. The book appeared in 1543, a quarter of a century after the Reformation began, and just one year after the Roman Catholic Church launched its Counter-Reformation at the opening of the Council of Trent.

It was Osiander who added the famous preface stating that Copernicus' system is not offered as a true description of the universe, but as an heuristic intended only to ease the mathematical task of calculating planetary movements. He did not sign the preface with his own name, thereby allowing it to be assumed that Copernicus himself had written it. Osiander's motive is not hard to grasp: he saw that the implications of the system, and its direct contravention of Scripture if claimed as true, would be controversial. And despite the cautious preface, his fears soon enough proved to be justified.

Yet an oddity is that when Copernicus first developed these ideas he made a synopsis of them and circulated them in manuscript under the title *Commentariolus* (*A Little Commentary*). That was in 1510, and it attracted admiring attention, even in the Vatican where it was discussed in a talk given by a papal secretary called Johann Widmanstadt in the presence of Pope Clement VII. Nikolaus von Schönberg, a cardinal who was also present, wrote to Copernicus to persuade him to publish a fuller version; when Copernicus' book at last appeared in 1543 the cardinal's letter was printed at the beginning.

The year 1510 lay in the quiet period of Erasmian influence, in the lull after the horrors of the Spanish Inquisition and before Luther's disturbance of the peace. Few then were much minded to scrutinise recondite works of natural philosophy for heretical implications, but thirty years later the situation was different. Copernicus' reticence about publishing during those thirty years is, however, significant; even more so is his taking the precaution to include the cardinal's letter with the book when it was eventually published. And the fact that Osiander was moved – with or without Copernicus' agreement, we do not know – to try to disguise the heliocentric theory as a mathematical heuristic speaks volumes by itself. For he knew his Bible, and knew that in the tenth chapter of the book of Joshua it is reported that the Sun stood still for a whole day, and the Moon with it; the word of Copernicus and the word of God were at odds, unless Copernicus could be made to say that he was not impugning the veracity of Scripture but only toying with mathematics.

Something was bound to bring the unacceptable implications of Copernicus' model to the Church's notice eventually. It is surprising that it did not happen sooner, but that is most likely because the second half of the sixteenth century was a time of many distractions for everyone, not least of war and anguish, and until a particular incident thrust the implications of Copernicus' theory under the nose of Rome, they were ignored by default. The incident in question was the trial and execution for heresy of Giordano Bruno in Rome's Campo dei Fiori in the year 1600. Bruno was an indiscreet eclectic with interests in occult sciences and mysticism and much besides, who happened also to profess adherence to the Copernican system as a true description of the universe. When it became apparent during the fifteen years after Bruno's execution that an increasing number of savants and philosophers were persuaded by the truth, not merely the utility, of the heliocentric view, Copernicus' *De Revolutionibus* was placed on the Index of Forbidden Books.

An incident that was partly instrumental in this was the attempt by a Carmelite friar called Paolo Antonio Foscarini to persuade the Church that Copernicus' system was consistent with Scripture. In 1615 he sent a memorandum outlining his arguments to the Vatican, and received a polite reply from the great Cardinal Bellarmine thanking him for his efforts but pointing out that 'If there were a real proof that the Sun is in the centre of the universe, that the Earth is in the third heaven, and that the Sun does not go round the Earth but the Earth round the Sun, then we should have to proceed with great circumspection in explaining passages of Scripture which appear to teach the contrary.' Lest there was any likelihood that Foscarini would take this cool irony the wrong way, Bellarmine had already said, 'As you are aware, the Council of Trent forbids the interpretation of the Scriptures in a manner contrary to the common opinion of the Holy Fathers. Now if your Reverence will read, not merely the Fathers, but modern commentators on Genesis, the Psalms, Ecclesiastes, and Joshua, you will discover that all agree in interpreting them literally as teaching that the Sun is in the heavens and revolves round the Earth with immense speed, and that the Earth is very distant from the heavens, at the centre of the universe, and motionless. Consider, then in your prudence, whether the Church can tolerate that the Scriptures should be interpreted in a manner contrary to that of the Holy Fathers and of all modern commentators, both Latin and Greek.'[47]

The Church was of course not willing to tolerate theories that controverted Scripture, but as it happened they no longer had much choice, and their silencing of Galileo on this point was effectively the last shot in their locker on the subject.

*

Galileo had been promising to become a thorn in Church flesh for more than two decades before he was finally arraigned before the Inquisition. He had given a series of lectures on a supernova observed by Kepler, showing that it had to be as far from the Earth as the rest of the stars, and therefore that it was evidently one of them undergoing change of some kind. This contradicted Aristotle's view that the stars are unchanging, and it also had implications for questions of the size of the universe.

More dramatic developments came when Galileo fashioned a telescope for himself and used it to make startling discoveries. In December 1609 he saw things through it that changed the world utterly. It revealed to him mountains on the Moon, spots on the face of the Sun, innumerable individual stars in the Milky Way, and satellites orbiting Jupiter. He promptly named these latter 'the Medicean stars' and sent news of the discovery and this baptism, together with a good telescope, to the Medici ruler of Florence, Cosimo II, the Grand Duke of Tuscany. Galileo was appointed 'Ducal Mathematician and Philosopher' as a reward, and given a handsome salary.

Galileo published the discoveries he had made with his telescopes in a short book called *Sidereus Nuncius* (*The Starry Messenger*), and this made him famous throughout Europe. Yet some of his most fascinating discoveries came after its publication. He made more accurate observations of Jupiter's moons, and while mulling over inconsistencies in the data thus collected realised that he had to include variabilities in his own position relative to the planetary and satellite motions he had seen, variabilities which could only be explained by the motion of the Earth – specifically, by its movement round the Sun. This was powerful evidence that Copernicus' model was not after all an heuristic convenience for simplifying mathematical calculations, but a literally correct description at least of the planetary system.

Galileo of course had been convinced of this since as early as 1598, in which year he told Kepler in a letter that he was a Copernican. But he did not advertise his now confirmed view, allowing himself to receive the plaudits of Rome and election to a fellowship of the Accademia dei Lincei, which satisfied him enormously.

The Copernican theory could not be left unaddressed for long. A former pupil of Galileo called Castelli, who was professor of mathematics at Pisa University, was invited by Cosimo II and his mother, the Grand Duchess Christina of Lorraine, to lecture on the conflict between the Copernican model and Scripture. Castelli defended the Copernican model in his lecture, and afterwards wrote to Galileo to tell him of the occasion and what had been said. In his letter of reply Galileo wrote that Scripture should always be interpreted according to the discoveries of science, and not the other way round. Copies of this letter fell into unfriendly hands, and one was shown to the Inquisition. The inquisitors took no action, perhaps waiting for a more propitious moment, perhaps undecided about how to proceed. Galileo was emboldened by their inaction, and in 1616 wrote to the Grand Duchess Christina saying, 'I hold that the Sun is located at the centre of the revolutions of the heavenly orbs and does not change place, and that the Earth rotates on itself and moves around it. I confirm this view not only by refuting Ptolemy's and Aristotle's arguments, but also by producing many on the other side, especially some pertaining to physical effects whose causes perhaps cannot be determined in any other way, and other astronomical discoveries; these discoveries clearly confute the Ptolemaic system, and they agree admirably with the Copernican position and confirm it.'[48]

This letter also reached the wrong hands, and at last the Church felt that it must do something. Pope Paul V instructed Cardinal Bellarmine to refer the issue to the Sacred Congregation of the Index, this being the Inquisition's official designation. The cardinals of the Sacred Congregation took evidence and deliberated on the matter in February 1616, and came rapidly to a conclusion. They invited only theologians to speak before them; neither Galileo nor any other savant was called, or even offered a chance to submit evidence bearing on the matter. The cardinals' unsurprising conclusion was that the Copernican theory must be condemned, describing the view that the Sun sits at the centre of the universe as not only 'foolish and absurd' but heretical, and also that the claim that the Earth moves through space as 'at very least erroneous in faith.'[49]

Cardinal Bellarmine summoned Galileo and informed him that he was thenceforth forbidden to hold, defend or teach the Copernican theory.

A twist to this story is suggested by some historians, to the effect that neither Pope Paul V nor Bellarmine wished Galileo to be punished, and they had contrived to have the instruction to him phrased in such a way that he was not to hold or defend the theory, but with no prohibition against teaching it. This meant that he could have taught it while yet professing not to believe it, by this subterfuge being able to continue de facto to promote it. But when Bellarmine delivered the Sacred Congregation's ruling to Galileo, its members were present and waiting for an opportunity to catch Galileo out so that he could be prosecuted further. It was they who had inserted the prohibition against teaching, and they wished to see whether he would agree. Because the inquisitors were present he indeed had to agree; thus Bellarmine's ruse failed. This version of the story further says that Paul V invited Galileo to an audience and assured him that while he, Paul, was on the throne of St Peter, Galileo would come to no harm.[50]

This charming tale does not ring true. If Bellarmine and Paul V were so friendly to Galileo, and by implication to Copernican theory, they would not have admonished Foscarini as they did, and Galileo would not have been so silent for the remaining years of Paul V's papacy. Nor would he have waited to publish his next important work, *Il Saggiatore* (*The Assayer*), a treatise on scientific method, until a new and genuinely friendly pope was on the throne.

That new pope, Urban VIII, was elected in 1623. He had been Cardinal Maffeo Barberini, and had long been a friend to Galileo's work. Galileo immediately dedicated *Il Saggiatore* to him and published it. It contains a passage that became famous: 'Philosophy is written in this grand book, the universe, which stands continually open to our gaze. But the book cannot be understood unless one first learns to comprehend the language and read the characters in which it is written. It is written in the language of mathematics, and its characters are triangles, circles, and other geometric figures without which it is humanly impossible to understand a single word of it; without these one is wandering in a dark labyrinth.' The statement was a barbed one; it was prompted by a fanciful explanation published by a group of Jesuits concerning three comets seen in 1618. (The Jesuits were not the only ones to give the apparitions fanciful explanations; they figured also in the decision of Frederick V of the Palatine to accept the crown of Bohemia, thus providing a trigger for the Thirty Years War.)[51]

Despite the tendentious nature of Galileo's comments in the dedication to Urban VIII (or perhaps because of them: Urban is said to have laughed uproariously at Galileo's digs at the Jesuits when *Il Saggiatore* was read to him), the pope invited Galileo to six audiences in all, showing him great consideration and thereby encouraging him to believe he could return to teaching the Copernican theory openly in the *magnum opus* he was engaged upon, his *Dialogo dei due massimi sistemi del mondo* (*Dialogue Concerning the Two Chief World Systems*). Galileo's labours on this book proceeded slowly because of repeated ill health, so it was not completed until 1629. He sought permission for it to be published by the Accademia dei Lincei in Rome, but because the academy was in turmoil following the death of its president (the 'Chief Lynx'), and even though he had the censor's approval, he transferred publication to Florence, where after delays caused by outbreaks of the plague it eventually appeared in 1632.[52]

At first there were no signs of trouble, but Galileo's enemies – principally a Jesuit named Scheiner, rather aptly named given that he had written about sunspots, thus attracting Galileo's scorn, to which Scheiner responded with enmity – were alert for an opening. They found it in the fact that Galileo had printed the censor's preface to his book in different type to distance himself from it, and that he had put into the mouth of the defeated disputant in the *Dialogo* the comment that the Copernican system was a mere hypothesis. It happens that these words had been recommended for inclusion by the pope himself, the hitherto friendly Urban VIII, as a way of protecting the book. Galileo's enemies pointed out to Urban that attributing the words to the less intelligent and unsuccessful party to the debate was an insult, and Urban was duly infuriated. The Jesuits now had open season. They trawled through the files to find matter for an indictment, and found it in the judgement of 1616, which had forbidden Galileo not merely to hold or defend the Copernican system, but to teach it; and here he was manifestly teaching it by giving it to the winning party in the *Dialogo*.

Galileo was summoned to Rome. Pleading illness he put off going for as long as he could. His former protector at Florence, Cosimo II, had long since died, and the new Grand Duke was still too young to know how to play politics with the Vatican. Galileo arrived in Rome in February 1633, and was put on trial. The outcome was scarcely in doubt; threatened with torture the 69-year-old Galileo, arthritic and increasingly blind, recanted. He was made to state that 'I abjure, curse and detest my errors' and to deny that the Earth moved. He thereby saved himself from the stake. He was condemned to life imprisonment instead, but the sentence was gradually commuted to house arrest at his home in Arcetri. There he passed the final decade of his life productively engaged in writing his last great work, *Discorsi e dimostrazioni matematiche intorno a due nuove scienze (Discourses and Mathematical Demonstrations Concerning Two New Sciences)*, which summarised his lifetime's work, including investigation into the pendulum, inertia and mechanics, and setting out his views on scientific method. He was visited by many distinguished men, among them Thomas Hobbes and John Milton.[53]

With a mind like his, Galileo assuredly knew that although he had lost a battle he had won the war. His *Dialogo* and especially the *Discorsi* were hugely influential in the rest of Europe, and served as a major inspiration for the rapid scientific advances that followed. Italy, by contrast, scientifically frozen and paralysed by the Inquisition's condemnation of Galileo, became a stagnant backwater. The whole story affords vivid proof of the fact that liberty of thought and enquiry is essential for progress, now a cliché but then perceived as a danger to what were held as precious truths, all the more precious because they were bulwarks to an established order that did not wish to change.

To secure liberty for enquiry in an age in which religion was still a potent force, and when all were believers apart from a very few (and those few kept their non-belief secret), the most urgent need, as the case of Galileo showed, was to separate the sphere of religion from the sphere of science. The aim of most of the leading thinkers contemporary with Galileo, such as Descartes, Marin Mersenne, Pierre Gassendi and others, was to allow religion and science to cohabit by making them cease to be competitors for the truth over the same range of considerations. If religion could be shown to apply to things of the spirit and heaven, and science to the world of matter, there would be no need for religious authorities to be alarmed by scientific discoveries, and science could proceed unhindered.

The task of separating the combatants was undertaken by two outstanding figures, René Descartes and Francis Bacon. Descartes made substantial contributions to mathematics and science in addition to his philosophical work; Bacon did not, but his writings on scientific method were to prove influential, and he was cited with admiration in the incorporating documents of the Royal Society in London, whose founders regarded him as their inspiration.[54]

Descartes was professedly a devout Catholic all his life, and indeed wished that his scientific works would be adopted in their schools by the Jesuits (of whom he had been a pupil in his youth) for they were still teaching Aristotelianism and Thomism. In his *Meditationes de prima philosophia (Meditations on First Philosophy)* he argued that mind and matter are essentially different substances; mind is thinking stuff, *res cogitans*, and matter is spatial stuff, *res extensa*, and they require to be thought of in two quite different ways. Famously, the essential division he proposed between mind and matter caused his successors in the philosophical tradition endless problems over the question of how they interact. How, they asked, do thoughts cause bodily movements, and how do bodily events issue in feelings of pain and pleasure, thoughts and memories, in the private inner sphere of consciousness? It was a problem only solved by assimilating mind to matter, that is, taking mental phenomena to be the output of physical (specifically electrochemical) activity in the brain.[55]

But the question of interaction aside, Descartes' theory offered a solution to the problem of whether religious orthodoxy was controverted by regarding the material realm as amenable to description in

terms of wholly physical laws. In seventeenth-century science a dominant model was that of mechanism, the prime example being clock-
work. The structure and properties of matter were hypothesised in
terms of relations between atoms or 'corpuscles' ('little bodies') interacting according to the principles of mechanics. Unless this way of
thinking about the world could be sealed off from implications for
supposed religious truths, except in the sense that God had made the
mechanism and set it going, trouble would ensue. Descartes' views were
intended to effect that separation and avoid that trouble. In the end it
did not persuade the Church; his publications ended up on the Index of
Forbidden Books, as many of the world's best and most important
works have done (including the Bible). But this gesture by the Church
was empty; it was now in no position to stop the fast-rising tide of
science. No one who mattered took any notice of the Index, and
Descartes' separation of the realms served as a further licence for
scientifically minded people, who were already considering the possibility that if religion was not merely antique superstition now super-
seded, it applied to a different – and perhaps metaphorical – sphere
altogether.

Francis Bacon was more specific in his strictures on the science–
religion relationship. His chief aim was to outline methods of enquiry
that would arrive at truth, in contrast to the mystical and magical routes
to knowledge that 'occult scientists' – Hermeticists, Cabalists, astrol-
ogers, alchemists and others – claimed to know or be seeking in their
hunger to discover how to transform base metals into gold, concoct
elixirs of eternal youth or long life, foretell the future, control others or
fate, cure diseases, and in general crack the arcane secrets of the
universe.

Bacon's contrasting desire to specify routes to genuine knowledge
was shared by Descartes, as the latter's *Discours de la Méthode (Discourse
on Method)* shows. This work urged the rational procedure of starting
from clear and distinct ideas and progressing by small and wholly
certain deductive steps (which are constantly checked and reviewed) to
conclusions that would thereby be guaranteed to be true. But Bacon,
writing before Descartes, was an empiricist, and said that science must

be based on facts from which theory could be generalised by inductive inference. His view has been caricatured as suggesting that the enquirer is to accumulate observations randomly and then seek a theory to embrace and explain them, but obviously the gathering of observations has to be organised by having an hypothesis to test or a question to answer, so that one can know what observations will be relevant and whether they count as supporting or refuting the hypothesis. The caricature was an immediate and a persistent one; no lesser figures than Newton and Darwin subscribed to it. In the second edition of his *Principia* Newton wrote, 'hypotheses . . . have no place in experimental philosophy. In this philosophy particular propositions are inferred from the phenomena and afterward rendered general by inductions.' In his *Autobiography*, describing the development of his views about natural selection, Darwin wrote, 'it appeared to me that . . . by collecting all facts which bore in any way on the variation of animals and plants under domestication and nature, some light might be thrown on the whole subject. My first notebook was opened in July 1837. I worked on true Baconian principles, and without any theory collected facts on a wholesale scale.'[56]

It is clear enough that Bacon intended his advocacy of fact collection and inductive generalisation to be an advocacy of the experimental method, and as such it admits of interpretation as a putting-the-question-to-nature model. In fact Darwin's 'Baconian' method is precisely that, for in amassing data on variation in plants and animals he was looking for a pattern, so the quest for observational data was organised and not truly random. If this is Baconian method then Bacon's view was not quite as crude as the caricature suggests.

In fact the contrast Bacon intended is instructive. Science before his time had been largely based on deduction, an armchair enterprise premised on the supposed greater wisdom of the ancients and the indubitability of revelation. Between these two sources all truth was to be found. Bacon insisted, to the contrary, that enquiry should aim to establish how things actually are, by means of observation and experiment. He also argued that the results of such enquiry should be applied to the benefit of mankind. It is now a commonplace of applied science, as the very label suggests, that discovery, invention and the improvement of technique aim at utility; and it is also a commonplace that purely theoretical work, and the pursuit of knowledge for its own sake, might and very often does turn out to have practical applications also. But when Bacon made this point it was far from the standard view. Knowledge, if permissible, was for its own sake or the support of the prevailing orthodoxy.

Of course practical folk have always engaged in observing the world, learning from it, and on that basis inventing and improving technologies on farms and in manufactories, in blacksmiths' forges and ship-building yards. The idea of humanity as the tool-using ape par excellence captures this general truth. It is probable that for most of human history there was no sharp division between knowledge for its own sake and useful knowledge, between theory and practice. That had to wait until something like a leisure class could detach what at some point one of them described as 'higher learning' from the necessities of making and producing. Bacon's proposal restored the direct link, and implied that theory had as much if not more to learn from practice as the other way round.

Bacon was aware of the fallacies inherent in inductive inference if not properly controlled, and addressed the question of how reasoning about matters of fact and experiment was to be best done. This is the most controversial aspect of his work, and initiated a debate in philosophy that continues. But as the quotation from Darwin shows, practising scientists took his ideas seriously and applied them, not least in his own century when science came into its own.

There were other significant consequences of Bacon's views. One was that they changed the perspective on the nature of knowledge. The standard view was that the ancients were superior in knowledge and wisdom, for theirs was a golden age to which the sixteenth century could only look back in wonder and, to its best ability, emulate. A mark of this is that some people described Copernicus' model of the heavens as the 'Pythagorean system', regarding it as a restatement of a view from the treasure house of antiquity. Moreover God had come to earth in those ancient times to save mankind, which was another reason for thinking that history since had been a story of decline and regress.

Bacon's attitude was the opposite of this. He was typical of the side of the Renaissance that did not think of itself as engaged in backward-looking recovery and emulation only, but as literally a rebirth and therefore a new beginning. Science was progressive; it consisted in finding out new things, making improvements, promising to put mankind on a better footing higher up the scale of knowledge and capacity.

The crucial point is that none of this is possible unless scientific enquiry is genuinely free. Since at the time Bacon wrote it was anything but free, he found it necessary, as Descartes had done, to seek a way of separating religion and science so that the latter could progress. One task was to contest superstition, a natural and perennial adjunct of religion. He wrote, 'it was a good answer that was made by one who, when they showed him hanging in a temple a picture of those who had paid their vows as having escaped shipwreck, and would have him say whether he did not acknowledge the power of the gods, "Aye," he answered again, "but where are they painted that were drowned after their vows?"'

An intimate relation of superstition is, in Bacon's words, 'blind immoderate religious zeal'; that too had to be abated, for it was 'a troublesome and intractable enemy' to science. He commented on how charges of impiety were laid against those in ancient times who said that thunder was not the work of gods but had natural causes; how the same happened to geographers in early Christian times who said the Earth was a sphere and that the Antipodes were probably inhabited; and finally how 'in our own days discussions concerning nature have been subjected to even harsher constraint'.[57]

It was not enough to try to diminish superstition and zealotry; more direct defences of science were required, and Bacon attempted as much in saying that theologically agreeable philosophy, namely the doctrine of the four elements endorsed by Aristotle, was more likely to promote atheism than the atomism then being revived in the early seventeenth century. His argument was that a system of only four elements interacting to form all nature's phenomena was more likely to arise by chance than the right arrangement of infinities of minuscule atoms, which surely needed the wise government of an omniscient and omnipotent being to form the macroscopic objects of the visible world.[58]

The conclusion of all this for Bacon is that it is wrong to try to 'commix together' religion and science; doing so only perverts both, making for heretical religion and fanciful science. That indeed was what was happening anyway, and it was, said Bacon, a 'disastrous confusion'. His conception of an unfettered scientific community – whose aims and methods are described in *The Advancement of Learning* (1604) and the *Novum Organum Scientiarum* (1620) – working in laboratories and observatories freely, without supervision by religious authorities, has come to pass in the modern world; but as the conditions of Bacon's own time suggest, they would not have done so if the (sometimes dangerous) effort had not been made to wrest intellectual authority from the Church. The words Descartes quoted from Bacon in his own *Discours de la Méthode* – 'rightly conducting one's reason and seeking for truth in the sciences' – in themselves constitute a manifesto for liberty of enquiry. 'One's reason' – one's own reason – and 'seeking for truth' are concepts directly at odds with the idea of a religious orthodoxy dictating what one can and cannot reason about, and what the truth anyway is.

The upshot of the liberation of science from the control of religion is that science – or more accurately, the scientific attitude, the attitude of rational enquiry controlled by fact and applied to the good of human existence – came to replace religious belief as the source of authority over thought and action. Recognising the aspiration to that change of authority is the key to understanding the Enlightenment, informed in its very essence by the idea that the spirit of science should be extended into all domains. Newton ended his *Optics*, published in 1704, with the words, 'if natural philosophy [science] in all its parts, by pursuing this Method [i.e. scientific method], shall at length be perfected, the bounds of moral philosophy [ethics, politics, economics, psychology, history] will be also enlarged'. That was what the Enlightenment was: an enlargement of the scientific approach – to put it at its most general: the

empirically controlled, responsible, non-dogmatic exercise of reason –
to wider domains of concern. One major exemplification of that
approach is to be found in the *Encyclopédie* of Denis Diderot and
his colleagues; major examples of its consequences, to speak again in
general terms, are all the revolutions of the eighteenth century. Writing
in the middle of that century David Hume was able to say that there
had been 'a sudden and sensible change in the opinions of men within
these last fifty years, by the progress of learning and liberty'.[59] This was
more true of Britain than most parts of Europe – Voltaire had to live
within fleeing distance of the Swiss border in case his sometimes too
sharp writings got him into trouble, and Immanuel Kant in Königsberg
had his career inhibited by the Pietists of his city; however enlightened
the despots of Prussia and Russia claimed to be, they were still despots –
but the mental climate of the eighteenth century was such that it made
possible the two great liberty-claiming revolutions that distinguish it as
an epoch, as we shall see in a later chapter here.

4

The Fight against Absolutism

ONCE PEOPLE ARE FREE to think for themselves, it becomes inevitable that many among them will desire a greater control over their own actions too – or at very least, to have a share in decisions that affect their lives. The connection between the two types of liberty is so obvious that it comes as no surprise to find that just as liberty of conscience in matters of religion was swiftly followed by increasing liberty of thought and enquiry, so the latter was as swiftly followed by movements towards greater liberty in the political sphere. Nor does it come as any surprise that the justification for its opposite in the early centuries of the modern era was theological, in the form of the doctrine of the Divine Right of Kings.

Nor yet again does it come as a surprise that one of the main centres of the Enlightenment in the eighteenth century was France, given that the paradigmatic example of an absolute monarchy, justified by the purest form of Divine Right theory, was the France of Louis XIV.[1] Just over sixty years passed between the Sun King's death and the French Revolution, six momentous decades in which the lessons, sometimes painful, about government and power learned in England in the seventeenth century – the lessons of its Civil War and the events surrounding and following the abdication of James II – came to be applied in both the theory and practice of the American and French revolutions of the eighteenth century. The seminal ideas of rights and representation applied (although only partially achieved, and in the

French case only temporarily achieved) in those revolutions came to be fundamentals of contemporary Western self-definition – that is, the self-defining aspirations on which Western societies now, in our present day, take themselves to be based.

Most histories describe the events surrounding the English Civil War, premised on the conflict between Parliament and Charles I, as 'the English revolution', but that phrase actually denotes something longer and larger: not just the conflict between the rising middle classes and the absolute powers of the Crown as embodied in the armed civil conflicts of the 1630s and 1640s, but the crucially important sequel to them. This was the 'Glorious Revolution' settlement of 1689, when Parliament chose who would wear the Crown whose powers had been significantly limited by the Bill of Rights passed in that year (embodying the rights of Parliament vis-a-vis the crown, not the rights of the people), and the much longer-term results that flowed from it.[2]

The actual historical events of the decades between 1630 and 1690 in England have their contrasting theoretical reflection and justification in the political writings of Thomas Hobbes and John Locke.[3] The seminal contribution of the latter gave the new dispensation its intellectual imprimatur. And as the importance of both Hobbes' and Locke's reflections imply, the English political experience of the seventeenth century is a key event in Western history, because it opened the way to the series of major anti-absolutist, pro-representative revolutions which followed in the next three centuries: the American, French and (in its first inspiration) Russian revolutions – and equally importantly, the evolutions of democracy and representative government first in North America and then in Britain, which paved the way for the development of liberal democracy in other parts of the world.[4]

To get a measure of the immense change wrought in the seventeenth century, one need only compare the England of Elizabeth I and Shakespeare with the England of Queen Anne and Newton. In almost every respect the transformation from the world of the late Renaissance to the beginnings of true modern times is made manifest by this contrast. In Shakespeare's *Macbeth*, written in the century's first decade, the killing of a king is deemed so horrific, so against the divine disposition of things, that unnatural events and portents appear on the night of the murder, and hag-ridden magic permeates the tragedy. In 1649 the English beheaded their king, and in 1688 changed another for a more acceptable replacement – acceptable to the governing class, that is – and then the latter chose to whom the Crown would devolve thereafter, at every step limiting its powers and reinforcing their own hold on government. It took until 1929 for full adult suffrage to be instituted in the United Kingdom, but the incremental widening of the franchise that occurred throughout the nineteenth century was an inevitable, if slow, result of these first steps in the transfer of power from a monarch to the people. From the regicidal horrors of Duncan's 'taking off' in Shakespeare's imagination, to the reality of Parliament's handing the Crown to William of Orange, is a leap across an immense gap.

This degree of change seen in England between the beginning of the seventeenth century and the beginning of the eighteenth is not so obvious elsewhere in Europe. It is not so obvious, for example, in France, where the grip of the centralised Bourbon monarchy was, as Louis XIV's reign proved, not shaken but strengthened by the revolution of the Fronde, which occurred in 1648 when Louis XIV was still a child and a regent governed in his place.[5] The reinvigoration of the monarchy caused by the Fronde was due in considerable part to Louis' memory of suffering indignities during its course – he and his mother, Anne of Austria, had spent a hungry and frightened winter in circumstances resembling internal exile at the height of the troubles – which made him determined not to allow a repetition. When he could he established his court at Versailles, away from the Paris mob, and he weakened the nobility by obliging it to disperse its energies and money in time-wasting attendance at court. Moreover he diluted the nobility by creating thousands of new peers, so that by the time of the Terror following the 1789 revolution – inevitably provoked by the absolutism Louis practised in response to the earlier revolution – the aristocrats who went to the guillotine were of a different vintage from the Fronde nobles who had sought to oust Cardinal Mazarin, the chief minister in Louis' regency government.[6]

As Louis XIV's reign is the paradigm of absolute monarchy in practice, so the views of Locke are the most significant contribution to theoretical rejection of absolutism. Locke was not the architect but the justifier and explainer of what happened in the anti-absolutist settlement of the Glorious Revolution, but that is exactly why his writings on the subject proved to be seminal for the political movements in North America and France nearly a century later. It is one thing to urge major political change, another to provide an exposition of the principles on which major political change has successfully occurred. Locke's career as secretary and physician to Lord Shaftesbury – involving danger and a period of exile in the Netherlands before and during the reign of James II – put him at the heart of the crucial events that made England a constitutional monarchy. It is a mark of their impact on the justification of this development that his writings are quoted verbatim and at length in the documents of the American and French revolutions, and that the French Enlightenment thinkers regarded him as one of the gods of the new pantheon.

To see what the task of political liberation was up against, nothing could be more instructive than the absolute monarchy of Louis XIV and the doctrines that purported to justify it.

An absolute monarch is one over whom there is no higher authority than himself (other than God; some thought they were God – Caligula; and some are God – the Japanese emperor), and who therefore, in theory at least, acts without any restraints except for his own conscience and what he accepts of tradition. He is above the law, and has no legitimately recognised opposition. His power over his subjects is technically unlimited. The terms of qualification in this definition – 'in theory' and 'technically' – convey the reality that absolute rulers are rarely without some constraint, even if it is the ultimate constraint of assassination or rebellion provoked by cruel or arbitrary use of their powers: witness Caligula and the like.

Absolute monarchy in the form relevant here emerged from the demise of medieval feudalism. In that dispensation kings were in effect chieftains among chiefs, the senior member of a clique who maintained power jointly by force. The term 'peer' to describe a nobleman preserves what was once a reality, namely, the near-equality of the great barons with the king (or more rarely queen) to whom they were related politically and by blood. In this arrangement it was not only the constraint of degrees of baronial loyalty required by the king to stay in power, but an evolved framework of traditions, customs, rights and grants (the latter often made by the Crown in exchange for money or support) that kept the Crown's power in check. But with the development of more centralised government, finance and military organisation, the power of kings grew and that of nobilities decreased.[7]

The great question in political theory is always: what is the source of a governing agency's power or authority? In earliest times the source of authority was sheer might; in the feudal era might was jointly wielded by the self-serving cartel of noble families among whom the king was first among equals; in democratic theory it is the will of the people. For the increasingly centralised monarchical arrangements that evolved from the fifteenth century onwards a new justification was required. Might was no longer enough of a justification; the peers were no longer equals; the monarch both reigned and ruled – but by what right?

The answer was found in an adaptation of a practice that the Church had promoted during its period of greatest power in the later medieval era, that of sanctifying kingship by papal blessing. From Rome's point of view this was an expression of the principle that St Peter's throne is first among thrones, and Christendom is a single imperium from which devolves the authority of the local kingdoms within it. From the point of view of the 'local' kings themselves, despite not all of them being happy to go along with this papacy-aggrandising view, having the imprimatur of the Church could be useful at such times as disputed successions or violent changes in ownership of the Crown.

One can see a progression: at one point getting one's hands on royal insignia – the sceptre, the crown itself, the badges of office – had been a significant matter, because the symbols of power and the actuality of power were once so intimately connected. But then the mark of divine approval or election came to be a necessity. Shakespeare's conception of kingship is instructive here: as he describes it, kingship has a status that is part-holy, part-magical, far above the ordinary, untouchable except at peril, where everything normally human is magnified by that status into epic and – when things go wrong – tragic proportions.

But no sooner had the divine ordination of kingship become the basis on which kings claimed the absolute nature of their authority, than Christendom began splitting into many fragments, in each of which the rulers required their subjects to follow the ruler's own choice of religion – the Augsburg principle of *cuius regio, eius religio*, 'the religion of the ruler is the religion of his people' – and in some of which rulers went further and made themselves the head of the national Church (as Henry VIII did in England). It was no longer so clear who conveyed the divine sanction, if it was not the pope. In England the Archbishop of Canterbury officiated at coronations. Whatever the mechanics, the idea remained that a king was a divinely chosen and – as the ritual at the coronation actually showed – anointed head of state, to whom allegiance was therefore a religious duty.

The man who played Locke's role as justifier and theoriser in the absolute monarchy of Louis XIV, but to quite different effect, was Jacques-Benigne Bossuet.[8] Following an earlier French theoretician with similar ideas about monarchy, the sixteenth-century writer Jean Bodin, Bossuet provided the theoretical justification for Louis' arrogation of absolute power – most famously summed up in Louis' claim *l'état, c'est moi* – in his *Politique tirée des propres paroles de l'Écriture sainte* (*Politics Taken From the Very Word of Scripture*) (1679). Certain passages from Scripture had become commonplaces of the monarchical tradition: Proverbs 8: 15–16 says, 'By me kings reign, and princes decree justice. By me princes rule, and nobles, even all the judges of the earth.' In Romans 13: 1–2 St Paul says, 'Let every soul be subject unto the higher powers. For there is no power but of God. Whosoever therefore resisteth the power, resisteth the ordinance of God: and they that resist shall receive to themselves damnation.'

These are exceedingly useful passages for tyrants, and Bossuet found others. 'We have already seen that all power is of God,' he wrote. 'The ruler, adds St Paul, "is the minister of God to thee for good. But if thou do that which is evil, be afraid; for he beareth not the sword in vain; for he is the minister of God, a revenger to execute wrath upon him that doeth evil." Rulers then act as the ministers of God and as his lieutenants on earth. It is through them that God exercises his empire. Think you to withstand the kingdom of the Lord in the hand of the sons of David? Consequently, as we have seen, the royal throne is not the throne of a man but the throne of God himself. The Lord "hath chosen Solomon my son to sit upon the throne of the kingdom of Israel." And again, "Solomon sat on the throne of the Lord." . . . It appears from all this that the person of the king is sacred, and that to attack him in any way is sacrilege. God has the kings anointed by his prophets with the holy unction in like manner as he has his bishops and altars anointed . . . Kings should be guarded as holy things, and whosoever neglects to protect them is worthy of death . . . The royal power is absolute . . . The prince need render account of his acts to no one.'

Despite the slavish appearance of these views, and contrary to their implications, Bossuet was far from conflating the idea of absolute power with that of arbitrary power. Amid all this Louis-flattering theory were indications of the constraints implied by the theory itself, and they turn out to be severe: 'But kings, although their power comes from on high, should not regard themselves as masters of that power to use it at their pleasure . . . they must use it with fear and self-restraint, as a thing coming from God and of which God will demand an account . . . Kings should tremble then as they use the power God has granted them; and let them think how horrible is the sacrilege if they use for evil a power which comes from God. We behold kings seated upon the throne of the Lord, bearing in their hands the swords which God himself has given them. What pro-fanation, what arrogance, for the unjust king to sit on God's throne to render decrees contrary to his laws and to use the sword which God has put in his hand for deeds of violence and to slay his children!'[9]

There is a contradiction implicit in Bossuet's account. The king is absolute in power, yet if he misuses that power he has gone against God's law, and the question therefore arises whether in doing so he has forfeited the divine election. In such circumstances can the Church uncrown him? Can the nobility, the clergy, the people resist him? Once a priest has been ordained it does not matter whether he sins, he can still administer the Sacraments because the (so to say) magic in him is independent of him, once the laying on of hands has occurred. Is this true also of kings? It was certainly easy for Bossuet's king to claim to rule by Divine Right while living a venal existence.

'Divine Right': the very phrase would seem odd, as denoting a deity's disposition of rights to a mortal man or woman to rule a portion of earth, if belief in it were not an historical reality. It is surprising that those who invoked the notion did not see that it rested on nothing more elaborate than the primitive notion that might is right, for it is the deity's vast and inexorable power to punish and dispose that enforces the 'right' of a king to rule by supposed dictate of what that deity wills. As concepts of deity evolved, from animistically conceived nature spirits to tribal gods, to the Sun and Moon, to invisible anthropomorphic agencies above the clouds or in some non-physical realm – thus increasing in abstraction and remoteness as knowledge of the physical world made belief in animism or the divine nature of the Sun and Moon less tenable – so the idea of their power over nature and humanity went with them, their unlimited physical strength (they could shake the earth, raise the sea in flood, cause thunder, kill multitudes of humans at a blow) giving them irresistible power over creation. The only difference between these primitive gods and the Gods of the (relatively young) monotheistic religions that have been dominant in the last two to three millennia – Christianity and Islam – is that all the power in question, and the abstraction into something outside the world but somehow active within it, has been placed in a single deity.

In the theory of Divine Right this power is what elects and invests the anointed king, who is therefore its earthly representative and even (as the more outrageous of the flatterers of Louis XIV had it) its embodiment. Only when religious belief is general could such a claim persuade. It is a mark of the loss of religion's grip that the Divine Right theory itself was being questioned in the seventeenth century, even as it was having one of its last major manifestations in the majestic shape of Louis XIV.

Louis was fully seized of the Divine Right by which he ruled. In childhood he had a text called *Educatio Regia* read to him, in which he was encouraged to remind himself every morning that he had to play the part of God in his kingdom, and to ask himself each evening whether he had succeeded in doing so: *Hodie mihi gerenda est persona Dei . . . Deusne hodie an homo fui?* In a memoir written for his son the dauphin he wrote, 'holding as it were the place of God we seem to participate in his wisdom as in his authority; for instance, in what concerns discernment of human character, allocation of employments and distribution of rewards.'[10]

History is divided over the question of how much divine wisdom Louis displayed: some comment that he appointed lesser men as ministers than he had inherited, which calls his judgement into question; others note his ability to grasp information and turn it to good use, which suggests that he was not without abilities relevant to his position. What is certain is that he had no time for the tangle of constitutional traditions and customs that had grown around the throne, and proceeded to dispense with them. The *Parlement* of Paris was given no share in the government of the realm, and within three years of Louis' attaining his majority and beginning personal rule in 1662 it had lost its status as a sovereign court. Louis did not bother to summon the States-General until late in his reign, during the War of the Spanish Succession, and even then he only called an Assembly of Notables. He gave no place to clergy and nobility in his government except in purely ceremonial capacities; his was personal rule, aided only by four ministerial councils and several secretaries of state. He was a classic absolute monarch.[11]

The secretaryships through which Louis governed were divided among two bourgeois families of professional civil servants, the Louvois and Colbert families, who owed Louis personal loyalty. They were not always competent; one of the worst misjudgements of Louis' reign was his revocation of the Edict of Nantes which, together with chronic mismanagement of the national finances and frequent and expensive wars, was a blow to France's economy from which it did not recover until the nineteenth century. The chief blow was sustained under Louvois management of the exchequer, following a period in which a Colbert had managed to stem the haemorrhage of public funds.[12]

Yet Louis maintained his absolutist grip by keeping the nobility weak and distracted, and the populace in love with him. His procedure on the first of these was simple. He never forgot the treachery of the nobility in the Fronde, and he took care to ensure that it would not be in a position to repeat the offence. Nobles by birth were expected to attend almost permanently at court, whose elaborate ritual and protocol required that scores of nominal offices had to be filled, from Grand Chamberlain downwards. Since an apartment in the palace of Versailles went with such appointments, nobles vied for them, and time and money were endlessly expended in keeping up appearances and carrying out empty duties. Moreover Louis kept bankruptcy away and the nobility in a state of ever-increasing dilution by selling large numbers of peerages, creating scores of new nominal offices with patents of nobility attached, and making the *noblesse de robe* hereditary and thus closer in status to the *noblesse d'épée*.[13]

As for the adulation of the populace, it is not so easy to explain; it happened that the French passed through a period of idolisation of their king, seeming dazzled by the theatrical splendours of royal pomp at Versailles – which the masses could know only by report and woodcuts – blind to the fact that Louis had his court there precisely to keep as far away from them as possible. He was a tall, humourless, outwardly emotionless man (though his attachments to his mistresses and their children show that he had an affectionate and indeed amorous side), and this gave him an air both regal and authoritative, which doubtless added to his people's admiration for him. But there is little in what he did for them, apart from imposing war and taxes upon them, that could explain the phenomenon of their affection, other than that they chose to give it.

The absolutism of Louis' kingship expressed itself in a variety of ways. He asserted that he owned all the land of France; what was thought of as private property in fact belonged to him, the titular owners merely having the usufruct. This was the logical conclusion of a view that absolute sovereignty is equivalent to absolute 'dominium', or ownership, of the kingdom. One contemporary critic of Louis (one of the few in France), Jurieu, claimed that there had been a scheme early in Louis' reign to confiscate all private property and rent it back to its former owners in order to fill the royal coffers, but that it was shelved indefinitely. Having the principle in place was obviously useful enough should a day of necessity for it come. As an expression of the doctrine of absolute monarchy it could not be more telling.[14]

Another aspect of absolutism was that since the king is answerable only to God, he is not bound by agreements with men, including other monarchs; and that meant that he was not bound by international treaties. Louis regarded treaties as stop-gaps for dealing with temporary circumstances, and as the history of his reign shows he abrogated them whenever convenient. In his memoir to the dauphin there is a blunt statement of this view; asseverations in treaties of eternal amity and alliance are, said Louis, merely diplomatic courtesies, and mean nothing beyond the treaty's useful lifetime.

A third aspect of absolutism is that the king is above the law, and this Louis certainly was. Among the legal traditions thought to be binding on the French monarchy was one to the effect that the succession descended through the legitimate male line only. Louis invoked it in decreeing that Philip V of Spain was entitled to his claim to the succession, thereby precipitating the War of the Spanish Succession, and then ignored it in saying that his bastards could stand in line to the succession in default of a legitimate heir. Laws and traditions thus stood on the same footing for Louis; they were conveniences at best, and never binding, existing as much for the breach as the observance at the dictates of expediency. Given this, it might be said that Louis was rather continent than otherwise in this respect, at least in domestic policy – another reason why he maintained his popularity among his own people.

With the Glorious Revolution of 1688 and the articulation of its principles by Locke, England emphatically repudiated the doctrine of

Divine Right. The principles were in essence those of parliamentary government founded on democracy, though actual democracy was a long time coming, and the true significance of the principles was only appreciated in England when George III acted in ways contrary to them nearly a century later.[15]

Locke provided a much-needed written defence to underpin the political authority which Parliament had arrogated to itself by declaring that King James' throne was now vacant, and then filling it with its own choice of incumbent, William of Orange, after protracted negotiations about what he could and could not do once on it. The de facto legitimacy of what Parliament did in these respects lay in the political turmoil of half a century before, when those who took arms on the parliamentary side in the Civil War did not see themselves as engaged only in settling a quarrel between King and Commons. The Independents and Levellers who called for adult suffrage and frequent parliaments were aiming for a genuine implementation of democracy; they represented a class insisting on its right to participation in the direction of their own and the country's affairs.[16] Other movements were enabled by the conditions of the time to speak out too: the Diggers of the seventeenth century argued for the common ownership of land so that all might have sustenance; the immediate history of their complaint was the enclosures that had been going on for over a century, in which landowners drove many people from the land, many of whom in turn died of starvation.

All the movements could trace a long history of a struggle for liberty in many guises, from Aelfric's pre-Norman Conquest Latin instruction book with its poignant conversation between an inquirer and a ploughman ('Master: And that is hard work? Ploughman: Yes, it is hard work, because I am not free') to William Longbeard of London, to William Holderby, the first organiser of agricultural labour against the landowners, and so on through centuries of intermittent attempted risings and rebellions stirred by hardship and injustice, by hunger in the belly and the hunger to be free. There is a long roll of honour naming those who acted for the rights, liberties and entitlements of the poor and oppressed – 'the poor and oppressed': such a glib formula; yet what a world of human suffering it encapsulates! – and the Diggers count among them.[17]

The Diggers' claims were symptomatic of how far the mood for change went. In other circumstances their movement might have effected what the rural poor needed, but in the event – though in the medium term intermitted by the Restoration – what happened was much more conservative and incremental, namely, the first permanent step in the transfer of power from Crown to Parliament. In practice the events of 1688 gave the great Whig families, and after a time their Tory equivalents, the levers of government; but the shift of power that had begun was to result, over the next two centuries, in its moving from the landed class to the middle class, and then onwards and outwards until full adult suffrage was attained.

The sophistication of English political dissent is evident in *An Agreement of the People for a Firme and Present Peace, upon the Grounds of Common-right and Freedome*, drafted by the Army Council in response to what the soldiers of the parliamentary army wanted, and printed on 3 November 1647. 'Having by our late labours and hazards made it appear to the world at how high a rate we value our just freedom,' it begins, 'and God having so far owned our cause as to deliver the enemies thereof into our hands, we do now hold ourselves as bound in mutual duty to each other to take the best care we can for the future to avoid both the danger of returning into a slavish condition and the chargeable remedy of another war; for, as it cannot be imagined that so many of our countrymen would have opposed us in this quarrel if they had understood their own good, so may we safely promise to ourselves that when our common rights and liberties shall be cleared, their endeavours will be disappointed that seek to make themselves our masters.' The Agreement then specifies that Parliament be reformed, with a proper distribution of seats by population in all counties, cities and boroughs, the franchise being complete adult male suffrage, that elections be held every two years, and that 'the power of this, and all future Representatives of this Nation, is inferior only to theirs who choose them'.

To this parliamentary democracy, imperfect only in excluding women from the franchise, is then added complete religious toleration, no conscription into the armed forces, a provision that laws must apply equally to all and must always conduce to the good, the safety, and the well-being of the people. 'These things we declare to be our native rights,' the *Agreement* continues, 'and therefore are agreed and resolved to maintain them with our utmost possibilities against all opposition whatever, being compelled thereunto by the examples of our ancestors, whose blood was often spent in vain for the recovery of their freedoms, [and] also by our own woeful experience who, having long expected, and dearly earned, the establishment of these certain rules of government, are yet made to depend for the settlement of our peace and freedom upon him [i.e. Charles I] that intended our bondage and brought a cruel war upon us.'

One has to admire the dexterity with which the ruling classes delayed implementation of these democratic demands for several centuries more, and how in some particulars they are delayed still; and how they were eked out in the smallest parcels capable of deflecting revolt (the mobs in the streets of London broke windows in their demand for reform of Parliament in 1832, yet were pacified by a grudgingly small measure). This is important background to understanding Locke's justification of (an unreformed) Parliament's seizure of power in 1688, something that Cromwell was unable in the end to do, as demonstrated by the fact that Charles II had serious hopes of instituting just the kind of government that Louis XIV began to construct when he came to his majority in 1662, two years after Charles' own restoration.

The two connected points permanently established by the revolution of 1688 were that Parliament is effectively sovereign, and that the concept of Divine Right to justify royal authority was dead. By placing William on the throne on the basis of a negotiated agreement concerning his privileges and powers, Parliament had asserted both points simultaneously, for it would have been impossible for anyone to argue that he ruled by Divine Right instead of by the pleasure of Parliament. Parliament controlled the national finances and the army, and had to be summoned annually to vote the former; by this simple move was its power assured. The independence of the judiciary and the right of petition were likewise secured, remarkably in the same Act that disinherited the formerly rightful heirs to the throne.

Locke's aim was to 'establish the throne of our great Restorer, our present King William, and make good his title in the consent of the people'. This is a frank statement of an intention to carry out the political art of what is now called 'spin'; but it was necessary in the uneasy circumstances of the time, in which some (the Tories especially) were unhappy about the constitutionality of what had happened. The blunder of Louis XIV in recognising James II's heir as rightful king of England also helped to allay a certain degree of popular doubt.

The key document is Locke's second *Treatise on Civil Government*. The first treatise is a detailed rebuttal of Sir Robert Filmer's argument in favour of Divine Right, Filmer being the English Bossuet in this debate. Filmer derived the rights of the kings of England from Adam in Eden, to whom and to whose heirs God had granted sovereignty over all things, thus (said Filmer) instituting absolute monarchy as a permanent political arrangement for mankind. Locke patiently followed him through the course of history to challenge his case. Some question why Locke gave Filmer's book so much attention; the answer is doubtless that it served as a stalking horse for bigger prey, in the form of Thomas Hobbes' version of absolutism.

Filmer's book is entitled *Patriarcha*, with the subtitle 'A Defence of the Natural Power of Kings against the Unnatural Liberty of the People'. It was written in defence of Charles I during his reign, but was not published until 1680 when moves were afoot to exclude James from succeeding Charles II, which fully explains its then appearance. His arguments in favour of absolute monarchy are similar to Bossuet's, basing themselves on Scripture and historical precedent. They lead him to say that he agrees with Hobbes about 'the Rights of exercising government', namely, that the sovereign power must be absolute, though he could 'not agree to his means of acquiring it', which for Filmer could only be done by legitimate descent from a predecessor on a royal throne occupied by Divine Right.

Locke did not address Hobbes directly because Hobbes was an atheist – *nom terrible* in the seventeenth century and for long afterwards

– whose views were such that they could be invoked equally to support the Stuarts or a republican polity. Given the practical task in hand, Locke was not minded to support King William on the throne by citing and engaging with Hobbes' work, in case its argument was invoked by the opposition because Locke had reminded them of it. So Hobbes is not mentioned; but his presence looms in the background.

Hobbes' fundamental concern was the security of individuals against the depredations and dangers they would suffer in a 'state of nature' – the hypothetical condition without law and institutions that exists before civil society comes into being, and in which each man is for himself alone – which in his view would consist and in a state of war of all against all, making life (in his famous phrase) 'poor, nasty, brutish and short'. Without a source of authority capable of ensuring the safety of all and the good order of their interrelationships, there is not even safety in numbers: 'be there never so great a multitude; yet if their actions be directed according to their particular judgements, and particular appetites, they can expect thereby no defence, no protection, neither against a common enemy, nor against the injuries of another'.[18]

To ensure safety their actions need to be guided by a 'common power' which Hobbes named the 'Leviathan' – the entity – and this might be a monarch, a unified republican oligarchy, or any other single governing entity. By a contract that each individual member of the commonwealth has with his fellows, this entity has the absolute power to direct affairs within it. 'For by this authority, given him by every particular man in the commonwealth, he hath the use of so much power and strength conferred on him, that by terror thereof, he is enabled to form the wills of them all, to peace at home, and mutual aid against their enemies abroad. And in him consisteth the essence of the commonwealth which is, to define it, *one person, of whose acts a great multitude, by mutual covenant one with another, have made themselves every one the author, to the end he may use the strength and means of them all, as he shall think expedient, for their peace and common defence.*'[19]

The contract underlying this arrangement is what carries men out of the dangerous and strife-torn state of nature into civil society. By their contract with each other men create a sovereign authority, and authorise it to act as an absolute power over them. The sovereign does not reciprocally have a contract with its subjects, but rather has two important 'rights' pertinent to its ability to carry out its function: one is that it cannot be set aside by its subjects, having been created by their mutual contract, and the other is that it cannot be accused of treating its subjects unjustly. The reason in both cases is that the sovereign is the embodiment of the will of the people expressed through their mutual contract for their own benefit, so for anyone to challenge the sovereign is in effect for him to challenge himself and thus to contradict the very reason for creating the sovereign in the first place. The example of injury illustrates the point: 'by this institution of a commonwealth, every particular man is author of all that the sovereign doth; and consequently he that complaineth of injury from his sovereign, complaineth of that whereof he himself is author; and therefore ought not to accuse any man but himself; no nor himself of injury; because to do injury to one's self is impossible.'[20]

These two 'rights' of the sovereign are what make it absolute in power. It alone can decide matters of foreign policy, war and defence; it determines what can be said and thought in the commonwealth; it adjudicates property rights, is the final court of appeal in all matters of law, decides all punishments, makes all appointments, and distributes all honours. These powers are 'the essence of sovereignty', Hobbes said; they are 'the marks whereby a man may discern in what man, or assembly of men, the sovereign power is placed and resideth'.[21]

Although all law is made by the sovereign which is itself above the law, nevertheless the exercise of sovereignty has to accord with the reason why it exists, namely, to ensure order and security for its subjects. The sovereign's 'office', says Hobbes, 'consisteth in the end, for which he was trusted with the sovereign power, namely the procuration of *the safety of the people*; to which he is obliged by the law of nature, and to render an account thereof to God, the author of that law, and to none but him.'[22]

There is an uncanny resemblance between Hobbes' 'Leviathan', or absolute sovereign, and today's British House of Commons. This is not a flippant remark, but a comment on the almost unbridled powers of that assembly, the checks on whose actions through judicial review, the delaying powers of the Upper House, and requirements in the Human Rights Act to revisit legislation not in conformity with its provisions, are all weak and not binding on the will of the House, which can in theory do almost anything it chooses by simple majority. In practice the restraint of public opinion, press comment, the prospect of future elections, tradition, recalcitrant back-bench Members of Parliament, and a sometimes surprising irruption of common sense and humanity, restrain it. But these are contingent restraints only, and the unwritten British constitution does not provide checks and balances in it as in the formal constitutions of the United States and other countries. For example: in other European democracies the equivalent of the Human Rights Act empowers courts to strike down legislation inconsistent with its provisions. Not so in the United Kingdom; courts can only require the administration to look again at inconsistent legislation, and Parliament has the power to repeal the Human Rights Act if it finds it inconvenient. In the short life of that Act, at the time of writing, it has indeed already proved itself inconvenient to the government, and Parliament is already considering repealing or weakening it. This, though with the addition of a due process for enacting its will (whose effect is to slow but not prevent that enaction), makes the House of Commons uncomfortably Leviathan-like.

It is easy to see the flaws in Hobbes' view. He slides from the implicit contract that rescues people from the state of nature to assuming that each individual is fully and consciously signed up to it; he takes this to entail that individuals cannot challenge the sovereign power thereafter, which means that he assumes that the authors of that power – the people – have no say in checking it, recalling it, or having an input into it once they have created it; and his grounds are the spurious ones that their being able to do so would subvert the point of their instituting it in the first place. The ultimate appeal to 'the law of nature' as the sole authority over the sovereign is weak and ill-defined, and in itself contradictory; if a law of nature exists that binds the sovereign to ensure the good of its subjects, specifically because its own end is the good of those individuals, then there is no obvious reason why it could not prevail in the 'state of nature' itself – its natural habitat, so to say – perhaps by the operation of a 'light of nature' (reason) in mankind. This would obviate the need for an absolute ruler altogether.

The concept of natural law, and with it that of natural rights, figures centrally in Locke's account of these matters, but with a quite different tendency. Like Hobbes, he utilised the idea of a state of nature before civil society, but he did not see it as a realm of strife in which each preys on each. Instead he thought of it as the locus of the natural freedom that individuals partly forfeit in order to gain the benefits of living in society with others, but which at the same time places limits on what those agreements can take away from people individually – in particular, their rights to life, liberty and property. It follows immediately from this that government by an absolute authority in Hobbes' or Filmer's sense is illegitimate, because it is inconsistent with the natural freedom of man that no contract establishing civil society can abolish.

Natural law and natural rights are closely interconnected. The latter rest on the fact that people in the state of nature have the free use of what the world provides; natural law is whatever people are enjoined to do and prohibited from doing in light of how things naturally are. For Locke, man is perfectly free in the state of nature: 'all men are naturally in . . . a *state of perfect Freedom* to order their actions, and dispose of their Possessions, and Persons as they think fit, within the bounds of the Law of Nature, without asking leave, or depending on the Will of any Man.' (His alternative formulation is, 'In the beginning all the World was *America*.')[23] This is because all men are equal in the natural state, and therefore none has any entitlement to dictate what others shall do. This meets Filmer's claim that hierarchy is natural because God gave dominion to Adam over his wife and sons, and thence by descent to all men. But for Locke because men are 'furnished with like Faculties, sharing all in one Community of Nature, there cannot be supposed any such *Subordination* among us, that may authorise us to destroy one another, as if we were made for one another's uses, as the inferior ranks of Creatures are made for ours.'[24]

This last consideration, says Locke, immediately entails a set of obligations binding on each individual, these being (in order of priority) self-preservation and active concern for the preservation of others. The latter includes not causing harm to others, and both involve ensuring that those who break these obligations, or in any way transgress the laws of nature, should be punished.

Now, in the state of nature it is difficult to ensure that these obligations can be fulfilled; Locke describes this as the 'inconvenience' of the state of nature; and if a sovereign were instituted with limitless and illimitable powers matters would be yet worse, for nothing could restrain it from waging war on its own subjects. In principle therefore it is wrong for people to submit themselves to an absolute sovereign, for they thereby render themselves incapable of carrying out the obligations imposed by the laws of nature. 'Freedom from Absolute, Arbitrary power is so necessary to, and closely joyned with a Man's Preservation, that he cannot part with it, but by what he forfeits his Preservation and Life together. For a Man, not having the Power of his own Life, cannot, by Compact, or his own Consent, *enslave himself* to any one, nor put himself under the Absolute, Arbitrary power of another, to take away his life, when he pleases. No body can give more Power than he has himself; and he that cannot take away his own Life, cannot give another power over it.'[25] This is Locke's answer to Hobbes, and to absolutism in general.

There is a dubious move here. It is that people do not (so to say) own themselves because (implicitly) God does, and therefore cannot convey ownership of themselves to another. In fact it must be a moot point whether an individual can enslave himself to another; the fact that the vast majority of people would not like to be enslaved does not entail that no right exists to volunteer one's freedom away. It would certainly be an odd situation for a person to claim the freedom to cease being free, but oddity is a human characteristic.

Still, the tendency of Locke's point is clear. The whole purpose of human beings joining together in societies is to ensure the preservation of their lives, liberty and property. Settled laws that everyone knows, independent and neutral judges to decide them, and power to ensure the implementation of their decisions, solves the problem faced in the state of nature of how people are to fulfil the obligations of the laws of nature. The sovereignty created to these ends has to be consistent with those purposes and obligations: a man 'having in the State of Nature no Arbitrary Power over the Life, Liberty, or Possession of another, but only so much as the Law of Nature gave him for the preservation of himself, and the rest of Mankind; this is all he doth, or can give up to the Common-wealth, and by it to the *Legislative Power*, so that the Legislative can have no more than this. Their Power in the utmost Bounds of it, is *limited to the publick good* of the Society.'[26] If the legislature acts in ways that run contrary to this, or oversteps its powers, it thereby ceases to be legitimate; Locke says it 'dissolves' itself. If it continues to exercise power nevertheless, it has become a despotism. In these circumstances it can no longer claim the loyalty of the people, who therefore have not merely the right but an obligation to overthrow it and replace it with a legitimate government.

These latter points, which occur in the final chapter of the second *Treatise on Civil Government*, are of course directly relevant to the deposition of James II and the installation of William and Mary in his place. At the same time they introduce a notion that has since been profoundly influential in the development of democratic theory, and indeed democratic forms of government. This is that power, whatever body or person it resides in, is a trusteeship held in behalf of those whose consent has endowed that body with that power in the first place. This is why rebellion is justified when the government trespasses beyond its contract with the people, for then the contract whereby it holds its power is at an end. '*Who shall be Judge* whether the Prince or the Legislative act contrary to their trust?' Locke asked; and answered, '*The people shall be Judge*; for who shall be Judge whether his Trustee or Deputy acts well, and according to the Trust reposed in him, but he who deputes him, and must, by having deputed him have still a Power to discard him, when he fails in his Trust?'[27]

Among the many important aspects of Locke's view is its contrast with Hobbes' view in respect of what the state of nature is like. For Hobbes the state of nature is a condition of dangerous and unsustainable anarchy characterised by an innate immorality of greed and carelessness about the welfare of others. For Locke the state of nature certainly lacks in effective means for ensuring that the dictates of the laws of nature will be carried out in regular, just and appropriate ways, which is why there is a need for civil society and the contract that establishes it; but still it is a realm of law, and the social character of human beings, and their possession of reason, is their inspiration for wishing to ensure that the natural freedom and equality of the natural state is preserved – hence the contract and the institution of civil society is itself a direct expression and outcome of the state of nature.

The selection of *life, liberty* and *property* as the three fundamentals to be protected by the political contract of society comes directly from the demands of the Independents in the Civil War. By liberty Locke meant the individual's right to make his own choices and live accordingly, subject only to compliance with the obligations imposed by the law of nature. This law, in turn, is a law of liberty, existing precisely to protect it; so there is no inconsistency here. A parallel is provided by traffic rules which require everyone to drive on the same side of the road, observe the speed limit, and obey traffic lights. The rules conduce to drivers' safety and their chances of completing their journeys. In the same way the laws of nature exist to safeguard the liberty of individuals, not to deny it.

Property is derived by Locke from an assumed original state in which all land and raw materials are in common ownership, but parts of which are taken into private ownership by the admixture of individual labour. This labour theory of property anticipates versions of socialism.

Whereas absolutist theories invested unlimited power in the sovereign, Locke's view is that the contract which creates civil society is specific and its specificity limits it. In Hobbes the contract yields all power into the sovereign's hands; in Locke the contracting parties are themselves the power, which they delegate on strict and limited terms and can recall or legitimately resist if recall fails. The entity created by the contract is the State. In fact Locke nowhere uses the terms 'sovereign' and 'sovereignty' at all, because of its association with absolutist theories. Instead it is expressly the *majority* of the people in whom power ultimately resides, and the mutual contract of *all* that creates the State. The State is not the same thing as the government; the former is the political society constituted by contract, the latter is what is deputed by the former to carry out the function of ensuring that the purposes for which it exists – protection of life, liberty and property – are met.

For Locke it was essential that the legislative and executive functions of government should be distinct. A legislature might meet, pass laws, and depart; but the laws in order to be effective have to be enforced, their application managed, and disobedience to them remedied. For this an executive arm is required, and it is desirable that the duties and the persons of the legislative and executive branches should be distinct, for if they were not the legislators 'may exempt themselves from the obedience to the Laws they make, and suit the Law, both in its making and its execution, to their own private Wish, and thereby come to have a distinct Interest from the rest of the Community, contrary to the end of Society and Government.'[28] This indeed is what happens when legislator and executor are one individual, as in the case of an absolute sovereign; which is why the lives, liberties and property of individuals other than the absolute sovereign are so typically at risk from him or it.

A question Locke had to address was, When can one say that the government has overstepped its proper powers? He had to allow that governments might make mistakes and occasionally mismanage affairs, and in such cases, he said, there are appropriate and legal means of redress. Insurrection on poor grounds or none is seriously wrong, and not to be countenanced. But in the kind of circumstances faced by England in the reign of James II, resistance was right; for James II had bypassed Parliament to make arbitrary law, failed to assemble it when he should, packed it with his hirelings, and betrayed the country twice over by attempting to reintroduce Catholicism and secretly treating with a foreign prince to further his absolutist purposes. These malfeasances constituted a breach of trust with the people, who had no means other than to use their reserve power of rebellion to put matters right.[29]

Locke is the point of departure for liberalism in modern times. True, he had many predecessors in his own country and Europe generally who felt and thought as he did, and his immediate forerunners in the Civil War era were themselves conscious of a long tradition of struggle for liberty, which they conceived as having formerly existed in a golden age (Locke's 'state of nature' was a suppositious version of the golden age) which had been lost and which their endeavours were aimed at recovering. In this Locke's predecessors were taking the standard Renaissance view that history was all declension from a long-lost better age; as Locke himself says, in the state of nature men enjoyed 'perfect freedom'. So it is not that liberalism springs from Locke's brow fully formed, as Athene had leaped from the brow of Zeus. Rather it is that he gathered and articulated a set of arguments which, though in aim a rationalisation for what had actually been done in the Glorious Revolution, was a potent expression of an outlook destined to become the basis for the Western world's political arrangements.

But this is not to say that absolutism was vanquished by Locke's arguments or by the application of them in the course of the following centuries. Absolutism continued in the monarchies of France until its revolution of 1789, and in Prussia (think of Frederick the Great) and Russia (think of Catherine the Great, and of the Alexanders and Nicholases) long afterwards, and found its twentieth-century avatars in the *Führerprinzip* in Nazi Germany, in Stalinism, and in Maoism – to say nothing of Pol Pot, Saddam Hussein, Augusto Pinochet, and a host of other pocket tyrants, who nevertheless caused the people they killed to be just as dead as those killed by the big names.

It might be said that a form of absolutism was only finally abolished in Germany in 1945, and that the constitutional inability of Russia to do without autocracy means that it is an absolutist state in all but name still. In a number of Second and Third World countries absolutism continues to flourish, sometimes in its naked form, sometimes under the guise of theocracy, sometimes (as in Saudi Arabia) in an ambiguous and cynical combination of both. These facts remind one that there are always desires and designs to return polities to a situation where the inconveniences to ruling groups or individuals of elections, rights, liberties, due process, and other slow-footed impediments to the enjoyment of power, always put these impediments at risk: even in democratic countries, where nibblings and chippings-away at rights and liberties which stand in the way of 'security' (or the economy) are a constant.

Moreover, democracy as the underpinning of Locke's conception of the liberal state did not generalise into a value as well as a policy until the revolutions of the late eighteenth century. Its chief momentum in the West owes itself to what happened in America and France in the final quarter of that century, under the influence of Locke's ideas certainly, but until then it was a value only for the Enlightenment intellectual elite. Among the political elites elsewhere in Europe, by contrast, the principle of democracy remained into the nineteenth century what it had been for Plato: the idea of the greedy anarchy that a vulgar, ignorant, appetite-driven rabble would speedily produce if given a chance. In describing the members of the Long Parliament as 'democratical' Hobbes had not been complimenting them; democracy for him implied disorder and instability, a return to the savage state of nature from which he saw absolutism as the escape.[30]

It is perhaps a mark of the suspicion with which Baruch Spinoza was regarded – in his own time and that which immediately followed – by all but the most intelligent of those who knew his views, that he was friendly to the ideas of equality and democracy, as his *Tractatus Theologico–Politicus* shows. His first objective was to secure the freedom of individual thought and speech, and he was prepared to accept any form of government that would ensure this; but he felt that a democratic and egalitarian dispensation was most likely to achieve it. And his reason was that the ultimate source of authority in a commonwealth is the agreement of the participants in it. This is democracy not just in effect, but in actuality too – even Hobbes' social contract is a democratic one-off act, as the contractors strip themselves of all autonomy and invest it in the sovereign. So all political arrangements are founded in democracy, and this, said Spinoza, makes it not only the most basic but the most natural of all regimes.[31]

Unfortunately for his contemporary reputation and the reception of his ideas, Spinoza's work showed, or fairly conclusively seemed to show, that he was an atheist. It is more than a mere point of interest that two of the seventeenth century's greatest thinkers about the political organisation of society – Spinoza and Hobbes – should have been atheists, for it suggests that the biblical doctrines which by reflex were taken to describe the basis of authority in society were no longer compelling. Locke was not an atheist, but his views – though paying the usual lip service, as even Hobbes' views did, to the deity as the author and (in Hobbes) guarantor of natural law – did not depend on revelation, biblical authority, or religious tradition. On the contrary, in expressly disputing absolutism Locke's theory rejected the religion-based arguments of those such as Filmer, and denied the central doctrine of Divine Right altogether.

The seventeenth century's revolutions – the scientific revolution, and the revolution in political thought – had as their first major fruit the Enlightenment of the eighteenth century. Before continuing the story of liberty and democracy in this latter century's own revolutions, its evolution and extension of the seventeenth century's legacy requires mention; for it is in this that the first epochs of liberty as canvassed to this point were given their largest impetus.

The Enlightenment – to speak for a moment as if this highly complex event had a single mind of its own[32] – engaged in the natural and, in the circumstances, inevitable work of defining what it was against, in order to define clearly what it was for; and although its definition of its opposite always looks like a caricature – and sometimes an irritated one – when described in summary, it in fact found the task an easy one. For there was indeed a clearly delineated opponent for the Enlightenment to hold in its sights, looming large in the unedifying spectacle of the preceding centuries. That opponent was the belief systems and institutions of religion which had resisted liberty of conscience, liberty of thought and enquiry, liberty of expression, and liberty of the individual in the political sense, and which were prepared to use every weapon to inhibit the growth of liberty, from torture and burning at the stake to elaborate arguments proving that absolute monarchy is divinely sanctioned.

What the Enlightenment asserted in opposition to the forces of reaction was the authority of reason and confidence in the powers of the human intellect to discover truths about man, society and the world, and therefore to make concrete progress towards the good of mankind. Enlightenment thinkers were inspired by the example of Newton's achievements to apply scientific method to social questions, reflected in the growth of theory in psychology, politics and economics, each motivated by an ideal of rationality governed by fact, observation and experiment.

The key Enlightenment concepts are reason and progress, the latter being the product of the former. The marks of progress are the growth of scientific knowledge and improvements to the condition of mankind through science's applications via technology; a correlative reduction of superstition and religious belief; and the replacement of tyranny both temporal and ecclesiastical by more just and democratic institutions of government. The '*philosophes*' – the Enlightenment thinkers – were not all utopians, and realised that the second of the marks of progress, namely, less superstition, was a longer-term goal. They therefore promoted the idea that religion should be as reasonable as possible in itself, that it should be kept quite distinct from questions of science and society, and that complete tolerance should reign as regards matters of personal belief.

The central years of the eighteenth century – between 1745 and 1755 – were the high point of the Enlightenment in France, marking both a culminating point of earlier endeavour and an impetus to later developments. At that time there appeared Montesquieu's *Spirit of the Laws* (1748), Rousseau's *Discourse on the Moral Effects of the Arts and Sciences* (1750), and the greatest monument of the Enlightenment, the *Encyclopédie, ou Dictionnaire Raisonné des Sciences, Des Arts et des Métiers* (1751), edited by Denis Diderot and Jean le Rond d'Alembert. The importance of this great work lies in the fact that it represents a defiant act of liberty in its own right, promoting against the active opposition of the Church and an absolutist monarchy what we now recognise (in the West at least) as the lineaments of our contemporary dispensation, characterised by secularism, freedom of thought, human rights, democracy and the achievements of science.

This triumphant characterisation doubtless reads more like advertising than a history of ideas. The fact remains that the intellectual spirit of that age was remarkable not just in its optimism on behalf of human possibility, but in its success. Its own definition of what it opposed – unreason, superstition, tradition, absolutism in the State and the perpetuation by religion of thraldom over the minds of many – it chose to sum up in two words: 'Christianity' and 'tyranny'.

The Marquis de Condorcet and Edward Gibbon were alike in thinking that Christianity – in their view an Oriental superstition that appealed in the first instance to uneducated women and slaves with its inglorious promises – had ruined classical civilisation and ushered in centuries of ignorance and darkness. From the classical age which, for all its faults, had been distinguished by its literature, art and advanced institutions, Christianity had reduced Europe to a peasant condition from which it laboriously and only partly recovered during the next eight centuries, and for most of this time no literature, no philosophy, little art and little culture of any significance was produced, apart from a few works of theology and devotion. 'When superstition is allowed to perform the task of old age in dulling the human temperament,' Diderot remarked, 'we can say goodbye to excellence in poetry, painting and music.'[33] It took the Renaissance to shake mankind out of the paralysis thus induced, for as Rousseau remarked, nothing less than a revolution of some kind could break the frozen grip of an imposed narrow orthodoxy.

A critic of this hard view might in response point to the glories of Gothic architecture and devotional art, and the achievements of the late medieval period in philosophy, theology, poetry and crafts, and might add that some of the finest literature of the early Renaissance itself was religiously inspired – Dante is the chief case in point. But this counterargument is unlikely to move an Enlightenment *philosophe*. Christianity was afraid of 'that spirit of investigation and doubt, that confidence in one's own reason, which is the scourge of all religious beliefs,' Condorcet wrote in his *Esquisse* of the early Church and its dire effect on human culture. 'It found the very light of the natural sciences hateful and suspect, for it is extremely dangerous to the success of miracles; and there is not a single religion that does not force its devotees to swallow a few scientific absurdities. Thus the triumph of Christianity was the signal for the complete ruin of the sciences and philosophy.'[34] In the same spirit Hume laconically remarked that early Christianity depended on miracles to recommend itself, and in his own day still did, for a miracle was required for anyone to believe it.[35]

In Voltaire's essay 'Whether it is Useful to Maintain People in their Superstitions' – ostensibly an effort to persuade religion to shrive itself of ignorant credulity in order to become 'pure and holy', but in fact a cut at Christianity's roots – he wrote, 'Finally the bourgeoisie began to realise that it was not Saint Geneviève who gave or withheld rain, but that it was God Himself who disposed of the elements. The monks were astonished that their saints did not bring about miracles any longer; and if the writers of the life of Saint Francis Xavier returned to the world, they would not dare to write that the saint revived nine corpses, that he was in two places, on the sea and on land, at the same time, and that his crucifix fell into the sea and was restored to him by a crab.' To drive the implicit point home Voltaire added, 'Each day reason penetrates further into France, into the shops of merchants as well as the mansions of lords. We must cultivate the fruits of this reason, especially since it is impossible to check its advance. One cannot govern France, after it has been enlightened by Pascal, Nicole, Arnauld, Bossuet, Descartes, Gassendi, Bayle, Fontenelle, and the others, as it has been governed in the times of Garasse and Menot.'[36]

Gibbon's view of the part played by Christianity in the decline and fall of Rome was intended not only as an historical judgement, but as a comment on his own day, aiming it at his contemporaries as Hume, Voltaire and Condorcet had likewise done. His thesis was that the two causes of Rome's demise were barbarian invasions from without, and the corrupting barbarism of Christianity within. They conspired as causes, for the Christians repudiated the public good in place of a private one, Gibbon argued, rejecting the commitments of citizenship that held the Roman polity together because their loyalty lay elsewhere, thus weakening the empire internally and increasing its vulnerability to external attack.

Thus once Christianity had taken possession of the Roman world there was little hope that classical civilisation could survive intact; not merely were the classical tradition's institutions and its basis in an imperial state undermined, but the prejudice against 'pagan' learning completed the wreck, which Gibbon describes by citing two instances. One is the destruction in 389 AD of the books in the library of Alexandria (200,000 volumes of the literature of antiquity, many of them the only extant copies and therefore irretrievably lost), ordered by Archbishop Theophilus, 'a bold, bad man, whose hands were alternately polluted with gold and with blood', says Gibbon.[37] The other was the abolition of the Greek schools of philosophy in 529 AD by the Emperor Justinian, who regarded their teaching of Plato, Aristotle, the Stoics, and the thinkers of the other classical and Hellenistic schools as incompatible with Christian doctrine. On this point, at least, he was right.[38]

It seems extraordinary that the editors of the *Encyclopédie* and their contributors should have been in a similar situation to the one that prevailed when Theophilus and Justinian were making the world safe for Christianity, in the sense that they were at risk from the authorities because their views controverted the prevailing orthodoxies governing State and Church. But so they were. The written word could get a man into prison in eighteenth-century France – as Voltaire and Diderot both knew to their practical cost – which is why the *philosophes* looked with admiration to England. By that time England had achieved liberty of thought and expression, and a greater degree of political liberty than anywhere else in Europe, if not indeed the world. Writing in 1733 Voltaire said, 'The English are the only nation on earth who have been able to prescribe limits to the power of Kings by resisting them, and by a series of struggles have established that wise government where the Prince is all powerful to do good, and the same time is restrained from committing evil; where the nobles are great without insolence, though there are no vassals; and where the people share in the government without confusion.'[39] This encomium, apart from being largely true, was intended as a tilt at the French state of affairs, unaltered from the reign of Louis XIV.

Voltaire was not alone in admiring the English and their contrasting arrangements. When Gibbon visited Paris in 1763 he found it seized by Anglophilia, and this despite the French having just been defeated by England in the Seven Years War.

The reason was not just England's political dispensation: Newton and Locke were inspirations; Diderot translated Shaftesbury; even the *Encyclopédie* itself had begun life as a translation of Chambers' *Cyclopaedia*, though Diderot quickly found – after being commissioned to reproduce it in French – that it was inadequate to the ambitious scheme he had for a major work of modern general education covering the whole field of knowledge and technology. What Diderot wished to convey was an attitude and an outlook: an attitude of enquiry untrammelled by dogmas, orthodoxies, or the restrictions of political control; and a correlative outlook based on reason, observation and experiment.[40] One good exemplification of it – apart from the scores of articles he himself wrote for the *Encyclopédie* – is his 'Conversation between d'Alembert and Diderot' of 1769 on the question of whether a purely naturalistic explanation can be given of life and consciousness. It is a tour de force of lucid argument in favour of a naturalistic view. 'Do you see this egg?' Diderot asks. 'With this you can overthrow all the schools of theology, all the churches of the earth. What is this egg? An unperceiving mass, before the germ is introduced into it; and after the germ is introduced, what is it then? Still only an unperceiving mass, for this germ itself is only a crude inert fluid. How will this mass develop into a different organisation, to sensitiveness, to life? By means of heat. And what will produce the heat? Motion. What will be the successive effects of this motion? Instead of answering me, sit down and let's watch them from moment to moment.'[41]

The conversation was begun by d'Alembert asking what alternative view there could be to the idea that there must be a deity to explain how there can be life and consciousness: 'I confess that a Being who exists somewhere and yet corresponds to no point in space, a Being who, lacking extension, yet occupies space; who is present in his entirety in every part of that space, who is essentially different from matter and yet is one with matter, who follows its motion, and moves it, without himself being in motion . . . a Being about whom I can form no idea; a Being of so contradictory a nature, is an hypothesis difficult to accept. But other problems arise if we reject it; for if this faculty which you propose as substitute, is a general and essential quality of matter, then stone must be sensitive.' By rather transparent subterfuge the argument against the idea of a deity is here summarised, and an opening given for the naturalism – in the eighteenth century the term employed was 'materialism', a synonym for 'atheism' – that opposes it.

The *philosophe*'s point in tirelessly controverting religious authority was that once it is undermined, there is no longer a barrier to the free exercise of reason and all that it reveals to be right for the flourishing of mankind. For religious orthodoxy attempts, in the interests of holy truth, to constrain not just enquiry and expression but thought itself. Furthermore, it underwrites the legitimacy of the absolutist state's constitutional arrangements and equates resistance to the sovereign with blasphemy against God, on the ground that the latter has instituted the king as his temporal representative. No one in mid-eighteenth-century France, other than those with a vested interest in doing so, accepted either proposition, but they were still in force as grounds for policing those who said or acted to the contrary. The *philosophes*' rejection of them opened the way for change.

Thus the ideological basis for the prevailing institutional arrangements of the eighteenth century was opposed, and room was sought for a new order of liberty in thought and politics. The intellectuals engaged in this project themselves called it 'the Enlightenment', in self-conscious determination to promote its values. And they well understood not just what they were trying to achieve, but where they were in the effort to achieve it. 'Enlightenment,' wrote Immanuel Kant in his 1784 essay 'What Is Enlightenment?', 'is man's emergence from his self-imposed immaturity. Immaturity is the inability to use one's understanding without guidance from another. This immaturity is self-imposed when its cause lies not in lack of understanding, but in lack of resolve and courage to use it without guidance from another. *Sapere Aude!* [dare to know] – "Have courage to use your own understanding!" – that is the motto of enlightenment.'[42]

Neither Kant nor his contemporaries thought that they actually lived in an enlightened age. By 'enlightenment' they meant a process – the process of lessening the darkness, the beginning of the spread of light. The human mind was starting to shrug off the rule of arbitrary authority in the spheres of thought and belief. Intellectual immaturity is characterised by a need for direction from others; intellectual maturity is characterised by independence. 'Nothing is required for enlightenment except freedom,' Kant wrote, 'and the freedom in question is the least harmful of all, namely, the freedom to use reason publicly in all matters.'[43]

In fact Kant and his fellow Enlightenment thinkers were asking for more than just freedom of thought. It had become difficult for the 'thought police' to act as effectively as they had done in Torquemada's time; that was a battle close to being won. What they more generally sought was to remove constraints on liberty as such. 'On all sides I hear: "Do not argue!" ' Kant continued. 'The officer says, "Do not argue, drill!" The tax man says, "Do not argue, pay!" The pastor says, "Do not argue, believe!" ' Whereas the officer and the tax man serve authorities which dislike anyone's questioning the political and social status quo, the pastor is a different matter: he represents authority which dislikes any kind of questioning, and especially the kind that is sceptical about received wisdom.[44]

As the flagship of this aspiration, Diderot's *Encyclopédie* declared its emphatic war on the authority of past pieties on the grounds that they were, and had always been, a barrier to intellectual advance. In this the Encyclopédistes were following Voltaire's lead, whose battlecry of *écrasez l'infame* had persistently rung out in his attacks on authority, against whom he used the weapons of logic and brilliant satire.[45]

Diderot's call to arms in the *Encyclopédie* is in the same spirit as Kant's and Voltaire's: 'Have courage to free yourselves,' he exhorted his age, 'Examine the history of all peoples in all times and you will see that we humans have always been subject to one of three codes: that of nature, that of society, and that of religion – and that we have been obliged to transgress all three in succession, because they could never be in harmony.'[46]

In fact, as these remarks show, the Enlightenment appeal was not merely to reason but to the necessity for individuals to stand up for themselves in the light of reason. Diderot quoted Dumarsais in his *Encyclopédie* article on the term 'philosophe': 'Reason is to the philosopher what grace is to the Christian.' And the authority accorded to reason meant that although one main aim was to understand man and the world through science, another was to change both by application of science's lessons. Reason itself dictated that there was to be not just knowledge but practice: in this sense the Enlightenment can also claim Marx as its own. It can certainly claim Jeremy Bentham, who in his *Fragment on Government* wrote, 'The age we live in is a busy age, in which knowledge is rapidly advancing towards perfection. On the natural world in particular, everything teems with discovery and improvement. Correspondent to discovery and improvement in the natural world, is reformation in the moral' (by 'the moral world' he meant the social and political realms).[47]

The unanimity of the eighteenth-century thinkers on essentials – despite the presence of large differences in other respects – is demonstrated by d'Alembert's comment in his *Essai sur les Éléments de Philosophie* (*Essay on the Elements of Philosophy*) on the fact that 'our century has called itself the philosophic century par excellence', where he says, 'from the principles of the profane sciences to the foundations of revelation, from metaphysics to questions of taste, from music to morals, from the scholastic disputes of theologians to commercial affairs, from the rights of princes to those of people, from the natural law to the arbitrary law of nations, in a word from the questions that affect us most to those that interest us least, everything has been discussed, analysed and disputed.'[48]

These remarks are especially interesting for two reasons, beyond the fact that they could serve very well as an advertisement for the aim and scope of the *Encyclopédie*. The first is that they in effect announce the victory of freedom of thought and enquiry. Almost nothing of what was discussed in d'Alembert's eighteenth century would have been permissible in the sixteenth century; much of it would have invited the death penalty. This is a dramatic change. Of course both Church and State in his contemporary France, as elsewhere in Europe, were capable of punishing people who in their view went too far, and indeed they did so. Nor were the underlying principles applauded by implication in d'Alembert's remarks secure. Even those who for a time profited by the new world that the principles introduced could reject them, as the Terror following the French Revolution proved, as did the reactionary and illiberal laws passed in England in the 1790s and subsequent decades for fear that a revolution and Terror would happen within its shores. But whatever is chargeable to the debit side of the liberation of thought, the liberation of thought had nevertheless happened.

The second point is that among the samples in d'Alembert's list of what free discussion – and therefore analysis and dispute – had ranged over, he includes 'the rights of princes [and] those of the people . . . the natural law [and] the arbitrary law of nations'. This was incendiary stuff: it took fire in the British colonies of North America, and on the streets of Paris.

––––––

'Mankind had lost its rights,' said Voltaire, 'Montesquieu found and restored them.' The Baron de Montesquieu was a wealthy French aristocrat whose seminal work on government was admired everywhere in Europe outside his native country, but most of all in America, where it had a great influence on the thinking of James Madison, one of the principal drafters of the United States constitution.[49] Montesquieu had experience of government in France as a member of the *Parlement* of Bordeaux, was a keen observer of affairs (his *Persian Letters* are a witty commentary on the foibles of French society), and had travelled widely; but his principal interest was the question of how power in a state could be so disposed that it would be impossible for any one man to harm or exploit another.[50] Louis XIV died in 1715, bequeathing absolute power to weak and incompetent successors; in their hands it ceased to be controlled and vacillated between ineffectiveness and tyranny, a circumstance that exacerbated the resentments felt by the ordinary people against clerical and aristocratic privilege.

Voltaire's comment on Montesquieu's *De l'Esprit des Lois* (*The Spirit of the Laws*) gives its author a place alongside Locke and Newton in the Enlightenment pantheon, though unlike them Montesquieu lived through it rather than preceded it. Some of the inspiration for the *Laws* came from Montesquieu's study of England's political institutions while visiting the country in 1729. His chief concern was political liberty, which he believed was achieved when individuals in a State had 'tranquillity of mind arising from the opinion each has of his own safety'. There cannot be such tranquillity if there is a risk that tyrannical laws might be passed by a governing power that is free to act arbitrarily: 'When the legislative and executive powers are united in the same person, or in the same body of magistrates, there can be no liberty; because apprehensions may arise, lest the same monarch or senate should enact tyrannical laws, to execute them in a tyrannical manner.'[51] There therefore has to be a sharp separation between legislature and executive, and Montesquieu further advised that the executive should be divided between a branch with responsibility for external defence and another for internal administration of justice. The legislature's powers are directed towards monitoring the executive, making law, and raising taxes for the purposes of government and defence.

A free country is, said Montesquieu, one in which each person is his own governor, and therefore the ultimate legislative power rests in the whole people. For efficiency there has to be delegation of the legislative function to an assembly of representatives, but the representation must accurately reflect both population and regional interests. The nobility are a special interest group which is likely to suffer in a democracy, so they should have a separate assembly, with no powers other than to react to what is proposed in the popular assembly. Like the monarch (if there is one) this separate assembly may be empowered at the utmost only to reject what the popularly elected assembly proposes.

One feature of the English system of government praised by Montesquieu was that it maximised the effectiveness of administration by achieving co-ordination of the legislative and executive powers. A critic might say that this was the result of the degree of subordination of the executive to the legislative, so that the former could never in any case act as an effective check on the latter in case of serious disagreement. When the executive branch managed to check legislative ambition it was by informal means rather than by a clear constitutional arrangement such as came into existence in the United States. Tom Paine and other commentators on Montesquieu pointed out that he had mistaken the source of English liberties: it was not their laws, as Montesquieu had claimed, but the character of the people. As Paine put it, 'The plain truth is that it is wholly to the constitution of the people, and not to the constitution of the government, that the crown is not as oppressive in England as in Turkey.'[52] And the character of the people was not proof against Parliament when, as in the 1790s, it found occasions to suspend some of the freedoms that had in fact been hitherto protected by law, as well as those sanctioned by custom.

It was indeed in the formulation of the US Constitution that some of Montesquieu's ideas found their first application. One anxiety that authors of the *Federalist Papers* felt was that even though the proposed Constitution had no place for a monarch or hereditary nobility, the kind of tyranny against which Montesquieu warned could happen nevertheless, unless separation of powers was expressly built into the arrangements. The resulting solution was to say that members of legislatures could not hold executive posts or appoint others to them, that the president could not legislate but could veto legislation, and that the independence of the judiciary would be secured by having the most senior judges appointed for life by the president subject to confirmation by the legislature.

The resulting three-legged stool looks optimal in theory, but as with all human constructions it proved less than perfect in practice, almost wholly because of the often ferociously partisan nature of party politics. If both houses of the US Congress and the president belong to the same party, and if the Supreme Court is given a majority sympathetic to that party's outlook by presidential nomination and senate confirmation, then the tendency against which Montesquieu warned becomes a reality. Moreover, when one party controls both houses of Congress and the president belongs to a different party, Congress and presidency can effectively paralyse one another by each invoking its checking powers and by (for example) Congress instituting enquiries and impeachment proceedings against the president. Recent history demonstrates both faults.

Madison in his contributions to the *Federalist Papers* saw the need for the checks and balances, and also the danger of partisan politics. The latter he discussed in Federalist No. 10, which had the twofold purpose of advancing suggestions on how to mitigate the effects of factionalism, which he regarded as inevitable, and of opposing the Anti-Federalists. The aims came together in his saying that the best defence against factionalism is a large republic and not a small one, as each individual state would be under the Anti-Federalists' preferred alternative. He went on to say that this is the only way of protecting liberty while allowing for a plurality of interests in the republic, the existence of which is itself a safeguard; the more such groups there are, the less likely it is that any one of them – any single faction – will be able to dominate the rest.

The Anti-Federalist reply, argued by Madison's opponent on the question, George Clinton – and relying on Montesquieu's claim that 'It is natural to a republic to have only a small territory, otherwise it cannot long subsist' – was that the United States is simply too diverse in its geography, climate, people and existing arrangements to admit of a 'consolidated republican form of government'. The principle of pluralism would be compromised by it, Clinton said, and far from interest groups proving a restraint on the dominance of any faction, they would be the more easily swamped.

The Montesquieu principle of separation of powers and the need for properly instituted checks and balances in the constitution was adopted by Madison in Federalist No. 51, unequivocally entitled 'The Structure of the Government Must Furnish the Proper Checks and Balances Between the Different Departments'. Apart from being important in its own right, the concept was in part also an answer to the factionalism problem. Subsequent debate about Federalist No. 10 in the United States – a debate that continues – includes focus on the question of whether Madison intended to say that government should be as non-partisan as possible. Certainly that is the reading given to it by the

Supreme Court in several rulings, among them one by Justice Byron White who remarked in the course of an opinion, 'the Founding Fathers [believed] that splintered parties and unrestrained factionalism may do significant damage to the fabric of government'.

The debate about the US Constitution is one of the most striking features of the Enlightenment, not least because the US is its first and to date most brilliant offspring. It was far more radical in its departure from tradition even than the French Revolution when this latter began; in 1789 the French revolutionaries' aim was to set up a constitutional monarchy after the model of England, not a republic, but in the revolted British colonies of North America the aim was bolder from the outset. Two among a number of reasons for this were that the colonies had been independent of one another, though not of the British Crown, until some form of federation or confederation was mooted as the alternative to the trans-Atlantic dependence, and a way of agreeing the relationship was necessary. The second reason was that not only the first colonists but many who had migrated to them in the centuries since had done so in order to be as independent as possible of the constraints, even tyrannies, of imposed religious orthodoxy and absolutist rule. When George III acted towards his North American possessions as Louis XIV had acted in seventeenth-century France, the independent-minded residents of the colonies quickly objected; the rest is history.

Opponents of the idea of a federation of the ex-colonies, most of whom favoured instead a looser confederation leaving political authority in the states themselves, argued among other things that it is a mistake to think in terms of a single overriding public interest that citizens of a state share, and which can be represented in its institutions accordingly. Different people have different interests, and wish to have those interests represented and indeed acted upon; they have a right to this, and to organise themselves into parties in order to ensure that their interests have the best chance of being promoted. This pluralistic view denies that the ideas of 'the many' or 'the majority' have political reality; there is instead a great number of individuals and groups, and whatever political structures are built must reflect this fact. This was the underlying case of the Anti-Federalists.

The Federalists, by contrast, argued that there is such a thing as an overall 'public good', and that it is possible to identify 'the *real* welfare of the great body of the people' (as Madison put it). In the debate over ratification of the proposed US Constitution, a debate that lasted from the autumn of 1787 until the Constitution was ratified in 1789, three of those closely associated with drafting it – James Madison, Alexander Hamilton and John Jay – wrote in support of it in a series of articles published under the name 'Publius' in a New York newspaper. (Their Anti-Federalist opponents used the name 'Cato'.)

The Federalist Papers together constitute a very remarkable document, not only because of the high quality of the writing and argument, but because they are the scripture of a novel order, actually setting up and arranging an entirely new republic on the best principles that experience and Enlightenment reflection jointly taught. When the Papers were collected and published in volume form, Alexander Hamilton (who wrote the majority of them) provided a general introduction, in which he began by saying, 'It has been frequently remarked that it seems to have been reserved to the people of this country, by their conduct and example, to decide the important question, whether societies of men are really capable or not of establishing good government from reflection and choice, or whether they are forever destined to depend for their political constitutions on accident and force. If there be any truth in the remark, the crisis at which we are arrived may with propriety be regarded as the era in which that decision is to be made; and a wrong election of the part we shall act may, in this view, deserve to be considered as the general misfortune of mankind.'[53]

It comes as a surprise to learn that the authors of the Papers were not in favour of a bill of rights to accompany the Constitution. When one was adopted it was in part because some of the Anti-Federalists' arguments in favour of one had prevailed. In Federalist No. 84, Hamilton surveyed the history of bills of rights, describing them as 'in their origin stipulations between kings and their subjects, abridgements of prerogative in favour of privilege, reservations of rights not surrendered to the prince.' For this reason 'they have no application to constitutions professedly founded upon the power of the people, and executed by their immediate representatives and servants'.

Only one statement was required to secure all the rights that a free people anyway possessed, as shown by the fact that it had instituted its own government, and it was expressed in the Constitution: 'We the people of the United States, to secure the blessings of liberty to ourselves and our posterity, do ordain and establish this constitution for the United States of America.' What could be clearer? Moreover, Hamilton said, bills of rights are not only unnecessary but a positive danger, by suggesting that they are protections from powers which do not exist – thus, protecting free speech appears to imply that there is a power somewhere that limits free speech, but there is in fact no such power, so no such exemption from it is required. 'Why for instance, should it be said, that the liberty of the press shall not be restrained, when no power is given by which restrictions may be imposed? I will not contend that such a provision would confer a regulating power; but it is evident that it would furnish, to men disposed to usurp, a plausible pretence for claiming that power.'[54]

The argument did not prevail for good reason. Thomas Jefferson, in a letter to Madison, said, 'A Bill of Rights is what the people are entitled to against every government on earth, general or particular, and what no just government should refuse or rest on inference.' Almost all the states already had their own bills of rights, and there had been a general outcry when it became apparent that none had been proposed alongside the Constitution. Hamilton's argument was regarded as especially sophistical. In the event five of the states voted to ratify the Constitution only on condition that a bill of rights would be subjoined, and almost all the states submitted lists of rights that they wished to see included in such a bill.

The states' bills of rights had a distinctively Lockean flavour – the Virginia Bill of Rights states that people 'have certain inherent rights, of which, when they enter a state of society they cannot by any compact deprive or divest their posterity'. But although the US Bill of Rights encapsulated the fundamental agreement between them all, it emphasised an extra dimension besides that only some of them specified: the right to pursue happiness. That is a very Enlightenment notion.

The immediate trigger for the American revolution was the colonists' perception of unjust taxation – 'no taxation without representation' – but it is arguably the case that even if the proposals advanced by Edmund Burke in favour of greater autonomy for the North American colonies had been implemented, the desire for genuine independence and a chance to fashion a truly modern constitution would have come to prove overwhelmingly attractive sooner rather than later. The terminology of 'Old' and 'New' Worlds captured far more than geography: it captured psychology, ambition, a sharply different perspective. And the colonists were where they were precisely because they had sought freedom from the outset. The taxation difficulties came to a head in the mid-1760s; in the decade that followed there was great opportunity for ideas of independence to ripen quickly in that fertile soil of liberty, and they did.

The wellsprings of revolution in France, and its outcomes, were different. The same ideas of liberty and rights that had once been mere aspirations and now in the eighteenth century were enjoying concrete realisation of course inspired both; Locke and the *philosophes* stood just in the background. But by the closing decades of the century the decay of the *ancien régime* and the unsupportable nature of the abuses, injustices and inequalities it presided over had passed any point of return. Bankruptcy of the national finances, the failure of the harvest in 1788, and the bitter winter of 1788–9, together with decades of increasing resentment and a sense of oppression in the populace, jointly induced collapse. A reluctant but optionless Louis XVI had to call the States-General, the first time that all three estates had been summoned together since 1610. The Third Estate – the commons – were adamantly determined on reform, and knew that if they could deliberate jointly with the First and Second Estates – the nobility and clergy respectively – they would have a majority for it. Repeated efforts to bring the estates together in a single assembly failed, so the Third Estate

Heretics being burned at the stake; sixteenth-century Flemish school.

Galileo on trial before the Inquisition in Rome, 1633; seventeenth-century Italian school.

Erasmus, by Hans Holbein, 1523.

Martin Luther, by
Lucas Cranach the Elder, 1529.

John Calvin; sixteenth-century
Swiss school.

Michael Servetus, by Christoffel van
Sichem the Elder, 1607.

Francis Bacon, engraving by William
Marshall, 1640.

John Milton, engraving by William
Faithorne, 1670.

John Locke, after Sir Godfrey Kneller.

Isaac Newton, after Sir Godfrey Kneller.

Absolute monarch: Louis XIV, by Claude Lefebvre, *c.*1683.

William and Mary receiving the Bill of Rights
and the joint crown, 1689.

The Declaration of Independence Committee: (*left to right*) Thomas Jefferson, Roger Sherman, Benjamin Franklin, Robert Livingston and John Adams; New York, 1776.

Tom Paine, engraving by William Sharp.

George III's statue being pulled down on 9 July 1776 at the bottom of Broadway, New York.

The Tennis Court Oath, Paris, 1789, by Jacques Louis David.

Mary Wollstonecraft,
by John Opie, c.1797.

The Peterloo massacre, 16 August 1819: the British government's
answer to the demand for working people's rights.

Chartist meeting on Kennington Common, London, 1848;
photograph by W. E. Kilburn.

Lord Acton, late nineteenth century.

John Stuart Mill, 1870.

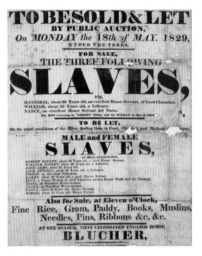

A slave auction poster, 1829.

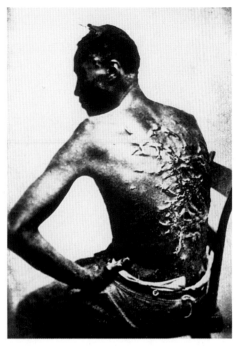

A slave's punishment scars,
Baton Rouge, Louisiana, 1863.

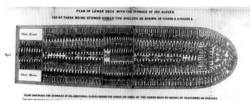

The infamous ship *Brookes*,
showing how slaves were
transported across the
Atlantic.

Abolition of slavery in the French colonies, 1848, by François Biard.

Women's suffrage on the march in America, May 1912.

Emmeline Pankhurst arrested while trying to deliver a petition to the king in May 1914.

Elizabeth Cady Stanton, 1900.

May Day rally of
the Hitler Youth,
Berlin Olympic
stadium, 1937.

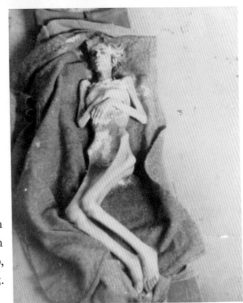

A victim of Nazism
in Bergen-Belsen
concentration camp,
May 1945.

The official inception of the United Nations, 1942.

Eleanor Roosevelt holding the 1948 United Nations
Universal Declaration of Human Rights.

An identity inspection by French troops in Algeria, 1950s.

An apartheid protest in Durban, South Africa, 1986.

A black American takes her children to school in Nashville, Tennessee, amid protests from whites, 1957.

Martin Luther King, 28 August 1963.

The World Trade
Center in New York,
11 September 2001, as
the second aircraft flies
into the south tower.

Demonstrators protest against
the Patriot Act, 2003.

107TH CONGRESS
1ST SESSION **H. R. 3162**

IN THE SENATE OF THE UNITED STATES

OCTOBER 24, 2001
Received

AN ACT

To deter and punish terrorist acts in the United States
and around the world, to enhance law enforcement inves-
tigatory tools, and for other purposes.

1   *Be it enacted by the Senate and House of Representa-*
2   *tives of the United States of America in Congress assembled,*

The first page of the 2001 US Patriot Act.

claimed power in its own name, which it changed to 'National Assembly'. The incompetence of Louis prompted first the Oath of the Tennis Court by the Assembly's members, and then the outbreak of rioting in Paris in July of that fateful year. This not only involved the sacking of the Bastille – an almost empty and actually irrelevant but still potent symbol of oppression – but also threw open the door to revolutionaries eventually less continent and more violent than the Assembly's first leaders could have dreamed possible.

At first the Assembly was intent on establishing a constitutional monarchy, and although it resembled at times the coarser revolutionaries who were soon to follow them in government – the events of 4 August 1790 come to mind, when the deputies repealed dozens of ancient laws in a night of frenzied and unconsidered exuberance – it nevertheless made serious efforts to devise a constitution that would solve the mass of problems under which France groaned. In America the drafting of the Constitution and the ratification debate that followed it had been sober, unhurried, thoughtful and replete with eloquence of mind and reasoning. In the difficult and heated atmosphere of Paris, the same endeavour proceeded very differently. Precisely a year after the fall of the Bastille a Constitutional Committee was formed, and its first task was the drafting of a Declaration of the Rights of Man. This they did in their first six weeks, and produced a remarkable and stirring document which, instinct with the spirit of Enlightenment, is a monument of its kind.[55]

But drafting a Declaration proved to be the easy part. A constitution was much harder to agree. All untutored enthusiasm in the streets of Paris was for the most primitive form of democracy, which the drafters recognised as unworkable. But their efforts failed to find a quick solution to problems such as whether to have two houses of legislature or just one (one was decided upon; Mirabeau warned – perhaps foresaw is the better word – that the unlimited power of a single chamber would be worse than the tyranny of a caliph), whether the king should have a power of veto over laws (Lafayette, thinking he was following American precedent, persuaded both king and Assembly to accept a much weaker power, that of suspending implementation; as the Crown had already been deprived of its power to dissolve the Assembly this was a nugatory provision); and so on across the range of necessities for a workable constitution.

The citizens of Paris were restive and violence kept breaking out, each time worse than the last. Eventually the king and Assembly were obliged to return to Paris from Versailles, a move which had the effect of weakening the moderates and soon delivering power to the more extreme elements in the Assembly. As arguments over a constitution continued, the Assembly created more and more committees to oversee the functioning of ministries, and their inexperienced meddling soon turned a crisis into chaos.

With domestic difficulties and foreign war to confront, the degeneration of France's revolutionary politics into bloodshed and turmoil seems inevitable to hindsight, as does the fact that repeated attempts to write a constitution and then to live by it failed in those first years. Many far beyond France's borders who had welcomed the onset of revolution with joy – 'Bliss was it in that dawn to be alive' wrote William Wordsworth – seeing in the fall of the Bastille especially a symbol of the planting of unqualified liberty in the soil of Europe, were deeply dismayed by the repulsive debacle into which it fell.[56]

With astonishing clarity Alexander Hamilton had recognised the dangers implict in revolutions and the factionalism and anarchy they could so easily degenerate into. In his introduction to the collected edition of the Federalist Papers, he wrote of what could happen when efforts are made to fashion new, principled but workable arrangements of government: 'And yet, however just these sentiments will be allowed to be, we have already sufficient indications that it will happen in this as in all former cases of great national discussion. A torrent of angry and malignant passions will be let loose. To judge from the conduct of the opposite parties, we shall be led to conclude that they will mutually hope to evince the justness of their opinions, and to increase the number of their converts by the loudness of their declamations and the bitterness of their invectives. An enlightened zeal for the energy and efficiency of government will be stigmatised as the offspring of a temper fond of despotic power and hostile to the principles of liberty. An overscrupulous jealousy of danger to the rights of the people, which is more commonly the fault of the head than of the heart, will be represented as mere pretence and artifice, the stale bait for popularity at the expense of the public good. It will be forgotten, on the one hand, that jealousy is the usual concomitant of love, and that the noble enthusiasm of liberty is apt to be infected with a spirit of narrow and illiberal distrust. On the other hand, it will be equally forgotten that the vigour of government is essential to the security of liberty; that, in the contemplation of a sound and well-informed judgement, their interest can never be separated; and that a dangerous ambition more often lurks behind the specious mask of zeal for the rights of the people than under the forbidden appearance of zeal for the firmness and efficiency of government. History will teach us that the former has been found a much more certain road to the introduction of despotism than the latter, and that of those men who have overturned the liberties of republics, the greatest number have begun their career by paying an obsequious court to the people; commencing demagogues, and ending tyrants.'[57]

In England Dissenters, working people, reformers and others had less cause than their French counterparts to revolt, but the example of what had happened in France, so glorious in its beginnings and so rich with promise for liberty, was an inspiration. To the governing class it seemed the very opposite, and fears of revolution produced repression. Edmund Burke, who had been a friend to American independence, was appalled by the events of 1789 and hastened to condemn them in his *Reflections on the Revolution in France*. He saw neither wisdom nor virtue in the revolutionaries and their demands, and three years before the Terror asked, 'What is liberty without wisdom, and without virtue? It is the greatest of all possible evils; for it is folly, vice, and madness, without tuition or restraint.'[58] Having always hitherto been a Whig of liberal principles, Burke was now made a conservative by the spectacle of all tradition, institutions, and respect for order and its symbols – including the monarchy – being overthrown and despised. 'The shallowest understanding, the rudest hand is more than equal to that task [of destroying institutions]. Rage and frenzy will pull down more in half an hour than prudence, deliberation, and foresight can build up in a hundred years.' Part of his hostility to the Revolution was sentiment; he had been charmed by the spectacle of Marie Antoinette at Versailles when she was the young dauphiness, and was horrified at the thought of disrespect being shown her by sans-culottes: 'in a nation of men of honour and of cavaliers, I thought ten thousand swords must have leaped from their scabbards to avenge even a look that threatened her with insult . . .'

But it was political principle that the events uncovered in Burke's thought, the principle that liberty, and the degree to which power can be entrusted beyond those with the capacity to wield it and a reason to wield it well, both have their limits: 'Where popular authority is absolute and unrestrained, the people have an infinitely greater, because a far better founded, confidence in their own power . . . they are less under responsibility to one of the greatest controlling powers on the earth, the sense of fame and estimation. The share of infamy that is likely to fall to the lot of each individual in public acts is small indeed; the operation of opinion being in the inverse ratio to the number of those who abuse power. Their own approbation of their own acts has to them the appearance of a public judgement in their favour. A perfect democracy is, therefore, the most shameless thing in the world. As it is the most shameless, it is also the most fearless. No man apprehends in his person that he can be made subject to punishment.'[59]

The 'crested rhetoric' of Burke's prose (as William Hazlitt called it) stiffened the resolve of those in Britain who were determined to see no sans-culottes on the streets of London or Edinburgh, but it provoked an outpouring of literature in response. Most famous was Tom Paine's *The Rights of Man*, published in 1791. In the same year appeared James Mackintosh's *Vindiciae Gallicae*. William Godwin published his *Enquiry Concerning Political Justice* in 1793, a few weeks after Louis XVI's execution, and it had an enormous effect, alarming conservatives and inspiring radicals. In it Godwin said that the American and French revolutions between them were a harbinger of a new era of peace and progress. He painted an optimistic and idyllic picture of the realisation of Enlightenment, envisioning rational autonomous people enhancing each other's well-being in a spirit of mutuality. Each of us is the arbiter of how he should act, Godwin said, under the sole proviso that our actions should aim at creating the greatest good all round. And he claimed that intellectual pursuits and feelings of kindness towards others are the chief sources of happiness.[60]

Godwin's views scandalised some of his readers because they were anarchic, atheistical and utopian. Others were inspired by their millennial optimism. To illustrate the points made in the *Enquiry* Godwin wrote a novel, *Caleb Williams* (originally entitled 'Things As They Are'), which became a bestseller immediately on its publication in 1794. It inspired imitation among a group of radical novelists, who accordingly came to be called the 'Jacobin novelists', among them Mary Wollstonecraft, Elizabeth Inchbald and Thomas Holcroft. Their publisher was the radical and Dissenter Joseph Johnson.[61] The public mind associated these writers with the group responsible for the Reign of Terror in France, Robespierre's Society of the Friends of the Constitution. But in fact the Jacobin novelists were advocates of peaceful reform, human rights, democracy, equality, and universal education.

Alas for the prospects of such views, England was in ferment because of what was happening across the Channel, and the government was not minded to entertain new ideas, even those that claimed to be peaceful. Reformist ambitions and political enthusiasm had never been at such a pitch. Many thought that it would only be a matter of time before the tide of liberty flowing in France reached England's shores – without attendant violence, as Godwin and the others hoped; but no one could be sure of that. Certainly the government was not prepared to take chances. Hindsight says that it need not have worried; historians such as Élie Halévy and E. P. Thompson argue that Methodism, the type of nonconformism most widespread among the working classes, was anti-revolution and pro-government, and its influence was too strong for revolution to be a possibility.[62] Few grasped this at the time, however, which is why the government acted as repressively as it did. It was roused by its own anxieties to do so, and by Burke's remark, 'Whenever our neighbour's house is on fire, it cannot be amiss for the engines to play a little on our own.'

Not all of the measures taken by the government worked. One of the great events of the day was the set of Treason Trials of 1794, the chief figures in which were the radical parson and reformer John Horne Tooke, the writer John Thelwall, and the secretary of the London Corresponding Society Thomas Hardy, a bootmaker by trade. The London Corresponding Society was one of the organisations, otherwise known as 'radical societies' or 'Jacobin clubs', set up on the model of the American Revolutionary societies to discuss and promote ideas of parliamentary reform and democracy. About forty of them were founded in the 1790s, all inspired by events in France. Some enjoyed considerable support among working people, and these included the London Corresponding Society, to the alarm of the government. It did not bother to interfere with certain individuals such as Godwin, on the grounds that his book was too expensive for working people to buy.

The government decided to take action against the increasing number of radical groups after the spring of 1793, from which time England was at war with France and the horrors of events there under Robespierre had hardened opinion among the Revolution's opponents. Prime Minister Pitt and his government believed that the war would be a short one; they thought that while the land armies of its continental allies defeated France, they would use England's sea power to help themselves to France's overseas possessions. Instead they got a serious fright: the French gave the armies of England's allies a beating; and England found that in lieu of being advantageously poised on the sidelines, picking up assets abroad as its continental neighbours were absorbed in battle, it was engaged in a serious war with a formidable enemy.

Determined not to be fighting on two fronts, one domestic and one against a possible invader, therefore, the government began to crack down on these radical societies, and found its opportunity when some of the latter set out to respond to Paine's call for a democratic alternative to Parliament. The idea was to establish a 'British Convention' which, because it would be democratically elected by the people and thus a genuine expression of its will, would have more authority than Parliament. This in effect is what the National Assembly in Paris had done, short-circuiting the impasse of the three estates by constituting itself the authoritative body.

At the close of 1793 an attempt to establish a Convention in Scotland was prevented by the arrest of its organisers, who were tried and transported in the following spring. As soon as they were out of the way the government took the same steps in England. On 12 May, Thomas Hardy of the London Corresponding Society and Daniel Adams, secretary of the Society for Constitutional Information, were arrested and charged with high treason, an offence punishable by death. At the end of May habeas corpus was suspended and many arrests followed. The government held as many as 800 warrants at one time for detaining suspected revolutionaries. Tooke and Thelwall were among those locked in the Tower with Hardy, and they accompanied him to the dock. The trial lasted eight days, and at its end, to the delight of the public, the jury took scarcely any time to dismiss the indictments against all three. As each man walked out of the court he was met by cheering crowds, held back with great difficulty by soldiers. The prosecution was obliged to drop the charges against the other nine who had been indicted on the same count.[63]

Godwin played a significant part in the collapse of the prosecution case. He anonymously published an article in the *Morning Chronicle* on 21 October 1794, at the very beginning of the trial, entitled 'Cursory Strictures on the Charge Delivered by Lord Chief Justice Eyre to the Grand Jury'. In introducing the charge against Hardy and the others to the grand jury, Eyre had invoked a statute of Edward III defining high treason as any act that imagined the death of a king. From this Eyre deduced that anything – other than parliamentary activity – that urged towards the overthrowing of a government was tantamount to threatening the life of a king; it was 'constructive treason' because that was the logical outcome, when pushed to its conclusion, of designs to overthrow a government headed by a monarch.

Godwin wrote, 'This is the most important crisis in the history of English liberty, that the world ever saw. If men can be convicted of High Treason, upon such constructions and implications as are contained in this charge, we may look with conscious superiority upon the republican speculations of France, but we shall certainly have reason to envy the milder tyrannies of Turkey and Ispahan.' The reason is that on this definition anything whatever can be defined as 'constructive treason' at the whim of judges, ministers, or anyone else in a position, or with a motive, to institute proceedings.[64]

The argument gave the chief defence counsel, Thomas Erskine, the ammunition he needed, and he persuaded the presiding judge, Lord Chief Justice Eyre, to change his opening direction to the grand jury. That in turn paved the way to acquittal.

The acquittals were a great achievement in themselves, but it was in fact a won battle in a lost war. The trials of October 1794 looked like a landmark in the story of liberty in England, but actually marked a serious interruption in the progress of reform for another generation. Things might paradoxically have been different if Hardy and his co-defendants had been hanged or transported, for then they would have become martyrs for the cause, and the government might have had a far harder task on the domestic front. But in any case the government's crackdown was taking effect, stifling radical political agitation and introducing a succession of 'gagging Acts'. The Treasonable Practices Act of 1795 made criticism of the government a 'high misdemeanour'; in the same year controls were instituted on public assemblies, and the licensing of meeting houses and itinerant preachers was introduced. The Combination Acts were passed in 1799 and 1800, and although they were then aimed at preventing seditious assembly, they proved useful over the next two generations in hindering the growth of trades unions.

These were not the last repressive measures introduced. Having got into the habit of illiberal legislation, successive governments (other than that of Charles James Fox and his companions in the short-lived Ministry of All the Talents, 1806–7) continued to introduce reactionary measures right into the 1820s. They brought in a bill to extend the death penalty to Luddites in the economic hardships of the last years of the Napoleonic Wars, again suspending habeas corpus in 1817, and then passing the infamous Six Acts following the Peterloo massacre of 1819. The Six Acts limited the right of public meetings, empowered magistrates to seize 'blasphemous and seditious' literature, and taxed newspapers to limit their accessibility to working people, for whom they were the principal source of radical opinion.

Among Godwin's friends was the portrait painter John Hazlitt, brother of the great essayist William Hazlitt. The latter was a pupil at the New College in Hackney at the time of the Treason Trials, and was not able to join Godwin and other friends of the accused radicals in the gallery in court. But each evening he heard Godwin, his brother and the others discussing the day's details, and shared in the public jubilation when Hardy and the others were acquitted. An added interest had been that a former pupil of the New College was among those arrested, but then discharged without trial following the acquittals.

The saga of the October trials was one of the motives for Hazlitt's lifelong radicalism. The contrast between the blissful early hopes of the French Revolution and the reaction of the authorities in his own country was something he could not bear, and he never forgot or forgave those whom he had known to be ardent reformers in the 1790s, but who later joined the Establishment and defended its repressions. This in his eyes was apostasy. They included his early friends Coleridge and Wordsworth, and his acquaintance Southey.[65]

A decade after the October trials Hazlitt was commissioned by Godwin, who had by then become a publisher, to edit and complete the autobiography of the playwright and novelist Thomas Holcroft, one of those indicted for high treason because he had been a member of the Society for Constitutional Information. His friends had been astounded at his arrest – though no more than he himself – for he was known to be an ardent supporter of peaceful and non-violent reform, always arguing that philosophy was the best route to reforming error and wrong, 'for' as he said, 'truth is powerful'. When Holcroft learned that he was on the bill of indictment along with Hardy and the others he immediately surrendered himself at the high court, saying that he wished to have the opportunity to defend himself. He was imprisoned in Newgate, and did not learn the details of his alleged treason until several days had passed. When charges were dropped against all those indicted, he was angry because it deprived him of a chance to clear his name. Thereafter he was described in the press by those hostile to him as 'the acquitted felon Holcroft', and he was obliged to live with the opprobrium of the mere fact of having been indicted for high treason.

Holcroft said of the trial, 'perhaps this country never witnessed a moment more portentous. The hearts and countenances of men seemed pregnant with doubt and terror. They waited, in something like a stupor of amazement, for the fearful sentence on which their deliverance, or their destruction, seemed to depend. Never surely was the public mind more profoundly agitated. The whole power of Government was directed against Thomas Hardy: in his fate seemed involved the fate of the nation, and the verdict of Not Guilty appeared to burst its bonds, and to have released it from inconceivable miseries, and ages of impending slavery. The acclamations of the Old Bailey reverberated from the farthest shores of Scotland, and a whole people felt the enthusiastic transport of recovered freedom.'[66]

Editing these words while completing the story of Holcroft's life gave Hazlitt a chance – another chance: he grasped them whenever he could – to dwell on the bright hopes for liberty and virtue that had captivated people at the beginning of the French Revolution. He remembered how, in its early days, and throughout the period when it was still possible to believe that great change would follow in England too, people treated one another with comradeship and fellow feeling, sympathy and tolerance. It is a frequent observation that community spirit breaks out in times of communal threat or endeavour, for example when peace is announced at a war's end, or when an unpopular government is defeated and hopeful new beginnings impend. 'Kind feelings and generous actions there always have been, and there always will be, while the intercourse of mankind shall endure,' wrote Hazlitt, 'but the hope, that such feelings and such actions might become universal, rose and set with the French revolution.' By the time he wrote those words, however, 'That light seems to have been extinguished for ever in this respect. The French revolution was the only match that ever took place between philosophy and experience: and waking from the trance of theory to the sense of reality, we hear the words, *truth, reason, virtue, liberty*, with the same indifference or contempt, that the cynic who has married a jilt or a termagant, listens to the rhapsodies of lovers.'[67]

Hazlitt's pessimistic tone was appropriate enough given the eclipse of reforming hopes and the backward steps taken by liberty, both in the debacle of the Revolution's Terror and in the close to half-century of reactionary government that it prompted in England. But it proved merely a temporary reversal in the longer pulse of history; the upward graph had received a considerable dip, but the tendency was still upward. That is proved by the fact that the main thrust of the political history of the West from 1815 onwards – taking the date of the end of the Napoleonic Wars as a not quite arbitrary marker – is one of widening democratic participation, growing recognition of rights, and entrenchment of the concept of liberty both in thought and practice.

In any case, even as Hazlitt wrote gloomily of the death of liberty's hopes, other shoots of liberty were still pushing upwards, first in the case of slavery, later in the case of workers' rights and – though only as a beginning – women's rights: these are the subjects of the next chapter.

The eighteenth century ended with the French Revolution's *Declaration of the Rights of Man and of the Citizen*, a Bill of Rights in America, Tom Paine's *The Rights of Man*, anti-slavery campaigns, revolutions against arbitrary government, and a ferment of debate about political representation and reform. In rhetoric alone the idea that the human individual has rights and entitlements just by virtue of being human, and is intrinsically free – though historically beset by forces that trap him in a variety of unfreedoms against which those rights have to be asserted – had scored a series of very remarkable triumphs.

Moreover the triumphs were not confined to rhetoric alone, but had actually been applied in important cases, and had become the stuff of conviction for many people across all classes in all European societies (including their extensions to North America). It had also thereby become the stuff of nightmare for those in the governing classes and their anxious supporters, who saw nothing but the dangers of Jacobin Terror lurking in them.

Cynics will point out, and quite rightly, that the century also ended in war, deep social divisions, reactionary measures prompted by talk of liberty and rights, and the actions – too many of them incontinent – that flowed from it. All this is true. The hard fact is that progress is almost always made at a cost, sometimes substantial; light throws its shadows, and the brighter the light, the darker the shadows. For every few steps forward there is at least one back at some point, for those with power, wealth, influence, and zealously held beliefs never give up easily. If anything, the reaction to the progress made by the idea of liberty in the eighteenth century is a measure of its power, and of its growing success.

Not all the reaction was misplaced. The French experience shows what Alexander Hamilton had predicted: that revolutions can be hijacked by demagogues and monsters, who then consume their own in ways more vile than the previous regime had practised. The contrast between the American and French revolutions in this respect is surely explainable by the degree of frustration in French society, growing for so long under the lid of absolute monarchy, and triggered by real hardships of starvation and anxiety in the years immediately prior to the explosion of July 1789. Marie Antoinette might not actually have said 'let them eat cake', but the contrast between the circumstances of the bloated, untaxed, parasitic nobility and the ragged hungry mobs is not a caricature. In it lies the explanation for the revolution's ferocity. What it should not do is detract from the principles at stake. When Paine wrote his *Rights of Man*, the first part of which was dedicated to George Washington, he singled out the first three clauses of France's *Declaration of the Rights of Man and of the Citizen* as the essence of the whole: '1. Men are born, and always continue, free and equal in respect of their rights . . . 2. The end of all political associations is the preservation of the natural and imprescriptable rights of man; and these rights are Liberty, Property, Security, and Resistance of Oppression. 3. The Nation is essentially the source of all sovereignty; nor can any individual, nor any body of men, be entitled to any authority which is not expressly derived from it.' Replace 'Nation' with 'People' – as suggested by clause 6 lower down in the *Declaration*:

'Law is expression of the general will' – and it is a close cousin of the American documents on which it is in part based.

The *Declaration* is a superb document. The fact that, not long after its publication, the revolution was hijacked by Jacobins who so comprehensively subverted its spirit, suggests that there was less political maturity in France than in America. In the older country men went from private life without any background in politics and government into the National Assembly. In America liberty did not collapse into licence; there was no euphemistically named 'Committee of Public Safety' guillotining dozens of people a day.

The problem in America was different: its heterogeneity of liberties, and the question of who held them, and why. It was partly solved, following the Civil War nearly a century later, by the compromises that ended that war and partly by the subsequent rapid expansion of its land area and economy (the effects described in Frederick Jackson Turner's 'Frontier Thesis'). In France the fact that experience of government had been reserved to so few, and the frustrations and indignities of the people had become so great, meant that the revolutionary process was almost bound to carry itself away, resulting in the creation of new and in some respects worse difficulties.

By themselves, obviously enough, fine pronouncements mean nothing unless they turn into realities. In 1936 Stalin's Soviet Union promulgated a new and beautifully liberal constitution, even as massacres of kulaks and show trials were happening. It enshrined freedom of speech, freedom of the press, freedom of assembly and meetings, freedom of street processions and demonstrations (all specifically permitted in clause 125). It stipulated 'universal, equal and direct suffrage by secret ballot' (clause 134), and gave 'each Union republic [the] right freely to secede from the USSR' (clause 17). These admirable provisions alone might raise a horse-laugh; history and Stalinism between them make the entire rambling document a comedy. The constitution was hailed by thinkers on the liberal left in Britain and elsewhere as a fresh dawn, adding to the popularity among them both of Communism and the Soviet system. In eighteenth-century revolutionary France the fine pronouncements were not masks of hypocrisy, but they turned into the wrong realities nevertheless. Lady Hester Stanhope reported that Prime Minister Pitt had said to her, after reading Paine's book, 'Tom Paine is quite right, but what am I to do? If I were to encourage Tom Paine's opinions, we should have a bloody revolution.'[68] Thus the example of French realities set back the cause of liberty, though only temporarily from the point of view of history. For the next two generations, at least, the setback was a painful one.

Pitt was referring to the second part of Paine's book, the part that attacked the hereditary principle and argued eloquently for representative democracy and the entrenching of rights. His views were themselves revolutionary; today they are largely commonplaces in the Western liberal polities. That is the success of the historical process described in this book.

PART II

THE EXTENSION OF LIBERTY

5

Slaves, Workers, Women
and the Struggle for Liberty

'ONLY CONNECT' was E. M. Forster's motto. The connecting link in the story of liberty lies in the life and work of a great-souled man, who by inheritance and principle constitutes the route through which any story must pass that begins with the religious persecutions of Torquemada and ends with the international adoption of human rights conventions.

The man in question is Anthony Benezet.[1] He was born in France in 1713 to Huguenot parents, who two years later were driven from their country by religious persecution, and went to England. Benezet received a good education there until the age of seventeen, at which point he was taken by his family to the North American colonies, where they settled in Philadelphia. Soon afterwards he became a Quaker, and joined the teaching staff at their school in nearby Germantown. There he established a reputation as an outstanding teacher distinguished by his humane principles, among which was his opposition to the then traditional preference for stick over carrot as a learning aid.

Early in his teaching career Benezet began to give lessons to the children of slaves in his spare time in the evenings. Later he started a school exclusively for girls, teaching them by day while continuing with the education of slave children at night. This experience provided one of his main motives for taking up an anti-slavery stance; in the slightly muted terminology of one knowing that he is announcing what the majority around him would see as heresy, he wrote 'I have found amongst the negroes as great a variety of talents as amongst a like number of whites; and I am bold to assert, that the notion entertained by some, that the blacks are inferior in their capacities, is a vulgar prejudice, founded on the pride of ignorance of their lordly masters, who have kept their slaves at such a distance, as to be unable to form a right judgment of them.'[2]

The Quaker movement was not opposed to slavery before 1750, though back in the 1660s its founder George Fox had urged his fellows in the movement to treat their slaves with kindness, and there were some among the Friends who had begun to question its morality. But it was Benezet who took up the cause with vigour.[3] He began by challenging his fellow Quakers to consider whether slavery was consistent with Christian principles. Apart from very few individual objectors, Christianity had never been opposed to slavery; indeed scriptural example in its favour could be plentifully cited – and was, right up to emancipation at the end of the American Civil War in 1865. But there were other texts that could be adapted well to the promotion of equality and universal brotherly love, and these Benezet urged.

His campaigning may have started in the 1750s, but his real influence spread later, in the 1770s, after he had begun writing. At his own expense he produced a number of tracts, one of which became the chief inspiration of efforts on both sides of the Atlantic to end the history-long atrocity of slavery. This was his *Some Historical Account of Guinea, Its Situation, Produce and the General Disposition of Its Inhabitants: An Inquiry into the Rise and Progress of the Slave Trade, Its Nature and Lamentable Effects*, published in 1771. It lit the touchpaper that was Enlightenment sensibility, and though the struggle it initiated took nearly a century and much bloodshed before it succeeded, its cause was unanswerable – the wonder is only that victory took so long.

The connection of Benezet's own motivations with the eighteenth-century temper of liberation, and his consciousness of his inheritance as one of those who had been victimised in the religious struggles of the sixteenth and seventeenth centuries, is apparent in the introduction to *Some Historical Account.* There he wrote that raising the question of slavery is appropriate 'especially at a time when the liberties of mankind are become so much the subject of general attention'. And he quotes Locke: 'Every man has a property in his own person. This nobody has a right to but himself. The labour of his body, and work of his hands are his own . . . For one man to have an absolute arbitrary power over another, is a power which nature never gives.'[4]

One of the compelling features of Benezet's book is its carefully documented but unflinching presentation of the plain but brutal truth about the slave trade and the life of slavery, which most people either did not know or did not care to think about. 'We have the relation of a voyage performed by Captain Philips, in a ship of 450 tuns, along the coast of Guinea, for elephants' teeth, gold, and Negro slaves, intended for Barbados; in which he says, that they took "seven hundred slaves on board, the men being all put in irons two by two, shackled together to prevent their mutinying or swimming ashore. That the Negroes are so loth to leave their own country, that they often leap out of the canoe, boat, or ship, into the sea, and keep under water till they are drowned, to avoid being taken up, and saved by the boats which pursue them." – They had about twelve Negroes who willingly drowned themselves; others starved themselves to death. – Philips was advised to cut off the legs and arms of some to terrify the rest (as other Captains had done), but this he refused to do. From the time of his taking the Negroes on board, to his arrival at Barbados, no less than three hundred and twenty died of various diseases.'[5]

These were among the first accounts of the horrors of the slave trade. As the abolitionist movement grew on both sides of the Atlantic, more and more of the scandalous and pitiable facts emerged: of how slaves were crammed into the holds of ships like sardines, and suffered there in appalling conditions during the weeks of the Atlantic passage; of how many died on the crossing or during the 'seasoning' process when they reached the other side, which prepared them for sale; of the vicious punishments and cruel treatment they endured. And then of the life of slavery itself, and what it could and did mean for the children and young men and women – they were invariably young – who had thus had their lives stolen from them.

The next important step was that Benezet's book fell into the hands of Thomas Clarkson, the person who, after him, proved to be the second most significant figure in the cause of anti-slavery.[6] Clarkson came from Norfolk, like Tom Paine, and was educated at Cambridge. While there he entered a Latin essay competition on the question *Anne Liceat Invitos in Servitutem Dare?* ('Is it lawful to make slaves of others against their will?'). The question had been devised by the university's Vice Chancellor, Peter Peckard, an Enlightenment figure who later wrote anti-slavery pamphlets himself. In preparing to write his essay Clarkson found that there was scarcely any reliable information available on the subject. Then he came across Benezet's book: 'I was in this difficulty when going by accident into a friend's house, I took up a newspaper there lying on the table. One of the first articles which attracted my notice was an advertisement of Anthony Benezet's *Historical Account of Guinea*. I soon left my friend and his paper, and, to lose no time, hastened to London to buy it. In this precious book I found almost all I wanted.'

It is of no surprise that the experience of examining the facts of slavery converted Clarkson to the cause of abolishing it, and he rewrote his essay in English and published it. It was immediately influential, and indeed appeared at just the right moment, for another individual who was to become notable in the abolition cause, Granville Sharp, was then setting up the Committee for Abolition of the Slave Trade.[7] Clarkson joined the Committee and became its tireless researcher, which involved the somewhat risky business of investigating the main slaving ports of Liverpool and Bristol, where anti-slavery campaigners were not welcome.

Granville Sharp had become involved in anti-slavery work as a result of an incident he witnessed in 1765 at the home of his brother, a surgeon in the East End of London. One night a black man called Jonathan Strong was brought to the house in a badly injured condition and close to death, having been severely beaten. He was a slave whose master, one David Lisle, had brought him to England from Barbados. It took several months for Strong to recover in St Bartholomew's Hospital, and when he was well Lisle sent men to get him back. Sharp took Lisle to court, on the grounds that no man is a slave in England; and, after a three-year battle, he won.

Most of those who gave their time, energy and money to the Committee were Dissenters – and most of these Quakers – which meant that none of them could occupy or aspire to occupy a seat in Parliament. Accordingly an MP was recruited to represent the campaign there, and in consequence came to be its public face. His name was William Wilberforce, and now, in the usual way of history's unjust apportionments, whether of praise or blame, he is the man most closely associated with the cause of anti-slavery.[8]

So successful were the Committee's efforts, and such the quality of the information Clarkson gathered and digested, that in February 1788 a Privy Council committee was convened to look into the matter. It found such evidence as that a slave ship (the *Brookes*) built to carry 451 people had 600 slaves packed into it. Briefed by Clarkson and the Committee, Wilberforce made a famous speech in the House of Commons on 12 May 1789, which, if the French Revolution had not started two months later, might have led to a far earlier abolition both of the British slave trade – then the largest in the world – and of slavery in the empire altogether. 'As soon as ever I had arrived thus far in my investigation of the slave trade,' Wilberforce said, addressing the Speaker of the House, 'I confess to you, sir, so enormous, so dreadful, so irremediable did its wickedness appear that my own mind was completely made up for the abolition. A trade founded in iniquity, and carried on as this was, must be abolished, let the policy be what it might – let the consequences be what they would, I from this time determined that I would never rest till I had effected its abolition.'[9]

In the event, abolition of the slave trade had to wait until 1807 for the brief and liberal government of the Ministry of All the Talents led by Charles James Fox, and abolition of slavery itself had to wait until 1833 and the Parliament elected after the passing of the 1832 Reform Bill.

Clarkson went to Paris in the autumn of 1789, full of hope that the new government there, with its declared championing of liberty and the rights of man, would be swift in ridding its own dominions of slavery. The French did indeed abolish slavery in 1794, only to have it restored by Napoleon in 1802 so that it had to be abolished again in 1848. But in England the anti-slavery question had dropped off the agenda for Parliament and the public alike – one reason being that Britain had captured the French colony of Haiti, only to be confronted by a slave uprising there led by Toussaint L'Ouverture. The dire struggle to put it down cost the British more lives than they had lost in the American War of Independence.[10]

Slavery had effectively been abolished in England itself since 1772 as a result of the case of James Somerset. He had been brought to Britain as the personal servant of a man who owned a sugar plantation in Jamaica. Somerset ran away and hid in London, where those who stood as his friends encouraged him to be baptised. On discovering his whereabouts his owner kidnapped him to return him to Jamaica, but his friends took out a writ of habeas corpus to recover him. The question for the Lord Chief Justice, Lord Mansfield, was whether Somerset's owner had a legal right to detain and dispose of him. On 22 June 1772 he concluded, 'Whatever inconveniences, therefore, may follow from a decision, I cannot say this case is allowed or approved by the law of England; and therefore the black must be discharged.' This in effect meant that slavery was not recognised in the common law. Mansfield's judgement resulted in the emancipation of between ten and fourteen thousand slaves who were in Britain at that time, and entailed that if any slaves were subsequently brought to Britain they would be free the moment their feet touched British soil.[11]

But what applied in the mother country did not apply in the empire at large; the British slave trade, carrying more than double the numbers of its nearest rival, was the largest in the world. This major industry poured money into the ports of Liverpool and Bristol, and fed a hunger for labour in the West Indies and North America that could scarcely be appeased. In the soon-to-be-independent North American colonies, plantation owners encouraged their slaves to breed, some even promising freedom to women who would produce fifteen children. Despite this, fresh imports of slaves were constantly in demand. And they were even more so on the sugar plantations of the West Indies and in the Spanish possessions of South America, for in both these places the death rate among slaves was so high that constant resupply was a necessity.

In the new United States abolition happened swiftly in the states of the North, but not of course in the South with its highly labour-intensive and at that time highly profitable cotton, tobacco and rice plantations.[12] It is not surprising that the conservative, traditionalist South should be more immune to eighteenth-century sentiment than the populous and varied North, which was more closely linked to Europe through travel and immigration.

The first article Tom Paine ever wrote, when newly arrived in America in 1774, was an attack on slavery. It was published on 20 November of that year in a Pennsylvania newspaper, and was entitled 'African Slavery in America'. In it Paine described slavery as a 'savage practice . . . contrary to the light of nature, to every principle of Justice and Humanity . . . the English are said to enslave towards one hundred thousand yearly, of which thirty thousand are supposed to die by barbarous treatment in the first year, besides all that are slain in the unnatural wars excited to take them . . . So monstrous is the making and keeping them slaves at all, abstracted from the barbarous usage they suffer, and the many evils attending the practice; as selling husbands away from wives, children from parents, and from each other, in violation of sacred and natural ties . . . Certainly one may, with as much reason and decency, plead for murder, robbery, lewdness and barbarity, as for this practice. They are not more contrary to the natural dictates of Conscience and feelings of Humanity, nay they are all comprehended in it.' And he asked, 'whether, then, all ought not immediately to discontinue and renounce it, with grief and abhorrence?'[13]

In 1775 the first anti-slavery society in America was established under the presidency of Benjamin Franklin, with a number of Quakers among its members including Benjamin Rush. It was called the Society for the Relief of Free Negroes Unlawfully held in Bondage, a title that ostensibly refers to freed slaves who had been kidnapped and returned to slavery. Among them were those who had escaped to northern states or Canada along what later famously came to be known as 'the underground railroad', a dangerous and clandestine route to freedom. But all 'negroes' were free by the rights of man, so the society's title usefully equivocated on the sentiments that prompted its formation. What those sentiments were was clear enough; one of its very first publications was Tom Paine's robust and eloquent 'African Slavery in America'.

The United States abolished the slave trade in 1794, in the sense that it forbade any citizen to engage in it, and in subsequent years outlawed slave trading by foreigners resident in the country (1800), forbade the importation of slaves into the country (1818), declared slave trading to be piracy punishable by death (1820), and in 1850 outlawed the sale of slaves in the District of Columbia. None of this abolished slavery itself in those (exclusively southern) states that still had it, where the maintenance of a slave population now relied wholly on 'breeding', and where the market in slaves continued.[14]

Slavery itself was abolished in New York in 1799, and the last northern state to follow suit was New Jersey in 1804. The method adopted was 'gradual' abolition, but it was abolition nonetheless. New York's abolitionist leaders included Aaron Burr and the Federalist Papers authors Alexander Hamilton and John Jay. These facts are significant. The United States is often indicted for having a grandiloquent preamble to its Constitution on the subject of man's equality and the value of liberty, while yet being the largest slave-based economy in what we now call the 'Western world'. The contradiction certainly existed, and not merely until 1865 but right into the 1960s, when the Civil Rights movement at last began to make a serious difference to the racism and de facto apartheid that existed especially in the US's southern states.[15] At the same time the examples of abolition in the northern states, and the conscience of the men involved, such as Anthony Benezet and Alexander Hamilton, Benjamin Franklin and Benjamin Rush, is testament to the fact that the effort to realise Enlightenment values in North America was not a sham.

Apart from the obvious intrinsic importance of the abolitionist movements on both sides of the Atlantic, and their eventual – but in human terms painfully slow – outcome, the significance of the anti-slavery chapter in the story of liberty is that, within a century of Enlightenment ideas about the rights of man becoming current, they had not only changed the political face of Western history, but had begun the process (not yet complete, but a long way forward) of dismantling ancient social, caste and racial divisions that justified the oppression of some by others – and usually the many by the few. When it is the few who dominate the many, oppression has to be effected by psychological means rather than force of arms, at least for the normal run of affairs. Religion has been the mighty adjunct here, making people believe that the few rule them by Divine Right, and that the order of their subjection is holy and just – or some such thing: history is also the story of grand lies and the captivity of mind they impose.

Resistance to anti-slavery campaigns took predictable forms, some of which followed this pattern. One species of argument had it that the black races were inferior, that both Aristotle and the Bible had delivered the inferior races over to slavery ('the sons of Ham shall be hewers of wood and drawers of water for ever' said the latter),[16] that they did not have the same emotions and sensitivities as white people, did not experience pain as much, and lacked both intelligence and imagination, and therefore neither regretted the past nor feared the future so much – in short, were beasts, and beasts of burden at that.

The third edition entry for 'Negro' in the *Encyclopaedia Britannica* (1798) makes educative reading on this score: 'Negro, *homo pelli nigra*, a name given to a variety of the human species, who are entirely black, are found in the Torrid Zone, especially in that part of Africa which lies within the Tropics. In the complexion of the Negro we meet with various shades; but they likewise differ far from other men in all the features of their face, round cheeks, high cheek-bones, a forehead somewhat elevated, a short, broad, flat nose, thick lips, small ears, ugliness, and irregularity of shape, characterise their external appearance. The Negro women have their loins greatly depressed, and very large buttocks, which give the back the shape of a saddle. Vices the most notorious seem to be the portion of this unhappy race; idleness, treachery, revenge, cruelty, impudence, stealing, lying, profanity, debauchery, nastiness and intemperance, are said to have extinguished the principles of natural law, and to have silenced the reproofs of conscience. They are strangers to every sentiment of compassion, and are an awful example of the corruption of man when left to himself.' It did not occur to the author of the *Encyclopaedia Britannica* article that if any of the imputed negative characteristics were accurate, it was because they represented the only resources open to subjected and oppressed people. Nor did he wonder whether he and his womenfolk might be found ugly by people of different experience and taste, blanched and soft as they were, the women needing padding to give them the steatopygia regarded as so charming in the tropics, but in which they were physically deficient.

The prevalence of the *Encyclopaedia Britannica* view of black people is evidenced by Thomas Jefferson's attitude. In a long essay he examined the respects in which black people were inferior to white people, and even though he did not defend the institution of slavery he wondered aloud how freed slaves were to be incorporated into society. One solution, adopted by the American Colonisation Society, was to return freed slaves to Africa, and to create a state for them there; hence the foundation of Liberia in 1821 after several false starts on other parts of the West African coast. Many freed slaves who had been born in America, as their parents and grandparents before them had been, did not wish to be sent to Africa, a strange land far away without the amenities of the country they were at least used to. Still, the very idea of a 'Liberia' is, for all the equivocality of it in practice, a striking mark of the era.[17]

Racist attitudes towards black people persist to this day everywhere, not least in the United States, and the myth of inferiority is part of it. But contemporaneous with the Enlightenment determination to end slavery was resistance to such attitudes, as shown by Benezet's remarks about the black children he taught.

The other species of argument used to justify slavery was that it amounted to rescuing 'negroes' from benightedness, from the savage, nasty and brutish life of the state of nature where they were no better than apes at war with one another. Evidently enslavement was a kindness to so 'unhappy' a 'variety of the human species', for (as many argued) they could thus be exposed to the saving influence of

Christianity, and could benefit from the example as well as the government of the superior white race. The thought of the infinite – literally – blessings of Christianity that they would have poured upon them by being rescued from their primitive state by enslavement and conveyance to the New World stirred the hearts of many with warmth. What a fine and noble endeavour slavery was, and how unfeeling of anti-slavery campaigners to try to stop rescuing the black man from the dangerous and hell-bound shadows of his jungles!

The answer to this pious and frequently disingenuous nonsense was provided first by Benezet, and then by others such as Paine, who stated the true facts of the case about Africa, and the nature of life and social organisation there. Part of the antidote to both the 'inferior being' view and the 'benighted' view came from no less a source than the Noble Savage thesis popularised by Jean-Jacques Rousseau, that ambiguous half-Enlightenment, half-Counter-Enlightenment figure – or perhaps he is more accurately to be described as something quite else, as one of the fathers of Romanticism.[18] Far from being inferior or sunk in a dangerous state of spiritual ignorance, said Rousseau, the alleged 'savage' is closer to nature, and therefore to truth, to the original golden age of man, and thus to the essence of being human, than the effete, bewigged, powdered, patched, mincing, overfed, tipsy, languishing, bored, lorgnette-waving dandy of the Paris salons.

This was a corollary of Rousseau's fundamental thesis that 'Man is born free but is everywhere in chains.' The sophistications of civilisation – 'sophistications' in its correct pejorative sense – are among the chains in question; the others of course are religion and monarchy and like tyrannies, but the useless elaborations of civilisation are chains because they mask and distort true feeling, true relationship, the true growth of the human heart. His *La Nouvelle Héloïse*, his account of the correspondence between Julie and Saint Preux, had an amazing impact on many who read it; William Hazlitt was one, who took himself off for a summer at Vevey, on Lake Geneva, to walk the paths of this story, and to visit the Castle of Chillon in whose dungeons had languished champions of liberty celebrated in the poetry of Byron.[19]

It was both right and inevitable that campaigns against slavery should make people see slavery in other places too: in the factories of the nascent industrial revolution, and in the kitchens of domesticity; the slavery – albeit of a different kind and order but slavery nevertheless – of workers and women.

'Slavery in Yorkshire' was the title given by Richard Oastler to a series of letters he published in the *Leeds Mercury* in 1830, describing the plight of workers in the mills of the town of Bradford, and attacking William Wilberforce, the local MP, for ignoring the slavery under his nose while basking in the glory of having led the abolitionist campaign in Parliament. 'Let truth speak out,' Oastler wrote, 'appalling as the statement may appear. The fact is true. Thousands of our fellow-creatures and fellow-subjects, both male and female, the inhabitants of a Yorkshire town (Yorkshire now represented in Parliament by the giant of anti-slavery principles), are at this very moment existing in a state of slavery more horrid than are the victims of that hellish system – Colonial Slavery. These innocent creatures draw out unpitied their short but miserable existence, in a place famed for its professions of religious zeal, whose inhabitants are ever foremost in *professing* 'Temperance' and 'Reformation', and are ever striving to outrun their neighbours in Missionary exertions, and would fain send the Bible to the farthest corners of the globe – aye in the very place where the anti-slavery fever rages most furiously, her *apparent charity* is not more admired on earth than her *real* cruelty is abhorred in heaven. The very streets which receive the droppings of an 'Anti-Slavery Society' are every morning wet with the tears of innocent victims at the accursed shrine of avarice, who are compelled, not by the cart-whip of the Negro slave-driver, but by the dread of the equally appalling thong or strap of the overlooker, to hasten half-dressed, but not half-fed, to those magazines of British Infantile Slavery – the Worsted Mills in the neighbourhood and town of Bradford! Thousands of little children, both male and female, but principally female, from seven to fourteen years, are daily compelled to labour from six o'clock to seven in the evening with only – Britons, blush whilst you read it! – with only thirty minutes allowed for eating and recreation.'[20]

The tone of outrage was justified by the fact that what Oastler described was the reality, and not just in Bradford. Throughout Britain the condition of these people was, to use Oastler's no less than accurate term, appalling. Enclosures and new methods of agriculture in the eighteenth century had driven huge numbers of people off the land; machine production and rapid industrialisation sucked them into towns which ballooned in size – between 1801 and 1831 the population of Liverpool grew from 82,000 to 202,000, of Manchester from 95,000 to 238,000, a pattern which repeated itself everywhere in the industrial regions of the country and even more in London. Yet even as machine and steam power moved tens of thousands from villages into industrial cities, it also threw many out of both; the Luddite riots that began in the closing years of the Napoleonic Wars were prompted by the reaction of frightened hand-loom weavers, faced with starvation, to the mechanisation of what had been their livelihood as a cottage industry.[21]

Everywhere there was agitation for action to be taken against the engulfing nightmare of unregulated, low-paid, slave-condition industrial labour, and in support of the distressed agricultural workers. In 1830 rebellion broke out among the latter in the southern counties of England – 'Have we no reason to complain that we have been obliged for so long to go to our daily toil with only potatoes in our satchels, and the only beverage to assuage our thirst the cold spring; and on retiring to our cottages to be welcomed by the meagre and half-famished offspring of our toilworn bodies?' asked a manifesto of Sussex farm labourers. A report from Hampshire said that 'nothing can be worse than the state of this neighbourhood. I may say that this part of the country is wholly in the hands of the rebels. Fifteen hundred rebels are to assemble tomorrow morning, and will attack any farmhouses where there are threshing machines. They go about levying contributions in every gentleman's house. There are very few magistrates; and what there are are completely cowed.'[22]

The uprising was put down by force, nine of its leaders were hanged, and hundreds of its participants were imprisoned or transported. A report from Winchester jail on 7 January 1831 described the scenes there of families seeing the last of their menfolk about to be transported: 'The scenes of distress in and about the jail are most terrible. The number of men who are to be torn from their homes and connections is so great that there is scarcely a hamlet in the country into which anguish and tribulation have not entered. Wives, sisters, mothers, children beset the gates daily, and the governor of the jail informs me that the scenes he is obliged to witness at the time of locking up the prison are truly heartbreaking.' Ten days later the local leaders of the insurrection were hanged on the jail roof for all to see: 'At this moment I cast my eyes down into the felons' yard,' says the anonymous author of the report, 'and saw many of the convicts weeping bitterly, some burying their faces in their smock frocks, others wringing their hands convulsively, and others leaning for support against the wall of the yard and unable to cast their eyes upward.'[23]

Imagine the hopelessness of these men, who had risen because they and their families were hungry, and had been hungry for a long time, and who knew the truth of why they were so. Yet they were defeated by a system against which there was no redress, and were now to be forcibly taken to Australia, on the other side of the world. One of the hardest things to bear, or even to hear about, is injustice so implacable and irremediable.

Following the troubles a member of the House of Lords moved that a subscription be raised to relieve the immediate distresses of the indigent in the southern agricultural districts. It was defeated by a large majority. Instead it was pointed out that the troubles had followed a visit to the region by several radical speakers, among them William Cobbett. It was decided to make the radicals an example to other would-be agitators, and they were put on trial. Cobbett was more than a match for the system; he defended himself with vigour, and was acquitted by the jury after it had deliberated for fifteen hours.[24]

Technological advancements can be a doubtful friend. Artificial lighting improved in quality, making it possible for factories to work longer hours. In many the workers were locked in after their dawn arrival, and the doors were opened only after darkness had fallen, twelve or more hours later. Ulstermen called factories 'lock-ups'.

A measure of the situation can be inferred from the first steps taken to address some of its worst aspects. In 1802 the working hours of poorhouse children set to work as apprentices in mills were reduced to twelve a day. The introduction of steam power made it unnecessary for mills to be situated alongside rivers and streams, so they were relocated to growing industrial towns where they were close to a plentiful supply of 'free' (that is, non-poorhouse) child labour. These children were not protected by the hours limitation law and could therefore be worked as many hours as the mill owner wished. In 1818 Sir Robert Peel endeavoured to extend the 1802 law's provisions to them too, initiating an interesting debate in Parliament about how many hours a day it was appropriate for children under ten to work. The Commons decided on eleven hours, but the Lords disagreed and postponed the bill. It was finally passed in 1819 with a limit of twelve hours for children aged nine to sixteen – but it included a first major step towards genuine reform, which was the banning of employment of children under nine.

More important than the actual provisions was the fact that they established a principle, namely, that government could legislate on matters of hours and conditions, thus trespassing on the privileges of parents and employers alike. This departure had an uphill battle against those in both houses of Parliament who thought the last thing that should be given to working-class children (or adults for that matter) was leisure: what would they do with it, other than make a nuisance of themselves? The thought anticipates the Duke of Wellington's lofty remark, some years later when the railways were burgeoning, that they would only result in 'the working classes moving needlessly about'. During a parliamentary enquiry into child labour Robert Owen was asked, in response to his statement that no child under ten should be at work, 'Would there not be a danger of their acquiring vicious habits for want of regular occupation?'[25]

The question might be thought by some to have a point: in the quickly growing cities of street after street of slums, there were no parks, no amenities, no entertainments within the affordability of workers – other than public houses, and, of course, not even they were genuinely affordable. A survey made as late as 1850 found that a third of all men and half of all women in the British working class were illiterate. The view of them as fodder for menial work and domestic service (this last one of the best fed and warmest of occupations, especially for women, although they were among the worst paid and not always safe from sexual harassment) did not allow room for thoughts of their education and culture – apart, that is, from proselytisation by inner-city evangelical missionaries and temperance groups.[26]

Of course working people made their own entertainment, and their communities were often close-knit and convivial.[27] But they were regarded by the middle and upper classes – who between them held all the wealth and political power in the realm, and therefore the competence to change things for the better if they chose – not merely with contempt because they were dirty and ill-educated, but with fear. This was the result of the French Revolution. The thought of mob violence engendered special horror. Given that there was no police force, and that the army was a cumbersome instrument when used in place of one, there was good reason for people to feel afraid if they had something to lose. All suggestions of moderate reform were accordingly met with the response that if the smallest of gaps were opened by making concessions, bloody revolution would be certain to explode through it. Walter Bagehot records a remark by the reformer Sir Samuel Romilly: 'If any person be desirous of having an adequate idea of the mischievous effects which have been produced in this country by the French Revolution and all its attendant horrors, he should attempt some reform on humane and liberal principles. He will then find not only what a stupid spirit of conservation, but what a savage spirit, it has infused into the minds of his countrymen.'[28]

It has to be said that the leaders of agitation for reform among working people did not help matters by the intemperate language of their pamphlets and speeches. The years between Waterloo and the Reform Act of 1832 were full of verbal and sometimes actual violence in political activism, to a degree that would be astonishing if replicated now. The employment of Jacobin and sanguinary language by the angry demagogues, even of French revolutionary symbols, was not likely to encourage different attitudes among conservatives.

The agitation and debate focused around one major point: the necessity of reforming Parliament, which was hopelessly unrepresentative, and mainly in the pockets of large landowners, the majority of them aristocrats. Old Sarum in Wiltshire with no electors returned two members to Parliament whereas most of the large manufacturing towns returned none. There were many such 'rotten boroughs' entirely in the gift of a local magnate, who could simply appoint whom he liked to sit in the House of Commons. On one calculation a third of the seats were in direct gift in this way. Eight noblemen between them appointed fifty-seven MPs. Only in Westminster and Bristol were there parliamentary seats elected by something resembling democratic means, and the former of them often served as a test case for public sentiment in the country. However, their existence did not appease, but rather inflamed democratic sentiment by their contrast with the rest.[29]

Viewed from the perspective of a history of liberty, the clamour for more representative government is precisely the next logical step in the tale, and in the case of Britain with its long tradition of focus on Parliament as the seat of reform and disputes with the Crown, it was altogether natural that the hopes of the poor and dispossessed should turn on making it more representative. Those who thought this were largely right; but once again the process of prising the fingers of vested interests off the handles of power took time. The reform of 1832 was followed by extensions of the franchise on four occasions – the first of them in 1867 – until at last in 1929 universal adult suffrage was achieved when the voting age for women was reduced from thirty to twenty-one, in line with men. (Its reduction to the age of eighteen in 1969 was not a further step of democratisation so much as a reflection of change in social attitudes – a paradoxical one, in this case, because as childhood has been lengthened and with it the span of years spent in education, so the onset of adulthood has been moved in the opposite direction.) But the key reform was the first one, even though it was relatively minor in effect, because it established the principle that the national system of representation was reformable, and it lanced a boil of near-revolution in the process.

Yet the manner in which that first reform came about was full of paradox, danger and black comedy. The country's politics were in a tangled state following the death in 1827 of George Canning, an able politician and minister who had held together a coalition government that no one else would have found possible to manage. That impossibility now proved itself, and for the next three years the administration of the country, not aided by the incompetence and personal animosities of George IV, passed uneasily from hand to hand among the quarrelsome and much-divided factions of both Whig and Tory, until the Duke of Wellington formed a government with Sir Robert Peel. Wellington was therefore the unlikely person to preside as prime minister over Catholic emancipation in the United Kingdom, an epoch, though a very belated one, in the history of religious tolerance.

Agitation for parliamentary reform in the country at large was not merely continuing, but growing. In 1830 a series of events brought the matter to a head. One was the death of George IV and the succession of his brother William IV, father of the future Queen Victoria. As was customary following a change of monarch, a general election was called, and in the constituencies where the result gave some indication of public feeling it was clear that there was a majority for reform.

The other event was the July Revolution in France, which threw out the last of the Bourbon kings, Charles X, and replaced him with the 'Citizen King', Louis-Philippe. This event revived enthusiasm for French methods of effecting constitutional change, to the alarm of the British Establishment. It was now clear to many of those returned in the 1830 election that reform of the system of representation which had brought them to Parliament could not now be delayed. Reform clubs such as the London Radical Reform Society and the Birmingham Political Union were energetically keeping the matter at the forefront of public attention. Wellington's government had to resign after he caused an outcry by expressing the view that the existing system of representation was 'perfect', and he was succeeded as prime minister by the Whig peer Lord Grey, who agreed to form an administration on the express understanding that it would introduce a reform bill.[30]

It is a remarkable fact that the cabinet put together by Grey for the task of introducing a measure for the reform of the country's system of representation was entirely composed of aristocrats, all but four of them sitting with him in the House of Lords. The four who sat in the Commons were the son of an earl, an Irish peer (Palmerston), an extremely wealthy English baronet, and an equally wealthy Scottish landowner who was soon elevated to the peerage.

A cabinet committee drew up a reform bill and presented it to the Commons on 1 March 1830. It surprised almost everyone with its far-reaching nature – using this phrase in relative terms – for it disenfranchised sixty small boroughs, redistributed seats to manufacturing towns and big counties, gave more seats to Wales, Scotland and Ireland, and of course abolished 'rotten' and 'pocket' boroughs in the process. The franchise was granted in towns to householders of properties worth ten pounds a year, and similar property qualifications applied in the counties.

The Tories vehemently opposed the bill, and their opposition focused support in the country for the Whig government. Tories blamed the Whigs for encouraging the popular ferment, and Peel in his speech opposing the bill presciently said that it could only be the first such 'levelling' measure, because for the first time it drew a sharp line between those with and without the vote, and the latter would campaign for it, until democracy (remember that this was then a word of horror, recalling the Jacobin rabble in the streets of Paris) was complete. Lord Macaulay made an equally impassioned speech, pleading with the House to save the country from revolution: 'Save property, divided against itself. Save the multitude, endangered by their own ungovernable passions. Save the aristocracy, endangered by its own unpopular power,' he said; 'The danger is terrible. The time is short.'

He was not being hyperbolic; the temperature of popular feeling directed at the Tories' opposition to the bill was running high. On 23 March the bill passed its second reading by just one vote, courtesy of the Irish members. In April the Tories voted the bill down in committee stage, and Lord Grey asked William IV to dissolve Parliament for a general election. William at first refused; but then was obliged to agree.

There was much reform excitement in the country, almost all of it confident of success, in the general election campaign. The reformers returned to Parliament with a larger majority in May, and the following month introduced a second bill, almost exactly the same as the first except that it made a concession to the landed interest by an adjustment to the rural franchise. In September the bill passed the last of its stages in the Commons. In the House of Lords in October, after five days of debate, it was defeated.

The mood in the country turned ugly. Two London newspapers were published with black borders to signify mourning, as they were when a monarch died. In Birmingham the city's bells were muffled and rung as for a state funeral. There was rioting in a number of towns. A Member of Parliament who had voted against the bill, and who was also a legal officer in Bristol, was attacked when he visited the city in the course of his duties. The Mansion House where he lodged was sacked, the city prisons broken into, the bishop's palace and a number of other buildings burned down. Squadrons of cavalry had to be sent to the city to quell the disturbances.[31]

Everywhere there were huge mass meetings, and authorities in towns around the country, with little in the way of police resources, were terrified that the Bristol events would repeat themselves in their own localities. Some of the political clubs began to talk of forming themselves into paramilitary units. Almost the only thing that held revolution at bay was the ministry's promise to persist with efforts to get a bill through. Grey discussed the matter with the king, who thought that the majority against the bill in the House of Lords was too large to be overwhelmed by creating new peers.

In December a third bill was introduced, containing a number of concessions chiefly made possible by giving up the idea of reducing the number of MPs in the Commons, which had been part of the first two proposals. The king did his utmost to persuade the twenty-six bishops in the House of Lords to support the revised bill. They were adamantly against, fearful that more democracy would threaten their privileges. (It has yet to happen, at time of writing.) Some in Grey's cabinet began to press for a mass creation of pro-reform peers, irrespective of the dilution to the peerage that would result. The king was prepared to create a dozen as a sign that he might create more, provided they were all sons of existing peers. (That meant that their titles would be subsumed into their fathers' titles when they inherited the latter, thus keeping the number of peers down and preserving their 'blue blood'). By such aristocratical means was democracy helped forward in the Mother of Parliaments, for the mere threat of the new creations persuaded enough peers in the Upper House either to support the bill on second reading there, or to abstain; and it passed.

But there was still the committee stage of the bill to get through, and the Lords began to interfere with its provisions. The ministers in Grey's government resigned in protest, with relief in most cases; the strain of work attendant on trying to get the bill through had been immense. Once again the country seethed dangerously. The king asked the Tories to form a government, on the understanding that they would introduce a moderate reform bill; Wellington, always obedient to the commands of his king, agreed; but Peel and other influential members of the party refused to join, on the grounds that they had opposed reform completely and were not now going to change their minds. The duke had to tell the king that he could not make a government.

King William then asked Grey to return to office, and he agreed on the strict understanding that he was to have his bill 'unimpaired in its principles and its essential provisions', which meant that the king had to promise – with immense reluctance – to create enough peers to carry the House of Lords if it still proved obdurate. To avoid the necessity William exerted all his influence on the Tories, begging them not to make a mass creation necessary. Wellington dutifully agreed; some of the other Tory peers did not. Because of abstentions (Wellington pulled his hat over his eyes and pretended to go to sleep when the third reading vote was called) the bill passed on 4 June 1832.

Grey asked the king to come to Parliament in person to give assent to the bill, the formulaic way of transforming a bill into an Act. He believed that this would repair the king's reputation in the country, which had been damaged by his reluctance to stand fully behind the reform. William refused, and the Royal Assent was given by messenger.

*

The passing of the first reform bill in the British Parliament was far from a local matter. The United Kingdom, as Britain had become in 1801 with the incorporation of Ireland, was the world's superpower in the nineteenth century, governing a vast extent of empire. As that century progressed its institutions and practices influenced the world at large in two ways. First, they were emulated, in various respects and to greater and lesser degrees, by smaller powers; and secondly, Britain endowed its imperial possessions with those institutions and practices, all the way from parliament and common law to education, sports and social mores (not all of these latter especially admirable, it has to be said; especially class snobbery). Arguably therefore it is the example of British evolution towards democracy in the nineteenth century that set a pattern for liberal polities in Europe, and it certainly established that pattern in its empire when later its components became independent – in the dominions of Canada, Australia and New Zealand, in the West Indies, less securely in South Africa, less securely still in other former African dependencies, and most remarkably in India, exemplary for being a genuine democracy despite its vast population, religious tensions, and problems of caste and diversity.

Of course the United States was already a democracy, and had been so for more than fifty years before Britain undertook its first and largely tentative parliamentary reform; but until the last third of the nineteenth century the United States was a minor player on the world stage. This status changed very quickly as its west opened up, and the combination of its vast resources, ebullient human energy, and almost limitless possibilities made it surge rapidly towards world status. By the time it achieved this status most parts of the Western world had or were adopting constitutions, bills of rights, and representative assemblies. The United States could be looked to as a model in some of these respects, though its too recent institution of slavery and its problem of establishing the rule of law on its frontiers made some observers sceptical.

The main point about the creation of the United States' fundamentally Enlightenment polity is that it was the outcome of revolution: the decks were cleared, a fresh start could be made, and to the infinite credit of the Constitution's founding fathers it was done with genius. But in Britain reform was not so easy. In one of the oldest of the Old World countries there was no sweeping of the decks clean; reform had to come in the midst of longstanding entanglements and many historical inhibitions. Thus the turning point for reform as opposed to revolution, for the idea of constitutional progression towards change, of accommodation of existing institutions to new demands, though forced on the conservative sections of a reluctant governing class in the first instance, was in its way an heroic achievement; and it became a norm of expectation after 1832, which is its greatest contribution. Prior to that time the only resource was revolutions, but from then on the hope was that reforming change could be achieved without them.[32]

Some will say that the revolutions of 1848 throughout Europe and especially in France and the Austro-Hungarian Empire are proof that the forces of reaction were still not prepared to let go without bloodshed, and that the bad old pattern persisted. But in one sense at least 1848 suggests the opposite. Soldiers opened fire, people died on barricades, others were imprisoned, yes; and this is another of the continuous stream of instances demonstrating how hard won each step in the progress towards liberty was, and how it remains always at risk of being reversed. But one result was that the governing powers of the affected European states submitted to the beginnings, at least, of reform processes internally, even as they also hardened under the impulse of a new monster on the block: nationalism, which was to offer a different threat to the lives, liberty and property of their people in the shape of the violent wars of the twentieth century's first half.[33]

Of course, as these wars and what happened after the two greatest of them – the First and Second World Wars – show, there have continued to be deviations from the norm. Several European countries succumbed for a time to bad old ways that consisted in a recovery of absolutism and the false rationales for dictatorial power – the worst examples of modern versions being Fascism in Italy, Spain and Portugal, Nazism in Germany, Stalinism in the Soviet Union – and several (including many countries in what came to be known as Eastern Europe) were captured for half a century by the Soviet perversion of a socialist dream.

But the norm from which these were deviations was constitutional adaptation, in which governments change smoothly, peacefully and in orderly fashion according to the expressed wills of electorates, a remarkable state of affairs so soon – in historical terms – after most of the countries of Europe were absolute monarchies, not much more than two centuries ago.

Still, the reform of Parliament in 1832 did not by a magician's snap of the fingers address the wrongs of working people, or enfranchise them. It left five out of six working men voteless, and they had to wait until 1867 before the next step was taken to widen the franchise. For basic rights in the workplace and a living wage – for an end to wage-slavery, in effect – a different hard battle had to be fought.

The question of the rights of workers is appropriately discussed in the British context because Britain was the world's first industrial power, and the problems caused by industrialisation were experienced and faced there in acute form before anywhere else. Some of the responses to those problems established a pattern for other countries, establishing a benchmark which shows how some economies to this day fail to protect either their workers or their natural environment from the harms that the behemoth of industrialisation can cause – the People's Republic of China being the egregious example.

Britain's industrial revolution was also the source of many of the facts and figures – gathered by Friedrich Engels, son of a Manchester industrialist – which constituted the material for analysis in Marx's *Das Kapital*, and it provided the model on which Marx, incorrectly as it proved, predicted the future course of history. As things turned out, the extension of ideas of rights into the workplace was a significant corollary of their application to politics and the individual in the evolution of Western liberal democracies – on the whole a more rather than less peaceful evolution – and this fact, which controverts Marx, is one of great moment. It effected a largely peaceful and gradual revolution; of course too gradual for those who lived through the early phases of the process, but a revolution nonetheless.

The Whig government of Lord Grey had battled to get the first reform bill through Parliament, and had thereby laid down a principle, and equally importantly an expectation, of further reform by constitutional means. But it matched this progressive step with a deeply retrograde one: the introduction of a new Poor Law in 1832 governing the treatment of unemployed and indigent persons. For many reasons the law's effects were especially harmful in comparison to the arrangements it replaced, but not least because it came in the midst of the increasing hardships caused by industrialisation.[34] The country was growing rich because of industry, but at the expense of the labourers at its literal and figurative coalfaces, whether they were in work, where they suffered harsh conditions and minimal wages, or out of work and hungry, made so by mechanisation and the shift from old to new industrial practices.

Until the new Poor Law the unemployed and indigent received 'outdoor relief' provided by the parish in which they lived. 'Outdoor relief' meant that they could remain in their own homes or, if they were homeless, in the fields and byways, which doubtless could not have been pleasant even if it were not cold and wet, but they would be better off than with the new Poor Law. This stated that there would be no help given to able-bodied unemployed people unless they went into a workhouse, there to live a regimented life as if in prison, doing long hours of menial work to justify a dole of food and shelter. The workhouses segregated men from women in different dormitories and workrooms, and therefore families were separated when they entered. That piled misery on wretchedness, but the alternative was starvation.

The workhouses almost instantly became hated and feared places, and the stigma attached to having to go into one, or having been in one, was enormous. Today one can still see some of the old workhouses in English cities – vast barrack-like buildings, looming prominently as if in admonition to the surrounding populace, like fortresses – now turned to different uses; hospitals in some cases, or 'lunatic asylums' as such institutions were once called.

The premise for the new harsh poor relief regime was the good biblical one that 'none shall eat unless he work'. There was an evangelical

Christian fervour stirring in the country of a moralistic and unchari-
table kind, its uncharitableness directly proportional to its vigorous
professions of charity, which consisted mainly in interference in the
lives of the less fortunate. It was also believed that too many people were
lazy and living on parish relief out of choice.

Working people were thus caught in a pincer. During the French
Revolutionary and Napoleonic Wars the government had passed a
succession of laws against 'combinations', that is, organisations promoting causes such as reform, workers' rights or wage demands. The
laws were aimed at nipping revolutionary movements in the bud, but
they had the direct corollary effect of making anything like a nascent
trade union illegal.[35] So the overworked, underpaid, half-starved, slum-
housed worker could not join with others to lobby for better conditions
and pay, and if he lost his job and could not find another, he had only
the choice of starving or entering the workhouse, because he was one
solitary man in the system without a support network of his own kind.

This was the dire background against which the struggle for
workers' rights began. Some among working people were heartened
by the passing of the first reform bill whose effect was, for them, a
promissory note for the future. But they wished to bring the hoped-
for benefits of that promise to fruition more quickly, and because
they knew that their circumstances would not finally and properly
change until the system of representation allowed them to elect their
own MPs, they were not prepared to go on slaving and starving while
they waited for the upper and middle classes to volunteer a greater
share of power to them.

The first efforts at industry-wide as opposed to purely local trades
unions began in the late 1820s, and were faltering affairs because the
organisational and financial skills for managing them were lacking. Far-
sighted individuals among the early unionists recognised that organised
labour could constitute a powerful weapon for bargaining with and
influencing employers and governments alike, and their aim was to
harness and channel that power in the direction of reform.[36] The first
significant such endeavour was the Grand National Consolidated
Trades Union. One of its main aims was the standard one of improving

the wages and conditions of its members; the other was to continue the campaign for reform of parliamentary representation.

The Grand National Consolidated was the brainchild of Robert Owen, the utopian socialist.[37] He was an experienced man of business, a wealthy factory owner and an avid reader of the eighteenth-century *philosophes*, who had become a factory manager at the remarkably early age of nineteen in one of Manchester's largest factories. Later he became a partner in a big Scottish mill, and went on to set up his own factories in Lanark, constructing them to the highest specifications and building model villages for his workers to live in nearby. From the Enlightenment philosophers he took the idea that human character is strongly influenced by environment; the housing and amenities he provided for his workforces, and the conditions in his model factories, were aimed at proving the truth of that conviction.

Owen was influenced by the nascent science of economics summoned into existence by the increasingly complicated nature of production and commerce since the seventeenth century.[38] Such indeed was the degree of their complexity that it had become necessary for good Enlightenment minds to apply themselves to it as systematically as possible. A generative classic of the new science was Adam Smith's *Wealth of Nations*. For Owen a more immediate impact came from the work of David Ricardo and Patrick Colquhoun. Ricardo argued that the value of commodities is largely a function of the amount of labour that goes into making them.[39] An answer was therefore required to the question, What is the right compensation to labour for its part in creating product value? One answer given by Colquhoun in his ambitious survey of the wealth of the British Empire, published in book form in 1814, was that labour's share is one quarter of the whole value. It was an approximation, but a reasonable one; and it gave reformers a benchmark to work to.[40]

For early socialists like Owen (he coined the term 'socialism' in 1817) the problem lay with the capitalist's claim to a share of the product value for his risk, and management's claim to a share for its endeavours. Both ate up too much of what was rightfully the worker's share, Owen thought, not least because management was under compulsion to maximise the capitalist's reward by every expedient, and was largely in control of determining its own. The solution Owen proposed was co-operative production. He believed that the economy could be wholly converted to the co-operative model by peaceful means. He was no revolutionary, and he dissociated himself from the radicals and demagogues to whom distressed working folk avidly listened, some of whom called for strikes and revolution to hasten reform.[41]

Given the difficulties of turning British practices round, Owen thought he would have a better chance of establishing a co-operative movement in the United States, and visited there in 1824 to investigate the possibilities. They did not prove promising enough. On his return to Britain he threw himself into the task of promoting co-operative societies and setting out what then and for a long time afterwards were thought utopian views on education, the health and safety of workers, care of the elderly, provision of parks in cities, the psychological effects of working and housing conditions, and much more – views which are now taken for granted though insufficiently credited to Owen's zeal. Works as widely separated in time as *The Social System* (1821) and *The Book of the New Moral World* (1842) show him tirelessly and con-sistently extolling his vision of good arrangements: 'To preserve permanent good health, the state of mind must be taken into con-sideration' . . . 'In advanced age, and in cases of disability from accident, natural infirmity or any other cause, the individual shall be supported by the colony, and receive every comfort which kindness can administer' . . . 'To obtain and preserve health in the best state to ensure happiness, pure air is necessary. It is at once obvious that large cities and extensive manufactories are not well calculated to permit pure air to be enjoyed by those who live in the one, or who are employed in the other' . . . '[In model workers' villages people] will be surrounded by gardens, have abundance of space in all directions to keep the air healthy and pleasant. They will have walks and plantations before them' . . . 'It is therefore the interest of all, that every one, from birth, should be well educated, physically and mentally that society may be improved in its character, – that everyone should be beneficially employed, physically and mentally, that the greatest amount of wealth may be created, and knowledge attained, that everyone should be placed in the midst at those external circumstances, that will produce the greatest number of pleasurable sensations, through the longest life, that man may be made truly intelligent, moral and happy' . . . 'There is but one mode by which man can possess in perpetuity all the happiness which his nature is capable of enjoying, – that is by the union and co-operation of all for the benefit of each.'[42]

It is easy to see why these sentiments were considered utopian in their day, and equally easy to see why they are no longer quoted: it is because they have become commonplaces. But Owen introduced them into his own factories and workers' villages, and conjoined a robust paternalism to his utopianism, encouraging illiterate adults to learn along with their children, specifying the evenings in the week when dances would be held in the community centre, specifying an eight-hour day when all other workers, including children, were labouring twelve or fourteen hours a day. 'Eight hours daily labour is enough for any human being, and under proper arrangements sufficient to afford an ample supply of food, raiment and shelter, or the necessaries and comforts of life, and for the remainder of his time, every person is entitled to education, recreation and sleep'; 'The lowest stage of humanity is experienced when the individual must labour for a small pittance of wages from others.'

Owen was mindful that not everyone shared the same tastes – 'The three lower rooms (in the Institute where the children are educated) will be thrown open for the use of the adult part of the population, who are to be provided with every accommodation requisite to enable them to read, write, account, sew or play, converse or walk about. Two evenings in the week will be appropriated to dancing and music, but on these occasions, every accommodation will be prepared for those who prefer to study or to follow any of the occupations pursued on the other evenings' – and he was mindful that not everyone shared the same religion: '[I]t is particularly recommended, as a means of uniting the inhabitants of the village into one family, that while each faithfully adheres to the principles which he most approves, at the same time all shall think charitably of their neighbours respecting their religious opinions, and not presumptuously suppose that theirs alone are right.'[43]

Owen was a remarkable man, a visionary, a philanthropist, and a shaper of the future. His model village of New Lanark is today a UNESCO World Heritage Site, as many of his humane and advanced principles are part of the world's heritage too – at least in the Western world. But one man and what in relative terms was a tiny experiment (though it has had these remarkable long-term effects) did little for the immediate situation. Impatience and necessity combined to make the desperate working population engage in more direct endeavours, which sometimes appeared to have a revolutionary character, but in fact were more in line with the precedent of constitutional reform set by the 1832 Reform Act. This was the attempt to organise a mass petitionary movement to press the government for further reform, and it is known as Chartism.

Owen's Grand National Consolidated Trades Union attracted half a million members and associate members, and startled the government accordingly. But it failed because its very existence raised expectations among working people that it could not meet. Its members became precipitate, starting disorganised strikes in different localities, and sought to extend union membership without proper supervision of its central officers. In 1834 in Tolpuddle, Dorset, six of its members were arrested, tried and sentenced to transportation for seven years because they had illegally administered oaths to others in their union. There was an outcry at the harshness of the sentences, and the six instantly became – and have since remained – martyrs for the cause of working people. As a result of a huge petition, one of the first in the strategy of mass petitions that the workers' movement now put into action, the six martyrs were pardoned and brought home.[44]

The collapse of the Grand National Consolidated reinforced the view of thoughtful leaders of the workers' cause that they had to get representatives into Parliament, which of course first necessitated further reform of the representational system. The idea of a mass petition was adopted as in itself a democratic and surely unanswerable means to call on the conscience of Parliament, asking it to open its doors to those who could truly speak for working men.

One of the leaders of the group which formed to pursue this aim, and which called itself the London Working Men's Association, was William Lovett. He was the son of a sea captain who had been a cabinet maker and then a member of a trading co-operative before becoming secretary of the British Association for Promoting Co-operative Knowledge.[45] With his fellows he drafted the People's Charter, calling for universal male suffrage, equal electoral districts, the removal of the property qualification for membership of Parliament, secret ballots, an annually elected Parliament, and salaries for Members of Parliament. With the exception of annual elections, this is what the system of representation was to become; indeed it was to become more with the inclusion of female suffrage. But in May 1838 when the Charter was drafted it was certain to get nothing better than a dusty answer.[46]

No sooner had the Charter been published than the cautious and moderate process envisaged by the London Working Men's Association was hijacked by enthusiasts. The Association's plan was to gather millions of signatures and present the Charter and its supporting petition to Parliament; the enthusiasts who clambered aboard were angry on behalf of working people, affronted by the Poor Law, and not interested in peaceful agitation for change; they proposed to back the petition with threats of civil unrest if necessary.

It did not take much for the demagogues among them to inflame popular meetings at which signatures for the Charter were being gathered. Workers were disappointed at the failure of the Grand National Consolidated, frustrated by exclusion from the political process, unable to get their demands met by employers, and scared of the workhouse. They wanted immediate action, and the demagogues were promising it. Chief among them was an Irish MP called Feargus O'Connor who owned a newspaper based in Leeds, the *Northern Star*, which served as the movement's mouthpiece. Because of this, because of having a seat in Parliament for an Irish constituency, and because he was a compelling speaker, O'Connor usurped the leadership of the movement and gave it a much more radical slant.

Meetings of the Chartists grew larger and noisier, and began to be held at night with torchlight processions. This alarmed the government, then led by Lord Melbourne, a prime minister engaged in coaching the very young Queen Victoria through the first years of her reign. But fearful of inflaming matters further, the government did nothing beyond monitoring the situation.

On 6 May 1839 a petition of 1,200,000 names was handed in to the House of Commons. The next day the government resigned, but over a problem affecting the government of Jamaica, a matter entirely separate from the petition. This meant that the Chartists had to wait until a new government was formed. They profited from the opportunity by moving their centre of operations from London to Birmingham, which strengthened the hand of the more radical among them.

Meanwhile some among the Chartist groups in the northern parts of the country had begun to drill, to talk of backing petitions with violence if their demands were not met, and to circulate instruction leaflets on the use of the pike. In response the government appointed General Sir Charles Napier to organise military security measures.[47] One of the first things he did was to invite leaders of the Chartists to a demonstration of artillery bombardment and musketry. The display had a sobering effect. Napier was himself sympathetic to the Chartist cause, but not to violent means of pursuing it, and he used the demonstrations as an effective way of cooling the hotter heads behind it.

Napier was largely successful, but some rioting occurred and two of the Chartists' leaders were arrested (even though they had been trying to stop the riot). Lovett was arrested too, despite being a moderate who deprecated violence, because he courageously undertook to publish a protest against the arrest of the other two. He was held for nine days, and was cheered by large crowds when released on bail.

On 12 July 1839 the House of Commons voted by 235 to 46 not even to consider the petition. This face-slapping decision amounted to calling the Chartists' bluff, for there had been much talk among the enthusiasts of a country-wide general strike if the petition were not accepted. No strike occurred, and as a result the Chartist movement effectively and rather lamely fizzled into nothing for the time being.

But the movement was not dead. Over the next couple of years its leaders regained their courage and set up a new body, the National Charter Association, determined to gather and present a new petition. The second version of the Charter attacked the Poor Law and listed a number of working peoples' grievances, and iterated the demand for universal suffrage. This time 3,317,752 signatures were gathered, and on 2 May 1842 brought to the House of Commons. A debate was held on the question of whether the petition should be received, and since its main demand concerned the franchise, the leaders of both sides of the House condemned it. Macaulay said that there could only be a universal suffrage if there was universal education, because a complete democracy 'could only be fatal to all purposes for which government exists'. He went so far as to argue that a universal franchise among an uneducated people was 'incompatible with the very existence of civilisation'.[48] In that climate the second petition was not likely to get any further than the first. The House refused to receive the petition by 287 to 49 votes.

This time there was no fizzling away of the Chartist movement. Strikes broke out in Lancashire and spread rapidly south to the Midlands and north to Glasgow. There were riots in a number of places, but the government was in no mood to be lenient; scores of people were arrested in the disturbances, and sentenced to transportation.

Moderates among the Chartists meanwhile had been organising separately from the main events, and at the end of 1842 some of them proposed to start a campaign for adoption of a bill of rights. Because this represented a shift from the main focus of the Chartist movement it caused a split, further weakening the movement's moderate section. With Feargus O'Connor once more able to direct its affairs, the movement was set for its last and greatest defeat. At first, though, it seemed on course for victory. O'Connor was elected to an English constituency, a mark of his popularity in the country, and he had begun to acquire a European reputation because of his contacts with German radicals and revolutionaries, whom he had met while on a visit to Belgium to study farming methods there. As an MP and leader of the radical movement in Britain he was admired by Engels and Marx, who wrote to say that they applauded his endeavours on behalf of working people. When the revolutionary events of 1848 in France and elsewhere raised political sensibility to fever pitch in Britain, O'Connor and the Chartists resolved to catch the tide and gather another petition, this time with a campaign of agitation in support of it.

When a convention of Chartists met to discuss the new campaign, hotheads among them rose to proclaim that the country was ready for revolution. O'Connor and other leaders would not support the call for violence, and in the end the convention decided to back the petition with an address to Queen Victoria asking her to dismiss the government and call a National Assembly to implement the Charter's demands. The Chartists agreed also that they would march on Parliament to present the petition en masse.

This last idea was one that the government would not tolerate, and it immediately invoked an ancient law that forbade groups of more than ten people from approaching the precincts of the House. The Chartists planned to meet on 10 April 1848 on Kennington Common and march from there to Westminster. When O'Connor arrived at the Common he found far fewer people than he had hoped, and moreover many of them were spectators and not activists. He was met by the police, who informed him that a march would not be allowed to cross any of the bridges into the northern part of the city. As the speeches began, so did the rain, and the event became a washout. But the extent of its failure only became clear when the petition – after being delivered to the Commons in a dismal little procession of three hansom cabs and a few men soaked by the rain – was found to contain many absurd forgeries, among them Punch of Punch and Judy fame, the Duke of Wellington, and the queen herself.

The comedy – worse, the bathos – of this end to the working class's great petitionary endeavour is interesting in light of the fact that every one of its substantive demands was eventually met, and in less than a century after they were made. It is remarkable and heartening how defeats turn out really to be victories in this way. This would be no consolation, if prophecy could have informed them of it, to the hungry and dispirited men who signed and marched and took the risk of being thrown out of work as troublemakers, to see their families starve because they had taken action, for that was the reality they faced. But quite a few of them, those that lived just nineteen years more, would witness the next widening of the franchise, effected in 1867; and they would perhaps have understood that history was moving gradually but inexorably their way.

Another indication that history was moving slowly in the right direction, independently of the political agitation of Chartism, was that the rights of workers were being incrementally secured through a series of Acts of Parliament concerned with working hours and conditions. A long-standing demand of workers was for a ten-hour day, and reformers concerned with the plight of women and children in factories had managed in piecemeal fashion to raise the age at which children were allowed to work, to reduce the working hours of women, and to have safety measures taken, for example to protect women from having their long skirts caught in the wheels and pistons of machinery.[49]

Each advance was bitterly contested by most of the manufacturers and their parliamentary representatives. An early move in the amelioration of working hours was a bill introduced in Parliament in 1831 to raise the age limit from sixteen to eighteen for girls to work twelve or more hours a day. Cobbett wrote scathingly of the fierce opponents of this proposal that they seemed to think the economy of England turned on whether or not '30,000 little girls . . . worked two hours a day less' in their factories. Opponents of working-time reform pointed out that because of the way mills operate, a ten-hour working day for children would mean a ten-hour working day for everyone, for the childrens' job was to assist the machine operatives who would not be able to continue working if the children were absent. A myth persisted for years that no regulation of men's working hours was needed because the men independently negotiated their hours with their employers. This was scarcely ever true; men worked the hours they were told to work, or they did not eat.

The working hours bill of 1831 became law in 1833 because a parliamentary committee of enquiry found that many children worked excessively long hours in appalling conditions, and their description of what they had learned shocked public opinion. Engels was, surprisingly, critical of the report when he discussed it as background to his *Condition of the Working Class in England in 1844*, because he believed the MPs who had drawn it up were hostile to the factory system (from which his family derived its livelihood). But apart from furthering the precedent of government intervention in regulating the activities of private companies, the 1833 enquiry had another important effect: it converted Anthony Ashley, Earl of Shaftesbury, to the cause of reform in industrial practices, and he became the leader in a gradual process of civilising the nature of industrial work.

Bottom-up agitation for access to the seats of power, and top-down piecemeal reform of industrial practices, constituted a significant part of the story; but a major place was taken by the trades union movement that grew out of the ruins of Chartism. A key fact was the almost uninterruptedly sustained economic growth in Britain between the late 1840s and the 1870s. In economic downturns the bargaining position of labour is weak relative to its power in periods of growth when demand for labour is high. Conducive economic circumstances enabled workers to organise more effectively than before.

A second important factor was that the model for the newly emerging trades unions was the craft organisation of skilled technicians, who among other things were better at administering their affairs and conducting their campaigns. The Amalgamated Society of Engineers, founded in 1851, served as a paradigm for others; it was a national union with a centralised administration able to employ paid officials because of a regular system of membership levies, and it profited from its legal status as a 'friendly society'.[50]

With the new species of union came an improved and more effective method of advancing the interests of working people. Instead of agitation, demagoguery and marches, which almost invariably stiffened rather than overcame opposition, the new unions employed negotiation and arbitration as a norm. There were indeed strikes at times, but unionists recognised that the technique of withdrawing labour was a double-edged sword, and best reserved for use as a last resort. When union power became overweening in Britain for a generation after the Second World War, the strike weapon was used far less responsibly. The damage inflicted by union leaders who had come to believe, not without justification, that they could hold the entire country to ransom, and therefore dictate terms to governments, eventually resulted in legislation that curbed their powers, having something of the effect of the Taft-Hartley Act passed in 1947 in the United States. That law limited strikes, which in effect emasculated the American trades union movement, because the strike weapon is, in the end, organised labour's main resource.[51]

A long and difficult strike of building workers in London in 1859–60 prompted the trades union movement to formalise co-operation between different unions on a national level. The eventual result was the Trades Union Congress, instituted in 1868. Just one year earlier Parliament had voted an extension of the franchise; the fact that more working men could vote, and that labour was more organised, meant that the major political parties had henceforth to take labour and popular sentiment even more seriously.

One reason for their doing so was a negative one. In the north of England there was a serious case of intimidation in which unionists had tried to force non-unionists to join them, with allegations of arson and even murder. The government set up a Royal Commission to investigate the wider questions prompted by this ugly affair. That was in 1867; in 1874 another Royal Commission investigated the entire question of existing labour law with a view to rationalising it and putting trades unions on a better footing. The combined outcome of the two enquiries was a significant improvement in the position of working people. New legislation made it possible for workers to sue employers for breach of contract (formerly it had only been possible the other way round), and a ten-hour limit was at last placed on the working day. Trades unions came within the protection of the law as officially recognised legal entities, and the sometimes acerbic debate over strikes and picketing was brought to an end by the legalisation of the latter.

These were all major gains and they generated the next development in trades unionism, which was a large increase in membership – but with it came increasing militancy. At the end of the 1880s two famous strikes, one by women match workers and another by dockers, heralded an era of turbulence. Wages were a central problem, of course, but so was the demand for an eight-hour day, a cause which had been adopted by international labour organisations.

Employers were not slow to fight back, and won some rounds in the battle; in the 1890s a railway company successfully sued a union for loss of income caused by a strike, and the picketing rights of unions came under renewed attack. The oscillating balance of advantage between labour and employers resulted in chronically tense labour relations that lasted all through the First World War and into the 1920s, when the labour movement attempted its largest throw of the dice yet: a General Strike.

In the background to the General Strike of 1926 lies one of the great events that shaped the twentieth century: the success of the Bolshevik Revolution in Russia in 1917. Working-class movements everywhere were inspired by the ideals of Communism, and felt a strong solidarity with the ordinary people of Russia, whose liberation from the world's last absolute monarchy they celebrated with joy. In this respect at least they were right to do so, and the ideals of Communism – no different in essence from the ethics of early Christianity – had a deep emotional appeal: the universal brotherhood of man, justice, sharing of all the good things of life, calling from each their best gifts, giving to each what they need for a good human existence, possessing in common the resources required for security in sustenance and shelter. The utopian dream seemed to be coming true.

How different the realities were did not emerge for some time, and the dismal fact that too many revolutions follow the model of the French rather than the American one was not likely to be appreciated by people motivated by hope that at last justice and equality would reign. Not all were starry-eyed about Soviet Russia. Sydney and Beatrice Webb had visited it, and were delighted; it filled all the wishes of their wishful thinking. Bertrand Russell, on the other hand, went shortly afterwards and saw with clarity the dangers, and wrote against them, attracting the hostility of the Left to which, as a moderate independent, he belonged. But some of those in Britain and elsewhere who were inspired by Communism had an additional reason for both their loyalty and their enthusiasm, which was their opposition to the growing and extremely dangerous menace of Fascism. The bristling hostility between Communist and Fascist stood in sharp contrast not merely to appeasement of the Fascist powers by Britain and other countries, but by the fact – unpleasant now to contemplate – that many in the British ruling class were sympathetic to Hitler's regime and (when they could get over the impression of him as a comic-cuts figure) to Mussolini.[52]

These are the features of another story, but they are relevant here because the effort to secure rights for working people had been a bitter one, against vested authority with little interest in making concessions at cost to themselves. Authoritarian and totalitarian regimes alike – distinguished from one another by the unideological pragmatism of the former, interested purely in power, and the ideological and dogmatic nature of the latter, interested in imposing conformity of belief and practice: both use violence as a means to their ends – posed a threat to the gains, partial and precious, that working people had made, so the latter were determined to fight to keep them. The first front line of that fight lay in the Spanish Civil War.

Again, that is another story; again, the relation of that other story to this is important. But for present purposes the efforts of working people are best understood by looking back at them through the lens of what was achieved. Think of the present day – with employment contracts, maternity leave, paid holidays, laws on working hours, compensation, equal pay, regimes of health and safety legislation, legal protections against harassment and unfair dismissal, redundancy terms, insurance, and much besides – and contrast it to just two hundred years ago, when eight-year-old children worked fourteen hours a day in filthy and dangerous factories. The contrast says everything; except, of course, that it is too easy to forget the hanged agricultural labourers, the transported Tolpuddle Martyrs, the marchers in the rain with their giant petitions, each of them many decades away from the basic human rights they were struggling for. If the idea of a struggle for liberty and rights could take on flesh and bones, it surely does so here.

And how much more so does it in connection with the greatest historical injustice ever perpetrated by one group of human beings against another: the subjection of women.

The roots of the effort to achieve female emancipation in modern times lie both in the anti-slavery campaigns that began in the eighteenth century, and in the fight for workers' rights that began in earnest in the nineteenth century. Women learned from them, participated in them, gave hugely to them, and did all this under the double handicap that being a woman in those circumstances imposed; for they had all the disabilities of the men alongside whom they fought, and yet all the disabilities of being women too.[53]

What women have achieved so recently in the West is great, but still not complete, because women are still trafficked and prostituted and subjected in the making of pornography; they still earn less than male counterparts in too many workplaces, still carry the main domestic and child-care responsibilities even while doing the same work as men; they are still woefully under-represented in senior management, government and education, and are still too often the object of demeaning or dismissive treatment and marginalisation, especially when elderly.

The thought that needs to be laid alongside these remarks is that a major reason for the slow pace of development in the Third World is the subjection of women there. Elementary education sufficient to make women basically literate and numerate is known to reduce rates of childbirth and infant mortality in Africa, to enhance the prospects of their children receiving education, and to reduce the rate of HIV infection among the women themselves. Where women are allowed to own property (as opposed to merely being property) HIV infection rates are lower too, because there women are not simply handed from father to husband, and from the graveside of one husband to another, but can if orphaned or widowed choose to make shift for themselves and their children autonomously.

If the world is to have a future, it lies in the hands of women. At time of writing nearly half of all women in the Middle East are illiterate; millions in poor countries are shackled to the most basic daily urgencies of finding water and feeding children; the majority of the world's women exist in various forms of bondage to necessity, to poverty, and to men. The story of Western women's ascent to a degree of emancipation cannot be a straightforward example for women still dispossessed and unemancipated elsewhere, because the process took too long. It is the point of arrival, not the journey, that matters to these latter.

Still, the story of women's liberation – the name for activist feminism in the 1970s is exactly the right one for the story as a whole – is an exemplary one, and demonstrates yet again the indivisibility of the striving for freedom and rights in modern America and Europe.

It was an immediate and natural step from the campaign to end slavery to a campaign for women's rights. What people said about the rights of slaves as human beings applied generally, and women who were engaged in anti-slavery activities – helping to organise meetings, collecting signatures for petitions, writing and printing pamphlets, and making public speeches – thereby learned how to organise efforts to improve the situation of women too, a situation which paralleled that of slaves in too many ways to ignore.

Describing the effects on women of their involvement in the anti-slavery movement, Elizabeth Cady Stanton and her co-authors wrote in *Anti-Slavery and Women's Rights*, 'In the early Anti-Slavery conventions, the broad principles of human rights were so exhaustively discussed, justice, liberty, and equality so clearly taught, that the women who crowded to listen readily learned the lesson of freedom for themselves, and early began to take part in the debates and business affairs of all associations. Women not only felt every pulsation of man's heart for freedom, and by her enthusiasm inspired the glowing eloquence that maintained him through the struggle, but earnestly advocated with her own lips human freedom and equality.'[54]

A second feature of women's involvement in anti-slavery work was that it helped give the lie to traditional views about women's supposed intellectual and physical incapacities. The one-time assumptions made about women are an embarrassment to recall now. Men – and alas too many women in support of them – said that women were incapable of understanding complicated problems or thinking logically about them, incapable of sustaining long hours of administrative or mental work, were too like children not only in being emotional, trivial, distractible, and ill-informed, but also in being physically and psychologically fragile, too much so to be given the responsibilities typically shouldered by men. All this and much besides was quite seriously believed, and was scarcely ever challenged even in the face of striking examples to the contrary. Not least among such examples were those of slave women labouring in the fields, working-class women labouring in factories, and the physical and mental demands of motherhood that many men would scarcely bear for a day.

One effect of the conjunction of these two features was that male protagonists of abolition, clergymen (whether involved in abolition work or not), and men in general became alarmed at the campaigning women in the abolitionist movement. Some of its leading male members attempted to silence women, and make them take a back seat again. 'Thus [women], in advocating liberty for the black race, were early compelled to defend the right of free speech for themselves. They had the double battle to fight against the tyranny of sex and colour at the same time,' wrote Cady Stanton.

The story of the struggle for women's rights goes back to isolated but remarkable voices in the seventeenth century and before – Aphra Behn is rightly held up as an early eloquent example – but the first major feminist voice belongs to Mary Wollstonecraft, whose *A Vindication of the Rights of Woman* marks an epoch in the cause.[55] She lived only until the age of thirty-eight, dying from complications in childbirth, but such was her brilliance that in her short life she produced a remarkable body of work. Her campaigning writing has great power, and focuses as much on the need to allow women education as to accord them the rights they lack. 'Contending for the rights of women,' she wrote in the dedicatory epistle to her *Vindication,* 'my main argument is built on this simple principle, that if she be not prepared by education to become the companion of man, she will stop the progress of knowledge, for truth must be common to all, or it will be inefficacious with respect to its influence on general practice. And how can woman be expected to co-operate, unless she know why she ought to be virtuous? Unless freedom strengthen her reason till she comprehend her duty, and see in what manner it is connected with her real good? If children are to be educated to understand the true principle of patriotism, their mother must be a patriot; and the love of mankind, from which an orderly train of virtues spring, can only be produced by considering the moral and civil interest of mankind; but the education and situation of woman, at present, shuts her out from such investigations.'[56]

Wollstonecraft is among the first to point out that the characteristics for which men asperse women – triviality, superficiality, and the like – are the result of lack of education, not of innate disposition. She criticised other women for their complicity in preserving the inequality, for example by cultivating 'sensibility' as a desirable man-attracting quality. 'Gentleness, docility, and a spaniel-like affection are, on this ground, consistently recommended as the cardinal virtues of the sex; and, disregarding the arbitrary economy of nature, one writer has declared that it is masculine for a woman to be melancholy. She was created to be the toy of man, his rattle, and it must jingle in his ears, whenever, dismissing reason, he chooses to be amused.' She soon after asks, '[But] do passive indolent women make the best wives?' Her plea is, 'Let their faculties have room to unfold, and their virtues to gain strength, and then determine where the whole sex must stand in the intellectual scale. Yet, let it be remembered, that for a small number of distinguished women I do not ask a place.'[57]

Wollstonecraft would not have asked a place for the formidable Margaret Brent, who owned large amounts of property in Maryland in the seventeenth century and acted on behalf of another landowner in the colony, Lord Baltimore. In 1647 she demanded the right to cast two votes in the Assembly, her own and Baltimore's, which he had delegated to her. She was refused; but she had raised the question.[58]

An oversight on the part of the framers of the 1790 constitution for the state of New Jersey allowed the vote to women and black people because it specified that anyone who satisfied certain property and residence qualifications could vote. Evidently the framers were victims of their own unthinking assumption that all human beings are (white) men. A state representative who had suffered the discouraging experience of being nearly defeated by the combined black and female vote introduced a bill into the state legislature in 1807 disenfranchising both groups, and it passed.

A turning point in the history of the American women's movement is the occasion on which the abolitionists Elizabeth Cady Stanton and Lucretia Mott were obliged to sit in the gallery at the World Anti-Slavery Convention meeting in London in 1840, because as women they were not allowed to join the delegates in the hall. It prompted them to address the question of women's rights directly, and the eventual result was the Seneca Falls Convention of 1848, when the American women's movement officially came into existence. It resolved that the surest way to secure equality of rights for women was to get the vote, and so the women's suffrage campaign was launched. But it subordinated itself to the abolitionist cause for the time being, especially during the Civil War, on the grounds that abolition of slavery, together with the ensuing enfranchisement of freed black men, would provide a moral dynamic on which the campaign for votes for women could ride.[59]

In the event Congress saw matters differently, distinguishing the issue of black male suffrage from women's suffrage and insisting on addressing the first only. When the Fourteenth Amendment was passed in 1868, citizenship and suffrage were explicitly conceived as male prerogatives; in 1870 the Fifteenth Amendment extended the vote to include black men only.

Cady Stanton and others had already set up the American Equal Rights Association in 1866, though as often happens in movements frustrated by lack of progress, it split in two for a time before reuniting in 1890 as the National American Woman Suffrage Association. In this guise it began its determined and ultimately successful assault on the suffrage by means of picketing, marching and petitioning. The vote was secured at last in 1919 with the Nineteenth Amendment, which tersely states, 'The right of citizens of the United States to vote shall not be denied or abridged by the United States or by any State on account of sex.'

As with all liberty struggles, victory in this essential was the beginning of a next major step: in the case of the United States, a battle for an Equal Rights Amendment, and from the 1960s onwards a determined effort to change attitudes as well as practices regarding women in education and the workplace. Getting the vote had not by itself shifted the deeply ingrained and institutionalised 'patriarchal' attitudes of society, in which women were persistently regarded as less robust and less able in the spheres of activity valued by men, namely, politics, business, the military, the professions, even in the arts where the facts had long been powerfully in women's favour.

The indivisibility of liberty struggles is exemplified yet again by the fact that feminist activism from the 1960s onwards was inspired by the Civil Rights movement in America, which had the same underlying rationale: that although slavery no longer existed, racism and apartheid still did a hundred years after its abolition. The business of getting rights, and the business of getting rights applied, are two different matters, and the examples of slaves and women in the United States suggest a pattern: that once a framework, usually of statute, is in place, the real task of changing attitudes and practices has then to begin, because they are just as imprisoning as the absence of enabling laws, or the presence of disabling laws. Getting the right laws in the cases of civil liberties is a first step only.

The experience of Elizabeth Cady Stanton and Lucretia Mott in 1840 at the World Anti-Slavery Convention is interesting as, among other things, an indication that consciousness of the unjust circumstances of women in society was rising. In 1841 Robert Owen invited controversy by denouncing the institution of marriage as a form of slavery for women. He envisioned a state of affairs in which 'Women will be no longer made the slaves of, or dependent upon men . . . They will be equal in education, rights, privileges and personal liberty.'[60] At the time he wrote, a woman's property automatically came to belong to the man she married; in the event of marital breakdown, custody of any children of the marriage went to the father; a woman had no remedy against her husband for ill-treatment, and because she was under an obligation to perform her 'conjugal duties' (accept sexual relations) the concept of rape within marriage was unrecognised. Divorce was difficult and carried great opprobrium for women. A divorced woman was regarded as 'damaged goods' – dangerous, infected and infectious – and invariably shunned by 'good society'.

The first step in remedying this situation of effective slavery in Britain was the Married Woman's Property Act of 1857, which ended the practice of automatic transfer of a woman's property to her husband on marriage. In this same year the laws of divorce were changed also; previously an Act of Parliament was required for a couple to divorce – exclusively a proceeding for the upper classes, therefore, where considerations of dynasty and great property were at stake – but now a divorce court was established, in the teeth of bitter opposition from the clergy (and William Gladstone). Although these were important steps which did much to improve the position of women, they were only fragments of the required whole. The main aim was still the vote, and following the lead of the Chartist movement in this regard, reformers such as John Stuart Mill and his wife Harriet Taylor Mill (whose article 'The Enfranchisement of Women' appeared in 1851) and others applied themselves to that goal.[61]

Britain's first women's suffrage organisation was set up in the city of Manchester in 1865, the year in which Mill was elected to Parliament on a women's suffrage ticket. In the following year one of the first women to qualify as a physician, Elizabeth Garrett, organised a petition for women's suffrage, and Mill moved an amendment to the 1867 representation reform act to extend the franchise to women. The amendment was massively defeated.

But the suffrage movement was encouraged by the extension of voting rights to women in local elections. In 1869 unmarried female householders were given the vote in municipal elections, on the somewhat illogical grounds that mothers should have a say in local government arrangements for education. Since marriage lost women the local vote, mothers evidently had to rely on their unmarried sisters to influence educational policy.

At the beginning of the twentieth century one part of the British women's suffrage movement took a radical turn. It was frustrated by the lack of response to the powerful and persuasive movement, supported by mass demonstrations, which under direction of the suffragist leader Millicent Garrett Fawcett had yet to register any progress. (Fawcett's organisation was the National Union of Women's Suffrage Societies, and it was a formidable body: it attracted the support of middle-class and working-class women alike, published a journal, organised meetings and sent distinguished speakers all over the country. One of the speakers was Bertrand Russell, who twice stood for Parliament as a women's suffrage candidate.)[62] The government remained unmoved, to the anger of Emmeline Pankhurst and her daughters Christabel and Sylvia, and they concluded that the only thing that would make an exclusively male Parliament take notice was a campaign of civil disobedience. Another motive was that some of the peaceful demonstrations and meetings arranged by Fawcett's organisation had met with rough handling not just by jeering jostling men who threw things at the women and their invited speakers, but even at times by the police; this angered the Pankhursts further.

Thus began 'suffragette' activism. 'Suffragette' was a derogatory term coined to denote the women who, unlike more moderate 'suffragists', set fire to buildings, broke shop windows, chained themselves to railings, and deliberately invited arrest and imprisonment to publicise the suffrage cause. In prison they went on hunger strike and were force-fed. As it proved, it was indeed activism that broke the logjam on women's suffrage, but it was not the activism of civil disobedience. When war broke out in 1914, all those engaged in suffrage campaigning turned their attention to war work instead, taking up nursing and ambulance driving, and going into the factories – empty now that men had been called up in huge numbers for the armed forces – to take over munitions production and other work. The change introduced into women's lives by the experience of this work and the independence it brought was an unanswerable fact, both in the country at large and in Parliament. An eloquent account of the dramatic changes that occurred in women's outlook, and the social acceptance of the change, is given by Vera Brittain in her *Testament of Youth*. The result was inevitable: in 1919 the franchise was extended to women aged thirty and over, and in 1928 the unacceptably condescending and paternalistic implications of the age restriction were abolished, and an equal franchise instituted.

It is interesting to contrast attitudes to women's suffrage elsewhere in the Western world during this period of struggle for its achievement. In some countries the barrier against women seemed higher than the mere absence of the vote; in Prussia in the nineteenth century 'women, lunatics and apprentices' were named together in a law forbidding any of them to join political parties or attend political meetings. The brief and ill-fated liberal republic of Weimar extended the franchise to women in 1919, and with it the right to hold public office. Hitler's Nazi regime did not deprive women of their votes, but it rescinded their entitlement to hold office. Mussolini's Italian government took away the limited suffrage women had inherited, and it was not until 1945 that the vote was given to all adult Italian women.

These facts contrast strongly with the situation in Scandinavian countries, which were more liberal far earlier; in Finland, Norway and Denmark women had the vote before the First World War. Perhaps most surprising of all the European countries in this matter is France, where women had fought on the barricades and taken leading positions in revolutions and in insurgencies against occupying forces, as in the Resistance during the Second World War. They were finally given the vote in a decree issued by the fiat of General Charles de Gaulle in 1944. Undoubtedly the franchise would have been extended by a post-war French government, but the usefulness of wartime short cuts makes itself obvious here. Frenchwomen had hitherto been denied the vote by an unholy alliance of the political Left and the Roman Catholic Church, the former anxious that women would be more conservative than men and therefore more likely to vote for their opponents, the latter anxious that having the vote would emancipate women too far, and thus interfere with their morals and family duties.

The same unholy combination stood in the way of women's suffrage in South America, but its reasoning has proved only half right. In most countries – with the exceptions of Britain, the United States and Norway – women do indeed tend to vote for right-wing parties, but since these standardly include religiously oriented ones it turns out that though the Left was right to worry, the churches were not. This might be a reason for Arab countries – where women still lack the vote, except in a few cases limited to local elections – not to fear an extension of the franchise.

None of this alters the fact that the right to vote is only a first step, as the United States and Britain proved by the necessity for vigorous feminist campaigns decades after securing women's suffrage. Even in the most advanced countries of the West today, women hold few senior positions in government and business, and the effort they have to make to break through the barrier into such positions is disproportionate in comparison to the career endeavours of men. Much injustice therefore remains; but it is a function of psychology rather than law or sanctioned social norms, which means that the process of reform is now chiefly an educational one.

An equally significant fact is that the right to an education, and not least to a university education, was an important corollary of the victories so far achieved in the field of women's rights. Mary Wollstonecraft astutely focused on the fact that while women were denied education, they were too easily made to fit the stereotype it suited men to impose. On the empirical evidence of educated women throughout history – think of women who had opportunities for education because of their social status: Queen Elizabeth I of England, a fine Latinist with a powerful mind; and the two brilliant royal women who corresponded with the philosopher René Descartes, Princess Elisabeth of Bohemia and Queen Christina of Sweden; think of them together with such writers as Aphra Behn, Mary Wollstonecraft, Jane

Austen and George Eliot (Marian Evans) – even this sampling of what could be a far longer list gives the lie to any man wishing to insist that women are less capable than themselves.

Nor alas was it just men who perpetuated myths about women's capacities and thus the social and political disabilities premised on them. Queen Victoria famously (infamously) wrote, 'I am most anxious to enlist everyone who can speak or write to join in checking this mad, wicked folly of "Women's Rights", with all its attendant horrors, on which her poor feeble sex is bent, forgetting every sense of womanly feelings and propriety. Feminists ought to get a good whipping. Were woman to "unsex" themselves by claiming equality with men, they would become the most hateful, heathen and disgusting of beings and would surely perish without male protection.'[63]

A turning point in the argument about education for women was acceptance of Mary Wollstonecraft's point about the role of women (as mothers) in the education of men (their sons). All the arguments to the effect that education would unhinge women's minds, cause them gynaecological problems, make them immoral, destroy the family, corrupt and pervert society, and so endlessly on, were brought up short by the observation that the first teachers of men are women, and therefore those women had better be well informed and clear-thinking if they are to make tomorrow's prime ministers, scientists, explorers and governors of empire fit for their duties.

In the United States a major step forward in women's higher education was the founding of Oberlin College in 1833. It was the first to open its doors to women and black people. In the declaration of women's rights adopted at the Seneca Falls conference of 1848, education plays a central part: '[The male] has monopolised nearly all the profitable employments, and from those she is permitted to follow, she receives but a scanty remuneration,' the Seneca Falls *Declaration of Sentiments* states. 'He closes against her all the avenues to wealth and distinction, which he considers most honourable to himself. As a teacher of theology, medicine, or law, she is not known. He has denied her the facilities for obtaining a thorough education – all colleges being closed against her.'[64]

The progress of women in education was thereafter rapid; the first PhD awarded to a woman came in 1877, and by then too 80 per cent of elementary school teachers were women. Nearly half of American college undergraduates by the beginning of the First World War were women – and more to the point, women constituted 20 per cent of college faculty. Since then the balance in education has generally been in favour of women, and in higher education it has been equal. This is one sphere in which equality of the sexes has been achieved in the United States.

It was not achieved so easily in Britain. At Cambridge University women were admitted to attend courses, but not to take degrees, after a sterling campaign by Emily Davies in the 1860s. Women undergraduates were not awarded equal status there, remarkably, until 1947. Anecdotes about the prejudice suffered by women undergraduates until the 1950s abound; at Oxford one of the professors, on seeing only women present in the lecture hall, muttered 'no one here' and walked out. A scathing attack on the presence of women in Oxford was written in the 1930s, mocking the enthusiasm with which they hastened on their bicycles to lectures, the basket on the handlebars crammed with books, while their far more sensible and superior male counterparts had their feet up in their handsome and ancient college rooms puffing their pipes and reading at their leisure (women students lived in modest accommodations away from the city centre).[65]

The great struggle for the rights of one half of humankind is emblematic of the struggle for rights in general, for rights of all kinds, and therefore for the freedoms that possession of rights makes possible. It is no surprise therefore that when the United Nations, in the key years of its formation after the Second World War, formulated and passed its Universal Declaration of Human Rights, it should have set to work to draft detailed and thoroughgoing conventions on all aspects of rights. And in this, in turn, a key matter was the place of women.

Eleanor Roosevelt, widow of President F. D. R. Roosevelt and chairwoman of the committee that had drafted the Universal Declaration of Human Rights, was especially keen on the question of women's political rights, so very recently made a discussible question by the extension to them of the suffrage. Her remarks on the draft convention for establishing the political rights of women remain a clarion call: 'I believe in active citizenship, for men and women equally, as a simple matter of right and justice. I believe we will have better government in all of our countries when men and women discuss public issues together and make their decisions on the basis of their differing areas of experience and their common concern for the welfare of their families and their world. In the United States, and in most countries today, women have equal suffrage. Some may feel that for that reason this convention is of little importance to them. I do not agree with this view. It is true, of course, that the first objective of this convention is to encourage equal political rights for women in all countries. But its significance reaches far deeper into the real issue of whether in fact women are recognised fully in setting the policies of our governments . . . too often the great decisions are originated and given form in bodies made up wholly of men, or so completely dominated by them that whatever of special value women have to offer is shunted aside without expression.'[66]

Half a century after these remarks they remain almost wholly true. Of all the Western world's liberation struggles described in this book, this struggle – the woman's struggle – is the one least complete. In other parts of the world it has scarcely begun, and that is a major factor in the world's continuing tragedy, for reasons Eleanor Roosevelt specified with such clarity. In the West, where possession of rights and liberties is meant to be the defining characteristic of our civilisation, much remains to be done in this sphere. It is as if women had reached a summit after a long hard climb, only to see the view for the first time, and for the first time to know the length of the journey ahead.

———

History as the complexity of actual events that take place in time, and history as the later written record of past time, are quite discrete entities. History in the former sense can be brimming over with experience characterised by struggle and limitation, not infrequently of hardship, benighted by superstition and lack of education, and confined by the rule of lords, priests and magistrates, while history in the latter sense is about kings, bishops, politicians and armies, with here and there a salient rebel. Thus history as lived actuality contains millions; history as recollection in tranquillity is about dozens, though thousands of soldiers march across the pages with dismaying frequency.

The excuse for the partiality of history in the second sense is that the dozens make the decisions and have an impact that, for most stretches of time, not even the millions en masse could possibly have. The dozens also write the contemporary records, and so have both the rub of the green and the wood's bias on their side. This last introduces true bias into history as record: history is victors' history, rich man's history, educated man's history. Its materials come so much from the side of the winners that it is easy to think in individual terms of (say) Lord Liverpool, prime minister of Britain in the years on either side of Waterloo, but only in mass terms of the starving, distressed, anxious poor in their hundreds of thousands, ruined by the economic collapse of the time, frightened that their livelihoods were being taken away by machines, desperate to see reform in the government of the country so that their very real grievances and sufferings could be addressed. Looking at history from their point of view, Liverpool's government is a tyrannous one; it met the anxieties and hunger of working people with the death penalty, transportation, laws that reversed recently and laboriously secured liberties, and – when the need and hunger of ordinary people prompted them to gather together to demand what they thought would help them – sabre charges such as the one at Peterloo in 1819. Looked at from Liverpool's point of view, by contrast, the economic problems and civil unrest were serious difficulties requiring alert and vigorous management, if the country were not to be plunged into chaos, with chaos's ever-present threat of turning into a Jacobin Terror.

The history books mainly look from Liverpool's point of view, not because they are on his side of the quarrel necessarily, but – to repeat – because that is where both the impact of decisions and the records lie. It is worth remembering this in connection with the history of attempts to achieve liberty.

*

The history books call the nineteenth century 'the age of reform'. For an historian of ideas about liberty and rights who has dwelt with the story of how the lack of both gradually led to an age when reform was not something to be resisted and punished but achieved, it is like surfacing for air. As the next chapter shows, despite the slowness with which liberty and rights came to be extended in the nineteenth century, the argument for them had at last been comprehensively won.

6

The Liberty Century

F OR CHAMPIONS OF the idea of liberty and the rights of man, the opening of the nineteenth century was a pessimistic time. Throughout the French Wars there were some in England who championed Napoleon because he seemed the best hope of salvaging some at least of the principles of that dawn, the French Revolution, in which it had been bliss to be alive; when he was defeated at Waterloo they were devastated. One of them, William Hazlitt, was drunk for a week in an effort to drown his despair.[1] It is not that he and others like him wished to see England defeated by France; rather, they wished to see Napoleon and his France survive. When Hazlitt was on his deathbed in the summer of 1830, and heard the news that the Bourbons had again been driven from France, he was roused to happiness; though in a whispered aside he told his son that he did not believe this latest new dawn would last.[2]

The grounds for Hazlitt's pessimism were good ones, given the experience of the preceding decades. But optimism would have been better justified, as the unfolding century proceeded to show.

The grounds for pessimism lay in the fact that from the early 1790s a succession of illiberal laws were passed, and repressive actions taken, by a British government afraid of revolution at home. When the wars ended the Tory administration of Lord Liverpool was in office. His party remained so until 1830, when the stalled pressure for reform, a pressure that had been building throughout the eighteenth century only to be frustrated at that century's end, was again making itself felt – and to such a degree that resistance was no longer feasible. Working men and women, and women in general, pinned their hopes on parliamentary reform, as already noted; and there was also a recognition that the disabilities imposed on those who would not accept the Thirty-Nine Articles of the Church of England were unjust. Repeal of the Test and Corporation Acts in 1828 and the first reform bill of 1832 were significant moments in breaking the logjam against reform that the Revolutionary and Napoleonic Wars had caused. From these cracks in the edifice, reform was able to leak through, gathering unevenly in force with time. This was the story of the preceding chapter.

So, despite its unpropitious beginnings, the nineteenth century began to see some major rays of hope, and not just in England. The United States, then still small and relatively insignificant, had achieved a post-revolution settlement that drew the interested attention of the Old World; it was soon to be visited by Alexis de Tocqueville. In Europe at large the shock waves of the French Revolution vibrated still: there were revolutions in 1830 in France, in 1848 in a number of major European countries, toppling several crowned heads – among them a French king for the third time in little more than half a century – and causing a major reconstruction of the Austro-Hungarian Empire. From Karl Marx to the Paris Commune, from Chartist marches in England to the Civil War in America, signs of the effects of deep changes in political and economic structures were everywhere apparent. One aspect of the changes was that it set the common man on the march, and woman with him, demanding participation, justice, destruction of old privileges in favour of new rights.

A passing observer from Mars would have been forgiven for thinking that 1848 was the year in which not just the nineteenth century but the whole of modern history was destined to break its back. From South America to the border separating the Austro-Hungarian Empire from the Ottoman Empire there were revolts and rebellions. A number of monarchs fell, others nearly followed, a rash of new and more liberal constitutions were announced across Europe, and as this shows the prevailing thrust that caused the tumults – and it is one of the chief pulses of modern history – was the demand for liberty and guaranteed rights.

In late March of that year the Niagara Falls dried up for an entire day – in fact because of ice upstream – but it was a portent of a kind: the old course of history was dammed, and damned, and an impending new flood was gathering to burst through.

The world survived the upheavals rather well, as it happened, from the point of view of bloodshed and disaster. There were some of both, but the reconfiguring of some of the world's major countries was almost wholly constitutional – and from the point of view of those wishing to see movement in the direction of constitutionality, democracy and liberty, the movement was in the right direction.

The year of revolutions got off to an early start. On 12 January in Palermo, Sicily, yet another revolt broke out against the Bourbon monarchy which had been instituted after the Congress of Vienna in 1812. The Kingdom of the Two Sicilies had briefly enjoyed a liberal constitution with a Westminster-style parliament until Ferdinand IV of Naples abolished it following Napoleon's final defeat in 1815. The Sicilians were understandably not pleased, and a series of attempted revolts followed at points in the succeeding decades. The Kingdom of the Two Sicilies did not expire until 1861, at the beginning of the Risorgimento that resulted in a united Italy, but the 1848 uprising saw the revival for sixteen months of the constitutional parliamentary arrangement in Palermo, and a call for a confederation of Italian states. The revolution was put down in 1849 by the army, but the warrant had been issued for the Bourbon monarchy's demise, and it came a dozen years later.[3]

Sicily set the rest of Italy and Europe vibrating. The king of Sardinia quickly agreed to a new constitution, and there was unrest throughout the Italian peninsula, the effects of which were still in full flow a year later; on 8 February 1849 the people of Rome overthrew the papal monarchy and a republic was declared under the leadership of Giuseppe Mazzini. It lasted only four months, but in its brief life it attempted a number of exemplary reforms. The Roman rebellion had begun in November 1848 with the assassination of one of the Vatican's ministers, causing Pope Pius IX to flee the city in disguise. Under Mazzini the short-lived republic introduced religious toleration, abolished capital punishment, and called direct elections on the basis of universal adult suffrage, the first in history. The euphoria of freedom might have sustained the nascent republic for a while, but its finances were in a plight, and even if the new head of state in France – Louis Napoleon, soon to make himself Napoleon III – had not decided to appease Catholic opinion in France by answering the pope's call for help by sending troops to put down the Mazzini government, it might anyway have run into difficulty. But one of the Roman republic's legacies was the blooding of Giuseppe Garibaldi, who went to Rome with an ad hoc force to help in the city's defence.

Revolution broke out in Pest in Hungary on 15 March 1848. It was to have far-reaching consequences for the structure of the Habsburg domains, such as greater autonomy for Hungary, and a continuing and unappeasable nationalistic hunger among the subject peoples of the empire, not least the Czechs. The turmoil in the empire was only stilled by the abdication of Ferdinand I in favour of his nephew Franz Josef I in December that year, and by promises of wide reforms. From then until the empire's collapse at the end of the First World War it existed under a gathering sense of doom, despite the decades of rapid development among whose symbols were the Ringstrasse development in the glacis of Vienna, the rebuilding of Pest as an eastern Paris, and the flowering of literature, art and architecture that marked the Austro-Hungarian *fin de siècle* so brilliantly.[4]

Three days after the events in Pest crowds demonstrated outside the royal palace in Stockholm, calling for the abdication of the king and the founding of a republic. Sweden's king, Oscar I, told his troops to open fire on the crowds if necessary.[5] In Bavaria two days after that, Ludwig I abdicated.[6] In England the Chartists were preparing for what they hoped would be their vast rally on Kennington Common on 10 April, ready to march on Parliament with their latest petition. The news pouring in from elsewhere in Europe might explain why the British government instructed the police not to let marchers cross any bridges into London north of the Thames.[7]

On 15 May the Chamber of Deputies in Paris was invaded by radicals. Three days later the first German National Assembly met in Frankfurt.[8] What Hobbes and Burke in their different ways had decried as 'democratical mobs' were proving insistent and, more to the point, were getting their way. Elsewhere older problems required solution in light of the new constitutional spirit: the Catholic cantons of Switzerland had reacted to anti-Catholic initiatives by the Swiss federation's governing Radical alliance by instituting a *Sonderbund*, a 'separate alliance', to protect their interests. After a short civil war between the seven cantons of the *Sonderbund* and the rest, the former were defeated and a new and liberal constitution was adopted. Its one illiberal provision was the banishing of Jesuits from Switzerland, a ban not revoked until 1973.[9] One of the civil war's positive outcomes was that there were few casualties in the fighting, and the victorious general, Guillaume-Henri Dufour, who had demanded that his troops treat their enemies with respect and consideration, went on to be a founder of the Red Cross.

If these had been the only events of 1848 it would have been a remarkable year by any standards. But it also saw, among other things, the beginning of the infamous Irish potato famine, insurrection against British rule in Ceylon, the California Gold Rush, and the Seneca Falls conference that launched the women's suffrage movement in America. It saw the publication on 21 February of the *Communist Manifesto* by Marx and Engels, a response to the early events of the year and what had been leading up to them; and it saw Henry David Thoreau's essay on civil disobedience, prompted by the experience of being jailed for a night following his refusal to pay taxes because of his opposition to slavery and the Mexican War, then in progress. The essay influenced Mahatma Gandhi.

The famous opening words of the *Communist Manifesto* could not have seemed more accurate – 'A spectre is haunting Europe' – a baleful remark for those with much to lose, a note of hope for those with everything to gain. It was however guilty of its own wishful thinking, in that it characterised the spectre as Communism: 'A spectre is haunting Europe – the spectre of Communism. All the Powers of old Europe have entered into a holy alliance to exorcise this spectre: Pope and Czar, Metternich and Guizot, French Radicals and German police-spies. Where is the party in opposition that has not been decried as Communistic by its opponents in power? Where is the Opposition that has not hurled back the branding reproach of Communism, against the more advanced opposition parties, as well as against its reactionary adversaries?'[10] Certainly, the unsteady governments of Europe were apt to lump together reformers, radicals, oppositions and Communists under the latter's label, but as the outcome proved – despite the tumbling kings and emperors, sops to the demanding crowds of democrats – the result was constitutional and gradualist rather than revolutionary in either the American or French eighteenth-century sense. But the direction was the direction of liberty; and liberty, having long found its voice, was establishing its reality.

Much of this was unequivocally progressive. But the multiple character of history – the negative with the positive – is rarely to be denied. From the time of the Treaty of Westphalia in 1648 the nation-state model had been maturing in Europe, and in place of old reasons for loyalty – to a king, to a religion – new ones were being created, notably those implicated in nationalism, whose idols were the Fatherland, the *Volk*, ethnicity and culture, and these were often wrapped in origin myths and clothed in patriotic jingoism. Nationalism was a political construct that proved useful to the unifiers of Germany and Italy, and to the leaders of independence movements at the end of the era of European colonialism.[11] Its usefulness stops there; the major wars of the twentieth century owe too much to it.

Demagogues preach nationalism for good reason. Hitler said, 'The effectiveness of the truly national leader consists in preventing his people from dividing their attention, and keeping it fixed on a common enemy.'[12] And he knew to whom the appeal should be addressed; Goethe had long before observed that nationalistic sentiments 'are at their strongest and most violent where there is the lowest degree of culture'.

Nationalism as a thesis confuses (almost always deliberately) certain legitimate desires with illegitimate ones. People like to run their own affairs, and most people value the culture they were raised in, are proud of its achievements and wish it well; a significant degree of their sense of personal and group identity derives from it. All this is unexceptionable. But nationalists try to persuade their fellows that the existence of other groups and cultures somehow represents a challenge, and sometimes a threat, to what the natives of the home culture value. To protect it they must be conscious of themselves as an entity, a distinct collective, whose identity is defined by ethnicity, geography, or sameness of language or religion. They appeal to 'our way of life', perhaps to 'our jobs', even 'our daughters'.

In some views nationalism is the direct result of industrialisation. In pre-industrial society people were defined by their place and function in a social order. The Enlightenment subjected that feudal conception to sharp criticism, affirming instead the rational autonomy of individuals. But Romanticism in its turn rejected what it saw as the coldness and isolation of the Enlightenment picture of man, and promoted in its place the idea of community: humans are social creatures, not in-dependent atoms, and their essence lies in belonging to a people and its culture. At the same time, the industrial revolution was creating a new social order, in which life is deracinated, mobile, anonymous and bureaucratic, characterised by new kinds of working practices and relationships. For the efficient functioning of this new society, political authority had to be centralised; as a justification, the Romantic rhetoric of culturally identifiable nation states aptly fitted the bill.[13]

The contrast between pre-Reformation Europe and the Europe of nation states is a very educative one. The medieval Church had sought to make Christendom a single papal monarchy, federal in structure with satrapies of local kings and princes, but a unity in faith and culture nevertheless. Although the papacy never succeeded in gaining quite the degree of hegemony it desired, Europe for a long time had a large measure of unity nevertheless; its rulers were members of an extended royal family, much intermarried and interrelated; its educated people all spoke the same languages – Latin, and also French – and the culture of those who travelled and communicated was in many respects a common culture, because religion and education were so closely allied.

Most of Europe outside England and France, which were the earliest continuous monarchies, was a shifting mosaic of princely states and republics – the German states of the Holy Roman Empire, the changing kingdoms of Italy and its city states, the fluctuating empires of Sweden, Poland and Lithuania, the advancing and retreating influence over south-eastern Europe of the Ottoman Empire, all the way to the walls of Vienna. What the Ottomans ruled ceased thereby to be Europe; when Elias Canetti was a boy living in Ruschuk on the Danube in Bulgaria in the early twentieth century, it was still the practice of members of his family to say, when they were going upriver to Vienna for shopping or a doctor's visit, 'I am going to Europe.'[14]

In the eighteenth century the University of Halle in Germany decided to stop using Latin as the medium of instruction in all subjects, and to use the vernacular instead. Others rapidly followed. The loss of a common European language of the intellect was one symptom of the widening gulf between nations, though the language of diplomacy continued to be French, and of the Roman Catholic Church, Latin.

Thus the partitioning of Europe brought about by the Reformation in the sixteenth century resulted in the Westphalian settlement of the seventeenth century, which in turn gave rise to the development of the nation state, a process essentially complete by the second half of the nineteenth century; and the tensions, rivalries and soon enough conflicts generated by these divisions resulted in the catastrophic wars of the twentieth century.[15] Some might say this is an example of history bringing in its revenges, and the sceptical might say that it is a process that at least sits at an angle to the increasing application of ideas of rights and liberties, an angle requiring explanation.

For some, such as Marx, who thought deeply about the kind of political and economic order necessary for the liberation of ordinary individuals, internationalism was the answer. After the World Wars of the twentieth century, multinationalism became the solution of choice, in the form of the European Union. One of the driving motivations for its creation was to render it impossible for the big nations of Europe, increasingly merging into a single entity, to go to war against one another ever again. Given how things were before the

Reformation, one could describe the unification of Europe as a reunification.[16]

The European Union embodies the reversal of large-scale nationalism's historical march. Small-scale nationalism might be described as a form of regionalism, but has sometimes been ill-described by its own votaries as nationalism, as in Scotland; the difficulty in the contemporary world of small economic and political entities flourishing outside a larger entity such as the European Union goes some way to explaining the difference. And a significant feature of the multi-nationalism that reverses nationalism is that it protects the growing regimes of rights and liberties that the worst forms of nationalism threatened. War, after all, is the most violent assault on all liberties, and nationalism is fruitful in war. The answer to the question, How was it that the application of rights increased even as nationalism, something potentially so inimical to them, increased also? lies in the fact already appealed to in connection with the Counter-Enlightenment: the Enlightenment generated, as all such movements inevitably do, an opposition to itself – increasing light throws darker shadows.[17]

Arguably, though, the evolution of regimes of rights and nationalism need not be adversaries, but might at a certain point or in certain ways be allies. It is easy to imagine an argument that says certain types and scales of political organisation favour the institution of rights regimes, because they are either more amenable to them, or more vulnerable to the activism that produces them.

The fact remains that as nationalism burgeoned in nineteenth-century Europe, so too did thinking about the idea of liberty – bearing much the same relation to the advance of liberty in the Western world as Locke's writings bore to the Glorious Revolution of 1688, namely, a theorising of what had already happened, thus clarifying it and securing its consequences, entering a feedback relationship with it in the way that theory and practice do at their best.

There are three significant figures in the period's discussion about the matter who brought about this reflective defence of the growth of liberty and rights: Alexis de Tocqueville, John Stuart Mill, and Lord Acton.

De Tocqueville's writings on America have endeared him to that country, which loves to hear itself praised, though he was not un-qualified in his admiration.[18] He believed in liberty under law and democracy, provided that it is for an educated people. In his last great work, *L'Ancien Régime et la Révolution (the Old Regime and the French Revolution)*, published in 1856, he argued that liberty is the only correct political condition for modern man, and pointed out that liberty is not a state which, once gained, can be left to look after itself; instead it is a dynamic condition, a process, whose achievement requires effort and whose maintenance requires vigilance. Of all the countries in the world, the United States of America was the one where the best hopes for democracy already seemed to be in process of realisation; and de Tocqueville was keen to learn as much from the example it set, good and bad, as he could.

His *De la Démocratie en Amérique* (*Democracy in America*), published in 1835, opens with the assertion that a fundamental reason for the success of political arrangements in the United States, and a determin-ing influence in the formation of its people, is what he called their 'equality of condition'. 'I then turned my thoughts to our own hemisphere,' he wrote, 'and thought that I discerned there something analogous to the spectacle which the New World presented to me. I observed that equality of condition, though it has not there reached the extreme limit which it seems to have attained in the United States, is constantly approaching it; and that the democracy which governs the American communities appears to be rapidly rising into power in Europe.'[19] As this suggests, for de Tocqueville part of the special interest of the United States was the light it cast on the prospects for Europe, where, he wrote, 'a great democratic revolution is going on among us', and moreover one that 'seems irresistible, because it is the most uniform, the most ancient, and the most permanent tendency that is to be found in history.'[20] For those who, as he did, counted among 'the partisans of liberty, not only as the source of the noblest virtues, but more especially as the root of all solid advantages,' the conditions of American democracy – setting aside the great fault of slavery – made a vital subject of study.[21]

And the reason is one we are now apt to forget, reading de Tocqueville as the leader of an American fan club in an era when the word 'democracy' is a feel-good term: namely, that 'democracy' was for many of his contemporaries still a name to be feared, not admired; it denoted the tyranny of uneducated, ignorant, poor and resentful masses who threatened social order, property, and their own safety. That is how ruling elites everywhere regarded the events of 1848. Knowing that the concept was highly equivocal in this way, de Tocqueville set out to describe the circumstances in which democracy can be a framework for flourishing and liberty, circumstances that he found in Jacksonian America, both in the positive sense of what produces it, and in the negative sense of the dangers inherent in it – dangers which have to be guarded against given, as he viewed it, the inevitability of democracy in Europe.[22]

Jacksonian America was the America of the period between 1824 and 1854 during which the franchise was extended among white adult males, and President Andrew Jackson, while increasing the power of the presidency relative to Congress, encouraged as much public participation in politics as he could. The ideal of a participatory democracy went hand in hand with the idea of a widened franchise, and that implied extending influence to people whose lack of property qualification (a supposed guarantee of sensible choices prompted by rational self-interest) and educational attainment brought the fact of genuine democracy closer.[23]

Equality, the sovereignty of the people, a free press, the expression of public opinion – all of these might be integral features of democracy, de Tocqueville pointed out, but their negative side includes extreme individualism, which threatens the cohesion of society, and ill-informed public opinion, which can lead to the tyranny of the majority.

This was a warning taken seriously by John Stuart Mill. In *On Liberty* (1859) he pointed out that the replacement of aristocratic government by popular government did not guarantee the end of tyranny, for there is no reason why majorities should not act with respect to minorities – especially as these almost by definition consist of people different from the majority – as any other irresistible authority behaves.[24] He discussed how this problem is to be best managed in his *Representative Government* (1861), there describing representative democracy as the 'ideal' type of government because it provides the best form of protection for individuals, namely self-protection, while fostering good personal qualities in them (self-reliance and the like) and at the same time promoting social cohesion.[25] Although he was in favour of extending the franchise to women, he was not in favour of a straightforward universal suffrage that would bring about democracy of the kind discussed by de Tocqueville – not, at any rate, until all the electorate were sufficiently equipped with rationality, self-possession and enough experience to avoid exercising their political power tyrannically.

Mill's anxiety about the risk of tyranny was a function of the importance he attached to individual liberty as a moral good of the first importance. In *On Liberty* he argued that if happiness is the highest good, and happiness consists in pleasure, and the best pleasures are those enjoyed by man's higher faculties, then it is essential that all should be at liberty to develop those faculties and to seek the pleasures that reward their exercise. Humans have a variety of higher faculties, and many pleasurable activities correlate to them; it would be wrong for anyone to legislate for others what faculties they should cultivate or pleasures they should seek. Therefore people must be free to develop their own talents and interests, for otherwise neither can be worth as much as they should be to them. Individual liberty is accordingly indispensable, a fundamental right, and as such it imposes an absolute restraint on political power: 'The only purpose for which power can be rightfully exercised over any member of a civilised community, against his will, is to prevent harm to others,' Mill famously wrote. 'His own good, either physical or moral, is not a sufficient warrant. He cannot rightfully be compelled to do or forbear because it will be better for him to do so, because it will make him happier, because, in the opinion of others, to do so would be wise, or even right.'[26]

In a society which respects the principle of liberty people can explore a variety of ways of living, and choose a diversity of goals, and from this will come creativity, the development of talent, and both moral and mental progress. *On Liberty* affirms 'a single truth,' says Mill, namely, 'the importance, to man and society, of a large variety of types of character, and giving full freedom to human nature to expand itself in innumerable and conflicting directions . . . The grand, leading principle, towards which every argument in these pages directly converges, is the absolute and essential importance of human development in its richest variety.'[27]

Mill's anxiety that liberty in all respects of thought, expression and choice of life can be threatened as much by majorities as by other forms of political tyranny surfaces here. 'If the American form of democracy overtakes us first,' he wrote, 'the majority will no more relax their despotism than a single despot would.' Worse, such a despotism would be one of 'collective mediocrity'.[28]

As noted, Mill did not take that to be a reason for being anti-democratic; rather, only as a warning to construct democracy carefully so that it safeguards the rights of individuals and minorities. 'Our only chance is to come forward as liberals, carrying out the democratic idea, and not as conservatives, resisting it,' he wrote, for he agreed with de Tocqueville's view that the onset of democracy was inevitable, a point further reinforced by the events of 1848. Accordingly he advanced various proposals about how democracy could best be instituted, in effect suggesting proportional representation and equal rights for women.

Given that the paramount consideration for Mill was that society's institutions should be so organised that they did not inhibit liberty of thought and freedom to experiment with lifestyles, it was inevitable that one target of his strictures was religion, more specifically the evangelical Christianity of his day, which vigorously sought to gain a control in the moral sphere that paralleled the one its forerunners had exercised in the political sphere. 'A state of things in which a large portion of the most active and inquiring intellects find it advisable to keep their general principles and the grounds of their convictions within their own breasts,' he wrote, 'and attempt, in what they address to the public, to fit as much of what they can of their own conclusions to premises which they have internally renounced, cannot send forth the open, fearless characters, and logical, consistent intellects who once adorned the thinking world.'[29]

The ideas and feelings Mill opposed to the attempted hegemony of religious morality were magnanimity, high-mindedness, a sense of honour and personal dignity, and a sentiment of duty to one's fellow men without thought of reward. These are, in short, the 'pagan' virtues of antiquity that also animated the Renaissance, and led to the first stirrings of liberty at the beginning of the modern period.[30]

The implication of this last remark would not be accepted by Lord Acton, for whom religion was precisely the source of the liberty that the modern epoch in history had seen grow with such persistence despite such opposition. One reason he thought this was that he believed the Church to be the only institution capable of protecting people from absolutism, not least the potential absolutism (as he saw it) of the modern bureaucratic state. And this mattered to him because he was passionately convinced of the value of liberty, about which he held the same view as Mill. He wrote, 'Liberty is not a means to a higher political end. It is itself the highest political end. It is not for the sake of good public administration that [liberty] is required, but for security in pursuit of the highest objects of civil society, and of private life.'[31]

When in 1869 the Roman Catholic Church, of which he was a member, accepted Pope Pius IX's decision to declare papal infallibility as a dogma, Acton was devastated: this portended the very absolutism to which he was vehemently opposed. The significance of this event was wider than the question of doctrine and faith, for it followed Pius IX's declaration in his *Syllabus Errorum* of 1864 that anyone who asserted that the holder of St Peter's keys should accommodate himself to 'progress, liberalism or modern civilisation' was in error. To an outside observer this is simply par for the course for the Church, as the paradigm of a reactionary institution, but while the pope was fallible it remained possible for ardent Catholics such as Acton to hope that a less emphatic pope might follow. Proclaiming papal infallibility was another matter entirely, not least by the increasingly obdurate and fallible Pius IX, scarred by his experiences of 1848–9.

Acton was energetic in opposing adoption of the infallibility dogma. He wrote a long review article extolling a German book which opposed infallibility, and travelled to Rome to combat the proposal on the spot. He had good contacts there: one was the British government's representative at the Council which had been summoned by Pius IX to ratify the dogma; another was a theologian who worked for one of the cardinals. With their help he was able to send accurate information to newspapers about what the members of the papal party in the Council were plotting, and how they were conducting their campaign of persuading – by some quite nefarious means – less amenable cardinals to support the pope's plan.

Acton's fear was that the dogma, once accepted, would centralise Church power far too much in Rome, and he was against all centralisation of power in any institution. From Rome he wrote to Gladstone, 'We have to meet an organised conspiracy to establish a power which would be the most formidable enemy of liberty as well as science throughout the world. It can only be met and defeated through the Episcopate, and the Episcopate is exceedingly helpless.' Almost certainly as a result of this letter and the subsequent action taken by Gladstone, the Catholic bishops of England and Ireland jointly wrote to the Council pointing out that the liberties of Catholics in the United Kingdom, very recently restored (in 1828), were contingent upon their having given solemn undertakings on various points, among them that their religion did not require acceptance of the dogma now being proposed, and it was only because of this that Catholics could now hold office in the United Kingdom and sit in Parliament.

That plea availed nothing; none of the governments of Catholic countries in Europe would do anything, and the pope had a majority – though a scant one – available to him among the bishops. In the event this provided him with his vote. The fact that the decision was not unanimous, or at very least overwhelmingly supported, was another cause of dismay for Acton, who was right in thinking that such a momentous innovation should require at least the latter.

The doctrine thus adopted read as follows: 'We teach and define that it is dogma divinely revealed: that the Roman Pontiff, when he speaks *ex cathedra*, that is, in discharge of the office of Pastor and Doctor of all Christians, by virtue of his supreme apostolic authority he defines a doctrine regarding faith or morals to be held by the Universal Church, by divine assistance promised to him in blessed Peter, is possessed of that infallibility with which the divine Redeemer willed His Church should be endowed for defining doctrine regarding faith or morals; and that therefore such definitions of the Roman Pontiff are irreformable in themselves, and not from the consent of the Church.'[32]

It is perhaps a matter for gratitude that infallibility has so far only once been invoked, and that was when Pope Pius XII in 1951 proclaimed the doctrine of the assumption of the Virgin Mary, that is, the doctrine that she did not die but was lifted bodily up into heaven. It is a remarkable fact that this should be taught, and presumably believed, some half dozen years after the world entered the nuclear age; but perhaps it is proof that miracles still occur, as David Hume observed – the miracle of belief.

The immediate effect of promulgation of the doctrine was political rather than doctrinal. Until Pope John XXIII reasserted the collegiality of the episcopate nearly a century later, the new dogma changed the relationship of the bishop of Rome to his fellow bishops by doing just what Acton feared, namely, by centralising Church authority. A wit summed up the situation by remarking that the bishops went as shepherds into the Council, and came out as sheep.

In Acton's view liberty is a moral matter, and that meant that anything that negates liberty is immoral. Absolutism negates liberty; the new dogma was an absolutist measure; it was thus immoral. His equation of liberty and morality was not an idle or arbitrary one in his view. Without liberty there could be no moral choice, which must be free; freedom of the will and liberty of the person in the social and political senses merged in Acton's conception of the matter. Moreover, he saw liberty in the latter two senses as a positive outcome of the right kind of political arrangements, something made possible by the right order and limitation of state power: 'By liberty I mean the assurance that every man shall be protected in doing what he believes to be his duty against the influence of authority and majorities, custom and opinion. The state is competent to assign duties and draw the line between good and evil only in its immediate sphere. Beyond the limits necessary for its well-being, it can only give indirect help to fight the battle of life by promoting the influences which prevail against temptation – religion, education, and the distribution of wealth.'[33]

Acton's devotion to history as a subject of study was actuated by the same moral purpose as informed his commitment to liberty. Like Aristotle and Burke before him he thought of politics as morality writ large and in action – 'The principles of true politics are those of morality enlarged' – and that it is the task of history to judge the moral quality of what it records. Its duty, indeed, is to 'suffer no man and no cause to escape the undying penalty which history has the power to inflict upon wrong.'[34]

That superb sentiment suggests the following thought: in the opening chapter here it was observed that one reason why Acton never completed his projected history of liberty is that the materials are so vast that the task of arranging them requires a work of encyclopaedic dimensions, beyond a single individual's powers. But I hypothesise another reason besides, namely, that Acton found it to be impossible to tell the version of the story of liberty that he wished he could.

This, to repeat, is an hypothesis. But Acton often reiterated his claim that religion is the source of liberty, and yet as the foregoing pages show, all the early effort to free conscience, thought and eventually the person from the toils of authority was effort that had first to be directed against religion – and not simply at religion as a man-made organisation somehow independent of verities that one could claim were perverted by local and temporal conditions. It was the tenets, the dogmas, the imposition of a world view that had to be fought to allow freedom of conscience, then freedom of enquiry, then freedom of action. Each successive freedom threatened the intellectual and moral authority of the belief system in the care of the churches, whose officers therefore struggled to prevent people from thinking, enquiring and acting in those ways.

The churches, and chief among them the Roman Catholic Church, thus resisted almost every step on the road of progress and liberation, a fact starkly and unavoidably clear in the record. Even the pope whom Acton resisted over the matter of infallibility proves this point; witness again his announcement that he was opposed to 'progress, liberalism and modern civilisation', in which he was merely echoing the great majority of his predecessors, to say nothing of Protestant evangelicals who in Acton's time were contesting the discoveries of Charles Darwin and their implications – as they still do to this day.

In the lecture 'The History of Freedom in Christianity' is to be found Acton's best effort to make liberty the product of religion.[35] He writes, 'The idea that religious liberty is the generating principle of civil, and that civil liberty is the necessary condition of religious, was a discovery reserved for the seventeenth century.' This is a telling remark. First, Acton does not explicate the notion of 'religious liberty' at the beginning of the sentence, a needful task because it collapses two stages: religious liberty as liberty of conscience, that is, liberty to think differently from a supposed orthodoxy about matters of faith; and religious liberty as the possibility of liberty from religious control or influence of any kind, as is required for scientific enquiry, or any enquiry unfettered by doctrinal prohibitions or limitations. Civil liberty requires this latter kind of liberty. To be realised in full, in other words, it requires secularism. Secondly, Acton does not address two significant points that arise out of the second part of his sentence, when he states that civil liberty is a necessary condition of religious liberty.

One is that, once again, the implication is that the civil order has to be secular – that is, one in which government and religion are separate, with the temporal sphere being indifferent to which private interest groups (including religious groups) exist within it provided they observe the law and do no harm to others.

The other point is that the existence of free religious organisations in a civil polity is potentially disruptive of it, given that they typically view themselves as possessors of final truth, and are under obligations of various kinds to promote or prevent activities, or beliefs, or the passage of laws and the like, as enjoined by their faith. A religious person must always have a greater loyalty to what concerns the fate of his immortal soul than to a merely temporal power, and thus he is potentially at odds with the latter. So the contract between the secular state and religious persons within it has to be that neither will disturb the other. This requires compromise and accommodation from the religious, for the reasons given. And it explains why, in the past, when there existed empty stretches of the world to go to with one's fellow believers, Nonconformists found it better to leave home and travel thither than to stay at home and compromise.

The history Acton wished to write starts not with the Reformation and the scientific revolution, with Locke and the Bill of Rights – on the contrary: he chose to represent the makers of the late seventeenth-century settlement in England as perfidious and self-serving – but much earlier, with the Church after the Norman Conquest, when the free though 'rude' institutions brought to the British Isles by Saxons, Goths and Franks from the German forests had suffered decay, and there was no urban middle class to resist the imposition of Norman absolutism. 'The only influence capable of resisting the feudal hierarchy,' Acton claimed, 'was the ecclesiastical hierarchy; and they came into collision, when the process of feudalism threatened the independence of the church by subjecting the prelates severally to the form of personal dependence on the kings which was peculiar to the Teutonic state.'[36]

This tendentious claim reverses the actual order of affairs. The Church was at the height of its power in Europe in the centuries after the Norman Conquest of England – this latter a relatively marginal affair from the point of view of the great powers on the continent – and the struggle taking place was one between local princes and the Church, the former resisting the hegemony of a papal imperium. If the Church had won its struggle in England to subjugate the temporal power, and if the same had happened elsewhere in Europe, establishing a papal empire in which the orthodoxies of the Inquisition were strictly enforced, there would have been no liberty anywhere, other than for princes of the Church themselves.

Acton's thesis thus astonishes. It does so all the more because he was as much against theocracy as he was against a polity in which religion has no place. He was a secularist (in the strict and literal sense of believing in separation of Church and State) because he believed that by giving neither Church nor State a hegemony of power, so that they can hold each other in check, the individual will be at liberty between them.

In a letter he set out his secularist view in plain terms: 'a religious government depends for its existence on the belief of the people – preservation of the faith is the *ratio summa status*, to which everything else must yield. Therefore not only the civil power enforces the religious law, but the transgressions of the religious must be watched and denounced – therefore espionage and religious detectives, and the use of the peculiar means of information religion provides to give warning to the police. The domain of conscience [is] not distinct therefore from the domain of the State; sins = crimes, and sins against faith, even when private, are acts of treason. Seclusion from the rest of the world necessarily follows, if the rest of the world has not the same religion, or even if it is not governed on the same principles. For liberty is extremely contagious . . . Poverty and stationary cultivation, that is to say, in comparison to the rest of the world, retrogression, [are] the price . . .'[37] This is a brilliant description of any totalitarianism, whether political or religious; the great totalitarianisms of the twentieth century share exactly the lineaments of a theocracy as Acton here describes; the methods and effects of the Taliban in Afghanistan and the systems of Soviet and Chinese 'communism' at their height are identical.

But for Acton the vital step by which secularism (or at least effective secularism) was attained in the seventeenth century by means of toleration, accepting liberty of conscience and observance under an implicit contract in which the tolerated will not disturb the peace of the tolerators, is neither the source of the diffusion of liberty into other spheres – entailing as it does freedom *from* religion as much as freedom *of* religion – nor is it desirable in itself. He believed that the non-religious state was as much a danger to liberty as a religion-dominated one. In particular he believed that democracy must collapse into anarchy – one of the worst forms of despotism, after all – unless the people are under the self-government of religion. In this he was at one with de Tocqueville and Edmund Burke. A religionless people would have no checks from within on their greed and aggression, intemperance and resentments, as they and Acton all thought, and therefore there must be checks from without.

There are two assumptions in this view. One is that human nature is intrinsically disposed to the bad. Without the 'checks' of authority, whether the internalised authority of religion or the external authority of the police, people will do wrong. This is a Hobbesian view of human nature, not a Lockean one in which the impulse to civil society, with its agreements and co-operations, is a function of the essentially social nature of humankind.

Secondly and correlatively, Acton assumes that unless people grasp that the state has a moral purpose, and indeed is 'divinely instituted' – thus the true source of his view becomes apparent – they will think it is merely a police organisation for the protection of property.

Neither assumption is the right place to start. The correct place is Locke's genealogy of social and political organisation, in which it is not the negative being controlled, but the positive being extolled, that underlies the contract. He has sociobiology as well as reason on his side. Humans are indeed social animals, with social instincts, needs and purposes. Primitively these issue in tribalism, and tribalism is a fruitful arrangement for conflict with other tribes – over territory, water, females (how much harm the view that 'females are resources' has thus done!) – until the tribes themselves need to socialise for yet larger reasons: and so on to civil society itself. The peaceful avocations of social life far outweigh the opposite, despite what the news media relentlessly tell us, for the constructions achieved by education, law and art long survive the destructions achieved by bombs.

The key to understanding Acton lies in identifying the point from which he looks at matters. That viewpoint is that God instituted the organisations, both State and Church, within which man lives. Church and State, Acton claimed, have 'the same origin and the same ultimate objects'. Neither must control the other, neither must obliterate the other; between them liberty thrives.[38] The Christian statesman's duty is to maintain that balance. Interestingly, Acton did not say that liberty would be extinguished under the thumb of either alone, although this is what his view entails. He wrote that 'all liberty consists . . . in the preservation of an inner sphere exempt from State power – that reverence for conscience is the germ of all civil freedom . . . liberty has grown out of the distinction of Church and State' – and he added that 'distinction' is a better word in this context than 'separation'.

The last part of this is of course right, that liberty has grown out of the 'distinction' between Church and State, together with the liberation of conscience and thought that this allowed. But it is hard to make this correct part of his view consistent with the earlier part, that the State is as divinely ordained as the Church. For what end? All those who agree with Acton on this point, namely the theologian theorists of God's government of the world through earthly vicars, are at one in seeing the State as the instrument of God's (that is, the Church's) purpose. It was only when this had ceased to be taken as fact that the first glimmerings of liberty shone through; until then the 'domain of conscience [is] not distinct therefore from the domain of the State; sins = crimes, and sins against faith, even when private, are acts of treason' – just as Acton had said.

Acton's admirable championing of liberty, whatever its wellsprings, comes to the same conclusions about the importance of liberty as John Stuart Mill's entirely secular and richly humanist account. This is a heartening fact. But from the viewpoint of getting the right account of the long hard struggle for liberty and its attendant notions of rights, it is important not to leave matters there. Mill essayed no historical account of liberty, but went straight to the philosophical point of its centrality to the good, his inspiration being the philosophical outlook of classical antiquity in which religion played no part in the formulation of ideas about ethics and politics. But he stands in the empirical tradition that stems from Locke, a tradition that underwrites the thought of the *philosophes* of the Enlightenment in recognising that rational accounts of man and his institutions must begin from the facts, including the facts of human nature and the human condition, and not from one or another system of suppositions about divine origins and destinies.

By contrast Acton sought to place the source of liberty in the history of the highly authoritarian Church, which tried for many centuries to control the thoughts, consciences, desires, feelings and activities of individual human beings right down to the minutiae of their daily lives. Acton's endeavour is a monument of special pleading. All the foregoing chapters here are a refutation of his view, and a paean to the opposite: namely to pluralism, secularism, and humanism. These, one feels pressed to argue, are the fields in which the harvest of liberty grows.

7

Rights out of Wrongs

S PEAKING IN 1953, Dwight D. Eisenhower, who knew something both of war and politics, said, 'Every gun that is made, every warship launched, every rocket fired, signifies in the final sense a theft from those who hunger and are not fed, those who are cold and are not clothed. This world in arms is not spending money alone. It is spending the sweat of its labourers, the genius of its scientists, the hopes of its children. This is not a way of life at all in any true sense. Under the clouds of war, it is humanity hanging on a cross of iron.'[1]

These are words that might have been spoken by anyone who had taken a leading role in the conflicts of the first half of the twentieth century in the hope that victory in them would not merely defeat aggression, but open a space for the best kind of development to follow. Had Eisenhower lived long enough to see the end of the Cold War, the increasing tensions of which prompted this remark, he would have recognised that in fact the struggle had not been unavailing; but as with liberal minds in the early nineteenth century, he instead felt he had reason to think that international affairs did not seem promising, and that the works of peace would be vitiated by the need to remain prepared for war. It does this Republican president and military man credit that when he left office he issued a warning (and in the process coined a term) against 'the industrial-military complex' which he had come to think was running his country.

There is indeed a dramatic contrast between the pictures one might draw of the Western world – Europe, North America, Australasia – in the first and second halves of the twentieth century. In the first half it plunged into the cataclysm of two World Wars, in the second it experienced a sustained period of growth, wealth, stability and internal peace the like of which it had not known since the second half of the nineteenth century. In part the West's peace and prosperity in the twentieth century's second half were a product of the reconstruction effort after so much cost and waste, and most particularly of the Cold War. This latter was in many ways good for the West, despite Eisenhower's anxieties; it proved the adage that it has to be a very ill wind indeed that blows no one any good. Defence spending and the disciplines of alliance together did much to make America richer than ever, and the West more closely knit and peaceful than ever: the joint outcome of the dollar's dominance and the 'Pax Americana' for which it paid. If anything, the West's half century following the end of the Second World War seemed to give the lie to Jeanette Rankin's remark that 'you can no more win a war than you can win an earthquake,' and no doubt explains the hubris – soon enough refuted by events – of Francis Fukuyama's 'end of history' claim.[2]

In the second half of the West's twentieth century there was a significant shift in thinking about three matters. One was the question of how the international community could best try to avoid wars and get along with itself constructively. The second was whether what governments do within their own national borders could any longer be thought no one else's business, especially if it involved attacks on the rights of individuals within those borders, even to the extent of genocide.

The third was a determination to collect together all the thinking of the past five centuries about rights and liberties, to organise it into a body of clear principles, and to affirm it as universally applicable to all human beings everywhere. All three were reactions to the horrors of war and human suffering that the first half of the twentieth century had piled up to unprecedented heights in world history.

After the First World War the creation of the League of Nations represented an attempt to address the first of these matters. It failed dismally, and so did the repeated efforts of peace and disarmament conferences in Geneva in the 1920s and 1930s. These were wrecked principally by the re-arming and war-planning Germans and Japanese, who walked out of Geneva when it no longer suited their purposes of disguise. The rest of the international community looked on, reluctant after so much recent slaughter to respond robustly; and they appeased and hoped all the way until the second catastrophe occurred. Winston Churchill, impatiently watching the appeasement process, remarked, 'An appeaser is one who feeds a crocodile hoping that it will eat him last.' Whereas the First World War had been grievously heavy in losses of young men on battlefields, the Second World War's squeamishness about military losses resulted in vastly greater civilian losses, through indiscriminate mass bombing of cities and other atrocities.[3] Worst of the civilian atrocities was the Holocaust of European Jewry carried out by the Nazis, an endeavour of industrial murder on a scale scarcely ever before imagined, let alone attempted.

It was the inhumanity of this last that most sharply impelled the greatest achievement in the sphere of rights and liberties that the world had hitherto seen: the drafting and adoption of a 'universal declaration' of human rights by the nascent United Nations just three years after the Second World War's end, while Europe and too many parts of the rest of the world still lay in ruins both physical and psychological.

A supremely important pair of facts about the Universal Declaration is that the committee which devised it was not merely international but drawn from all quarters of the world, and in its personnel represented the world's major traditions. When it was presented to the assembled United Nations in 1948, those who welcomed it most warmly were Third World countries who saw in it their hope of casting off colonialism's yoke. The great powers of the United States, Britain, France and the Soviet Union were, by contrast, less enthusiastic, because it threatened to interfere with their free hand in their 'spheres of influence', as the euphemism had it.

In the six decades since the Universal Declaration came into existence, to be followed by the two great Covenants on Civil and Political Rights, and Economic, Social and Cultural Rights, both of which are intended to have the force of law, plenty of voices have been raised to challenge them. Are rights universal, or are they Western Enlightenment notions that the dominating powers were trying to impose on the rest of mankind, who have their own traditions and ways? Are they meaningless pieties, of no use without the serious prospect of enforcement and an international court to try malefactions against them? Is the very concept of 'human rights' – the very idea of a 'right' itself – philosophically coherent? What is the basis of the idea of rights, and what is the justification for thinking that anything sub-stantive answers to it? Could it be that there is something arbitrary and even merely expedient about the idea?[4]

Sceptical questions about the *universal applicability* of the idea of human rights are asked by people for whom it is proving inconvenient – for example, by the leaders of the People's Republic of China, officially one of the most vigorously relativistic opponents of the idea because they are so often accused of violating the rights of their citizens. Sceptical questions about the *utility* of the idea in the absence of means to enforce it are asked by those impatient of mere talk, of hot air and well-meaning declamations that cut no ice, who instead think that infantrymen's boots on the ground are the only real solutions for real problems. Sceptical questions about the *basis* or *justification* of the idea of rights itself are asked by philosophers in safe, comfortable armchairs who have not been arbitrarily arrested and then subjected to electric cattle prods and imprisonment without trial.

Putting matters this way about three of the main sources of scepticism in relation to human rights should be enough to suggest rebuttals. But in fact the chief rebuttal comes from the history – sketched in the foregoing chapters – of how the rights were claimed and won with so much struggle. A mature, reflective exercise of gathering the hard-won lessons and even harder-won advances of five centuries into a single document distilling that experience is itself an achievement of the human spirit that dwarfs the naysayers, motivated as they seem to be by a lack of understanding of what it would be like to stand on the kindling at the stake as the fire is lit under you, as inquisitors practise the water torture on you, as you languish in prison for your beliefs, as you slave in the fields or go hungry and in rags to the factory before dawn, as you live a life on the margin of society excluded from the goods and possibilities available to the mainstream, as the midnight knock comes at the door, as your children are torn from you and marched towards the gas chamber. In the absence of direct experience of hardship, suffering and exclusion, enslavement and discrimination, persecution and murder, the next resource is moral imagination. The ground of scepticism too often lies in its lack.

The story of human rights – and its correlative story, not at issue here, of international law – could well start in 416 BC, when Athenian forces sacked Melos and massacred its inhabitants because the city would not side with Athens in its war against Sparta. Thucydides, who wrote his *Peloponnesian War* to illustrate the effect of war on morality, reported what happened when the Melians tried to negotiate with the Athenians to avert the sack; the latter rebuffed them with words that have rung chillingly down the centuries: 'You know as well as we do that right is only in question between equals in power, for the strong do what they can and the weak suffer what they must.'[5]

The principle that might is right was contested by Plato, Augustine, Aquinas, Grotius – to leapfrog through two thousand years and to mention a few salient names only – and by the time that the modern history of liberty began in the embers of Torquemada's fires, it was no longer acceptable as a principle, even though no rational person would deny that the Athenian's reply remained too often true in practice. Pragmatism, after all, is what Machiavelli preached, and among other things he saw the utility of principles in masking their own non-observance. One cannot be Machiavellian without overtly proclaiming a principle while covertly defying it, one's advantage being best served if everyone else continues honest.[6]

'United Nations' was the name coined by Britain and the United States during the Second World War to denominate the coalition of nations allied against Nazi Germany and militaristic Japan. At the end of the war the United Nations was intended by its founding members – the great powers – to be a revived and better League of Nations whose principal aim was the maintenance of international peace. But a variety of governments – noticeably those of Central and South America – and non-governmental organisations demanded that it should also sign up, as a body, to an explicit regime of human rights. These non-governmental organisations were the direct successors of those that had fought for the abolition of slavery, workers' rights, universal suffrage, freedom of speech and conscience, and more.

The human rights project, which was at first regarded as a side issue, proved to be the signal achievement of the new organisation. One of the factors that prompted this outcome was the Nuremberg Trials, which brought to world attention both the details of Nazi atrocities and the concepts of genocide and 'crimes against humanity' freshly devised in response to them. Footage of heaps of emaciated corpses, of dazed, starved, abused prisoners in striped pyjamas, of the Nazi war criminals on trial, of the ruined land of Germany, conspired to generate a mood among many that was ripe for a big decision in favour of talk about human rights, and of a world order premised on protecting them.

The fact that the Nuremberg Principles were a response to enormities and not an embodiment of pre-existing legislation gave rise to the anxiety that they constituted *ex post facto* law and thus a breach of principles of natural justice, which does not permit criminalising an activity retrospectively. But a way was found round the difficulty, and an important precedent was thereby set that encouraged the drafters of the Universal Declaration. The precedent in question was that the accumulated insight of mankind into what might be called an ethical bottom line was justification enough for stating and applying principles showing where it must be drawn.

In the summer of 1945, less than a month after the war in Europe officially ended, delegates from the United States, Britain, Russia and France met in London to discuss putting Nazi leaders on trial for war crimes. The *ex post facto* problem was addressed by noting that, in starting the war, Germany had violated several conventions and treaties to which it was a signatory: the Hague rules of 1907; the Treaty of Versailles at the end of the First World War; the Kellogg–Briand Pact of 1928 outlawing war; and the Locarno Pact of 1926 which fixed

Germany's eastern border – to the annoyance of Hitler. The Third Reich's invasions of Poland, Norway, Holland, Belgium, France, Greece, Yugoslavia and Russia breached all its treaty obligations.

That was one starting point. Secondly, all countries have laws against murder, torture and enslavement, and the delegates recognised that drafting a charter for an International Military Tribunal would simply be an application of such laws. It was not that the International Military Tribunal was applying laws created retrospectively, but rather bringing well-established law to bear in the special circumstances it faced. The International Military Tribunal was accordingly set up as an instrument of enforcement, not of legislation.[7]

By the beginning of August 1945 the Charter of the Tribunal had been agreed and signed, and it specified four crimes for which Nazi leaders would be tried: conspiracy to carry out aggressive war; the launching of aggression; killing and destroying beyond the justification of military necessity; and 'crimes against humanity'.

The concept of crimes against humanity was new, having been born in the course of the war itself. It addressed the Holocaust and other crimes against civilians. In the Nuremberg Indictment it was defined with precision to include 'murder, extermination, enslavement, de-portation, and other inhumane acts committed against any civilian population, before or during the war, or persecutions on political, racial or religious grounds in execution of or in connection with any crime within the jurisdiction of the Tribunal.'[8]

The idea of crimes against humanity implies the idea of human rights. There cannot be crimes against people unless there is something the people possess of which they can be criminally deprived, or in respect of which they can be criminally injured. The connection between the Nuremberg concept and the idea of human rights is implicit, though the former did not appeal overtly to it; but by reciprocity the rhetorical case for human rights – and in particular the adoption of a declaration of principles enshrining them – was made very much easier by the fact that Nuremberg had made talk of crimes against humanity familiar, as had the trial of Nazi leaders for commit-ting them. The trials in effect said that serious violations against human rights had occurred, and action had been taken to punish them; and this implied the correctness of saying that there was a pressing need to make clear what was at stake to prevent further human rights violations if possible, and if not possible, to have a standard for holding violators to account.

'Whereas recognition of the inherent dignity and of the equal and inalienable rights of all members of the human family is the foundation of freedom, justice and peace in the world,' begins the Preamble to the Universal Declaration of Human Rights, '[and] whereas disregard and contempt for human rights have resulted in barbarous acts which have outraged the conscience of mankind, and the advent of a world in which human beings shall enjoy freedom of speech and belief and freedom from fear and want has been proclaimed as the highest aspiration of the common people . . .'

These ringing words not only state the immediate reason for adoption of the Universal Declaration, but they sum up and distil many of the achievements of the long liberty struggle set alight by Torquemada's fires. The proximate source of the Declaration itself, from the point of view of its wording, was more recent; it derived from the constitution-building that followed the example set by the United States of America at the end of the eighteenth century, and proceeded afterwards with the devising of state constitutions and bills of rights both in older countries requiring or desiring new forms of governance – for example, France in 1789 and Prussia not long afterwards – and young republics in the nineteenth century, such as the newly independent states of South America. The focus on individual liberty in the Anglophone tradition, and the focus on equality and solidarity in the Francophone tradition, were brought together in these initiatives, and provided the background of thinking about the universal bill of rights that was mooted at the Second World War's end.

Those who urged that such a bill be adopted were able to point to the fact that Allied powers had in effect made the provisions of such a bill their objective for war. In early 1942, when the Allies first called themselves 'the United Nations', they issued a joint statement declaring that they sought complete victory in order to 'defend life, liberty, independence and religious freedom and to preserve human rights and justice in their own lands as well as in other lands'. This statement echoed the central ideas in President Roosevelt's 'four freedoms' speech of 1941, which specified freedom of speech, freedom of religion, freedom from want and freedom from fear as the conditions for peace and security in the world.

When the United Nations Charter was adopted in San Francisco at the end of June 1945, its Preamble contained a paragraph which set the terms for the Universal Declaration's drafting committee. It announced the resolve of the United Nations to 'reaffirm our faith in fundamental human rights, in the dignity and worth of the human person, in the equal rights of men and women . . . [and] to promote social progress and better standards of life in larger freedom'.

The Universal Declaration's drafters had these statements in mind as well as the tradition of discourse about rights that all the liberty struggles had made familiar. But such discourse embodies large generalities, and to make them more precise the drafters sought and found the common fundamentals that lay at their base. They saw the Declaration as a whole, all the enumerated rights together providing a portrait of the conditions for a good human life: they were likened to a temple whose portico is mounted on four pillars, one upholding rights to life, liberty and personal security (articles 3–11 of the Declaration), the second upholding rights in civil society (articles 12–17), the third upholding political rights (articles 18–21), and the fourth upholding economic, social and cultural rights (articles 22–27; see the full text of the Universal Declaration in Appendix 5). The rights in the third and fourth pillars are spelled out in greater detail in the two Covenants, adopted by the United Nations in following years, on civil and political rights, and on economic, social and cultural rights respectively.

Cold War realities did not conduce to the Universal Declaration's uptake as a map for the development of the post-war world. It became a menu rather than a portrait, a menu useful for accusation and counter-accusation and other rhetorical gestures on the international stage, instead of a coherent picture of the overall conditions for good and flourishing individual lives. At time of writing that remains largely the case.

The UN's rights conventions still suffer from too little discussion about the implications of the individual articles in the context of their joint aspiration. Does a right to life mean a right to a certain minimum quality of life? Yes, definitely, as the later articles and the two Covenants make explicit. Then does a right to a certain minimum quality of life entail a right to a good death, eased by medical science, given that dying is an act of living and can be painful, distressing and undignified? Immediately there will be controversy over this implication, and there already has been; but it makes the point that the Universal Declaration still awaits its Locke, so to say – the philosophical explication and justification of what is already the case.

But it has changed the world nevertheless. One example – drawn from a number of years' worth of personal experience of this author – illustrates how.[9] It is the example of how a major human rights violator, the People's Republic of China, views the opprobrium that indictment at the UN Commission of Human Rights would represent. At the Commission's annual spring meetings in Geneva – even before the reform of that largely ineffective talking-shop in which, too often, representatives of governments which were themselves perpetrators of serious human rights violations sat in self-importance at the central table and made speeches – the very large Chinese delegation would be actively at work deflecting censure for their human rights record, partly by smooth diplomacy and partly by promising small countries aid and weapons in return for a vote. They were so successful that they were never once censured in the years following the Tiananmen massacres of 1989, and have never been censured for their vast gulag of forced labour camps, or in connection with executions for more than sixty capital offences (more executions than all the rest of the world put together annually; they ensure a supply of corneas and kidneys for transplant purposes, and the family of the deceased had to pay for the bullet used). There they have never been condemned for their practice of arbitrary arrest and detention, or for censorship, invasion of privacy, and mail-tampering, or for their brutal and illegal occupancy of Tibet.[10] One reason – apart from the pusillanimity of the rest of the world contemplating the vast potential market China represents – is the large, smooth, well-oiled machine Beijing sent annually to Geneva to talk, persuade, prevaricate, explain away, lie and dodge on the question of human rights.[11]

The fact that China felt the need to invest so much in this endeavour is proof of the effectiveness of the mere existence of internationally agreed human rights standards. One could add the excellent work of Human Rights Watch, Amnesty International, International PEN, the International Labour Organisation and others, together with inter-governmental discussions of human rights regimes, as proof that the concept makes a difference.

It is, though, by no means effective enough. The atrocities go on: if one listed them from Cambodia to Bosnia, from Rwanda to the Middle East to Darfur, one would be out of date before the sentence was finished. Perhaps the most hopeful sign at the beginning of the twenty-first century is the coming into existence of the International Criminal Court, because the one big lack in the matter of human rights is enforcement of the covenants that articulate and enjoin them.

The principle underlying the concept of an International Criminal Court is that there should be for the world community what any civilised national community has, namely, a properly constituted means for dealing with crime and wrongs. The trials at Nuremberg and Tokyo after the Second World War provided precedents for bringing individuals to justice for human rights violations, but those tribunals, and later ones such as the Bosnian tribunal in the Hague, were ad hoc. The International Criminal Court was needed to provide a permanent and properly constituted institution for its purpose.[12]

No one claims that an International Criminal Court will stop crimes against humanity happening, although it will certainly prevent some – the deterrent effect on a would-be Hitler or Pol Pot cannot be underestimated. But, more importantly, it offers the alternative of justice in place of revenge for wrongs done; it offers the possibility of redress to the wronged; it offers an important contribution to processes of healing and reconciliation after conflicts, something not always possible without justice being carried out on behalf of victims or their relatives. And it offers a chance of truth, or something anyway better than rumour and legend, in the record of conflict and great crimes.

Some critics object to the idea of an International Criminal Court on the grounds of the practical difficulty it faces. This is rather like objecting to Montgolfier's balloon because it is not yet a jet airliner. Patience is required: just as the introduction of law to the Wild West was (so Hollywood tells us) a hard slow process, so much more so is the process of making the international arena a lawful domain. It is a noble aspiration to want to make it so; it cannot be the work of a moment.

Some object to the very concept of an International Criminal Court, declaring that, despite the principle of complementarity embodied in the Rome Treaty (which provides that where national law is sufficient for what the International Criminal Court might otherwise do, it takes precedence), it nevertheless impugns the sovereignty of nation states.

One answer is that a reduction of sovereignty in the appropriate respect and degree might be a good thing.

Others object that a process of 'judicial creep' will eventually extend the Court's powers to competence over, say, drug smuggling, environmental pollution, and beyond.

The answer is that some of these extensions would be a good thing too, given the globalisation of the world economy and the irrevocable interdependence of the world's communities. But anyway one rejects the implicit 'slippery slope' argument here; it is not beyond the wit of man to see where the jurisdiction of an International Criminal Court is most effectively applied, and where not.

Another objection is that the Court will involve a great deal of cost and bureaucracy.

The solution is, first, to manage it well; and secondly, to accept that peace and justice are worth paying for.

Critics of the Court insist on the difficulty of making it work in practice, and add the worry that it will make the United States less willing to serve as the world's policeman. In part this criticism rests on the argument that no such thing as an 'international community' exists, which if correct entails that only historically evolved national, ethnic or tribal frameworks of law can work. The hopes of human rights advocates are bound to be disappointed therefore, say the critics, because they rest on the mistaken view that mankind is a nation in large.

Critics also charge the Court with being undemocratic, and consider this to be a definitive rebuttal of its claim to legitimacy. These criticisms rest on the same commitment to the idea that only subdivisions of humanity, such as the nation state, can serve as the basis for law and government.

But this argument, the standard defence of the nation-state ideal, gets weaker the more globalised and interdependent the world becomes. Of course, in the opinion of some defenders of the nation state, the fact of globalisation makes the continued existence of such states more urgent; but one can only repeat that in fact their relevance appears, on the contrary, to be diminishing, as the demands of new global realities grow more exigent.

Democratic accountability can anyway be channelled through international organisations by representing the collective view of participating national governments; ultimately the authority of bodies like the United Nations rests on the agreement entailed by the participation of its members.

The point about the value of an international instrument of enforcement for human rights standards can best be put as follows. Suppose, *per impossibile*, there had been international human rights conventions in force, and an International Criminal Court, at various times in the story told in these pages. How would Torquemada have fared? Or Calvin, for that matter? Or the Vatican and its Inquisition? Or Robespierre? The harder questions would have been, Who would have been indicted before such a court, Charles I or Cromwell? How would the United States have fared in connection with slavery? Or the British government on the occasion of the Peterloo massacre in 1819, when six demonstrating workers were killed in a sabre charge by troops?

If someone were to say that these questions do not grip because the world has changed now, the response can only be: Yes, and despite everything, much for the better.

8

The Idea of Liberty
and the Verge of Betrayal

IT IS COMMON FOR politicians to talk of 'liberty' and 'freedom' without saying precisely what they mean by these terms. The case of 'freedom' is especially instructive. It is easy to be in favour of freedom as a value, a goal, a great good – but what does it mean? Until one has a specification, stating 'freedom *to* do so-and-so', 'freedom *from* such-and-such', 'freedom *of* this-and-that', the word is practically empty. It only begins to take on definite meaning when discussion turns to such practical matters as freedom to choose whom to marry, freedom from arbitrary and tyrannous rule, freedom of movement. And then it often turns out that such freedoms have to have limits, if only to protect a certain degree of freedom for others.

'Liberty' is not an exact synonym of 'freedom', though it can be used as such in many standard cases (for example, 'liberty of movement'), for it denotes a condition or situation in which groups or individuals have a set of specifiable freedoms *to*, *from* and *of*. Put like this it might appear to be chiefly a political concept, denoting immunity from arbitrary authority, and this is certainly one main sense. But it more generally means immunity from any form of external compulsion, not just governmental rule but also religious prescriptions and social pressures.

Famously, Isaiah Berlin distinguished between *positive* and *negative* liberty, defining the former as the freedom to avail oneself of rights and entitlements of given kinds, and the latter as protection from the arbitrary exercise of authority.[1] An alternative way of characterising the contrast he drew is to describe positive liberty as the freedom to seek and realise certain goals, and negative liberty as freedom from external compulsion. For Berlin negative freedom is the important kind; he thought positive freedom could tempt the state to prescribe and perhaps enforce ways of living and acting that it believed would be in the best interests of individuals, and thus what those individuals should desire (whether or not they in fact did so). This temptation has lately come to prove too great even for Western liberal democracies, which now routinely pass laws enforcing behaviour they think is in individuals' best interests to adopt: not smoking tobacco, not driving a motor vehicle without a seat belt, and so on for many such examples. By contrast, as Berlin phrased it, 'liberty in the negative sense involves an answer to the question "What is the area within which the subject – a person or group of persons – is or should be left to do or be what he is able to do or be, without interference by other persons." ' This might be called the classic conception of liberty; it is shared by John Stuart Mill, and is the principle of modern liberalism.[2]

This treatment of the concept of liberty places it squarely in the social and political domain, where its main meaning certainly lies. But it has a related employment in philosophy to denote freedom of the will as opposed to the strict causal constraint which determinism says governs all events, including human actions, in the world. It is the former not the latter sense of liberty which is at issue in this book, though it is important to note the allied meaning, because in antiquity the value accorded to liberty (by Aristotle and Cicero among a number of others) was in part associated with rejection of fatalism, the idea that each individual has a prescribed (in the literal sense) destiny; and this connects with the questions debated in Christian theology about whether human beings are free to make moral choices, or are pre-destined to salvation or damnation. The seriousness of such questions for Christian theologians can be seen in the problem that arises if humans have free will, because if they do, how can their freedom be consistent with the omniscience of God, which, as such, would have to include foreknowledge – which in turn seems to entail a predetermined course of history, and therefore lack of freedom for human individuals?[3]

The concept of liberty evolved throughout the period covered by this book by enlarging in scope and coming to apply to more aspects of human life and interests. To see how this worked, let us summarise the story told here from the viewpoint of the idea of liberty itself. Doing so also serves to gather the threads of the overall tale, in preparation for considering what is currently happening in the major Western liberal democracies which gained so much from this monumental endeavour to achieve liberty and rights.

The story began with the struggle to secure liberty of conscience, a struggle directed against the hegemony of a single religious outlook. It progressed into a struggle to be allowed to think and enquire, in philosophy and science, free of the demand that all such enquiry should conform to the prescriptions of that same religious outlook. Chapters 2 and 3 told this story. And once people had come to taste liberty in these latter respects, their desire for greater personal liberty, which is the same thing as greater control over aspects of their own lives once wholly governed by the state or its ruler, became insistent. By the Enlightenment, as Chapters 4 and 5 here showed, the idea of liberty had come to be closely associated with the ideal of the rational autonomy of the individual. This indeed is how Immanuel Kant saw liberty, and for him it was the key notion in his idea of human nature and therefore the ethical theory he erected upon it.[4] By this time, too, the concept of liberty had explicitly come to consist in a set of associated concepts, principally that of rights. Thus individual liberty was conceived as being constituted by such rights as entitlement to due process of law, to protection from arbitrary exercise of governmental power, to the secure possession of private property, to the expression of opinion without prior restraint, to private views on religious matters, and more. The great eighteenth-century expressions of this formative outlook were the American and French Revolutions.

The ideas motivating – and embodied by – these revolutions had grown out of the political theories of the preceding two centuries, which had been occasioned by a major historical shift, and made possible by a major intellectual shift. The historical shift was the need for new power arrangements following the failure of the solution to the end of feudalism, which had been monarchic despotism as a means of unifying humanly disparate and (given difficulties of communications) functionally widespread domains. An example is England, which after long and agonising struggles replaced feudal structures with the Tudor absolute monarchy, and which by the beginning of the Stuart period at the start of the seventeenth century was in need of another justification for the authority of the sovereign power. The proposed answer was the 'Divine Right' of kings, which was then rejected by England in the mid-seventeenth century at yet more cost of blood, including that of a king. How reluctantly power of any kind yields.

The questions at stake in this momentous event of the English Civil War, described by Christopher Hill[5] as the first of the great revolutions that shaped modern times (to the American and French he added the Russian Revolution of 1917), are at the heart of Thomas Hobbes' *Leviathan*, published in 1651. This work, the first classic of political philosophy in modern times, turns on two propositions: that all forms of government rest ultimately on a body, whether an individual or an institution, which has unchallengeable sovereign power, and that this sovereign power exists as a result of a primitive contract between individuals who found life 'solitary, poor, nasty, brutish and short' in the state of pre-social nature. In return for the sovereign's protection they have thereby implicitly agreed to obey it, thus trading some of their primordial liberty for the advantages accrued.[6]

There is another proposition of importance in Hobbes' doctrine, namely, that it is a 'necessity of nature' that human individuals should have their own best interests at heart, and that they cannot be expected to do other than promote them. This amounts in effect to a natural right. That is why, in the state of nature before civil society exists, there is an inevitable 'war of all against all', each pursuing his individual good against the rest. It is to escape this self-defeating situation that people voluntarily forfeit some of their rights and liberties for the benefits of political society.

The Civil War was not a final rejection of the doctrine on which Stuart monarchy supposed itself to rest; had it been so there would have been no Restoration in 1660. But though France was seeing, in the rule of Louis XIV, the greatest and most luxuriant manifestation in modern times of absolute monarchy, the English were not prepared to put up with its excesses, for them exemplified by James II's efforts to restore Roman Catholicism by piecemeal revocations of the existing non-Catholic settlement. The word 'piecemeal' is to the point: in France the Revocation of the Edict of Nantes in 1685 was anything but piecemeal, and Protestants everywhere looked with dismay at this reopening of wounds that the Thirty Years War, which had ended a mere thirty-odd years before, was meant to have stitched closed. The Revocation of the Edict of Nantes sent a shock through the polities of Europe, though to universal relief it did not restart the Thirty Years War. But in England James II's own tinkering revocations, taking the form of installing Catholics in university sinecures, packing Parliament, interfering with judicial processes, and other actions designed incrementally but un-questionably to secure an eventual reversion to the Old Faith, were not endurable. He was deposed from the throne like his grandfather, but unlike his grandfather he kept his head – a mistake, later cynics remarked, in view of the would-be coups attempted by the Old and Young Pretenders in succeeding generations.

The theoretician of this second seventeenth-century English revolu-tion was John Locke, whose *Two Treatises of Government* (1690) constituted its explanation and justification. Like Hobbes he premised the idea of a social contract as the underlying source of governmental authority, but unlike Hobbes he made government party to the contract too, and thus subject to limitations in the exercise of its powers. If the governing authority (whatever form it takes) misapplies its powers, the people with whom it stands in that contractual relation-ship have the right to resist and depose it. Thus was the theory of limited monarchy born from the practice of limiting a monarchy, though in the unsettled sequel to the latter it was some time – and another historical accident (the inability of George I, who ascended the throne in 1714, to speak English) – before it fully took hold.

These points, discussed at greater length in Chapter 4, are repeated here because implicit in them is the idea of *natural rights*. When Locke talked of the people's right to resist and dismiss the king or government if it acted beyond its contractual terms, he was applying an idea that had emerged from a much earlier conception of 'natural law', the idea that nature (or God) had produced people and their societies according to laws of its own, to which therefore both people and societies must conform. As individualism took increasing root in the post-Reformation world, the natural law doctrine was adapted to accommodate it, in the form of a view that individuals have natural rights that nothing and no one can violate. For Locke this meant that despite the terms of the social contract, individuals possessed certain inalienable basic rights brought with them from the state of nature, chief among them being freedom of conscience, the right to private property, and the right to a say in forming the laws that govern them.

In the contrast between, on the one hand, the idea of a natural right as an intrinsic endowment of human beings and, on the other hand, the idea of a legal right as an institutional artefact created by an act of the governing power, there is implicit the idea that in cases of conflict between them, the natural right must prevail. This further implies that natural rights are universal concomitants of the condition of being human, and as such are independent of time, place, and the accident of social developments, including the belief systems (among them religions) that history has produced in diverse circumstances.

Locke's writings are quoted verbatim and extensively in the documents of the great eighteenth-century revolutions, American and French, and these revolutions give the idea its fullest expression and application. From England's Bill of Rights (1689) through America's Declaration of Independence (1776), France's Declaration of the Rights of Man and the Citizen (1789), and the US Bill of Rights (the first ten amendments to the Constitution, 1791) to the United Nations Declaration of Human Rights (1948), the idea of rights has become the central organising concept among those of constitutionality, democracy, and the rule of law.

That this is so is independent of the philosophical debate that has surrounded the idea of natural rights, and indeed independent of its rejection (famously, Jeremy Bentham dismissed talk of them as 'nonsense on stilts'). Critics have focused on the arbitrariness of the claim that nature or a deity has somehow magically endowed people with rights to life, liberty, property and happiness, when in fact the idea of these things is a human invention, and their existence as rights (in those dispensations where they are indeed rights) is the result of *decisions* to regard them as such. I call this the 'arrogatory theory of rights': experience and rational reflection show what is required to give individuals the best chance of making flourishing lives for themselves, and these framework requirements we institute as rights in order to make the chance of such flourishing available. It is as simple, yet as profound, as that.

So we do not need to be wedded to the idea of 'natural' rights at all. The proceeding just described – of people coming to see what they should lay claim to as the basis of their social and institutional arrangements – is acceptable and justifiable on its merits; one can make an excellent case for saying that over time a consensus has been reached about the kinds of basic laws and principles required to so arrange things for individuals and groups that they can exist in ways we ('we' in those societies) recognise as desirable. It is for this that a robust and generalised concept of liberty is needed. As has often enough been pointed out (for example, by the philosopher H.L.A. Hart), if any idea of rights is to have content, the basic one must be liberty, for without it none of the others can apply.[7]

At the same time, though, one has to remain conscious of the powerful criticisms that these liberal ideas have been subjected to by Marx and the traditions of socialism and anarchism. Marx attacked the French Revolution's 'Rights of Man' as expressive merely of 'bourgeois egoism', and socialists and anarchists alike argue that without a state of equality between individuals, liberty will merely turn out to be licence for the strong to exploit the weak. So indeed it too often proves; and even in notionally liberal dispensations the practical illiberalities consequent upon poverty and the various disenfranchisements that flow from it mean that liberty is only real for those who manage to succeed among the complexities and expenses of modern life. By itself this thought would be enough to raise questions about how far the West had been successful in its long haul towards a situation where everyone is free and enfranchised, subject to the reasonable constraints required by a good society.

In the foregoing chapters the ideas of liberty and rights at issue are those that emerge from this long and complex debate about the nature of both, and their relation. Context makes clear what particular sense attaches to a given use. In general the default meaning is provided by the negative sense of liberty and the sense of 'rights' which revolutionaries, workers, women, and eventually the whole world community in the first hopeful moments of the United Nations' founding, came to adopt as a central idea.

Since 11 September 2001 at least two of the major Western liberal democracies, historically leaders in the progress towards securing liberty and rights for individuals, and through them in the forging of open societies under the rule of law, have begun to go into reverse on some of these vital matters. They are the governments of the United States and the United Kingdom. They have compromised some of their own civil liberties, and at time of writing threaten to compromise more. They are doing it, their governments say, in the name of security, necessitated by a new and dangerous brand of terrorism carried out by religious fanatics who use their own lives and bodies as weapons. This makes them harder to guard against, and vastly more dangerous than terrorists of earlier eras – for example, the anarchists of the late nineteenth century, who had small bombs and pistols only, or the bombers of the IRA, who usually gave warnings of an attack (but were habitual employers of murder nonetheless), or of ETA in Spain. Today's new breed of terrorist has access to technology which threatens the deaths of thousands or tens of thousands in the countries they attack, and they are driven by an ideology which places a quite different value on their own deaths and the deaths of those they see as enemies profoundly hostile to their own most cherished commitments. The supreme danger they pose lies in these facts.

Mass murder under any pretext is a contemptible thing, but the contempt which the new breed of terrorist invites is not a protection against them. Governments accordingly tighten security by introducing new measures of surveillance, giving security services new powers, granting themselves licence to investigate their citizens' mail, electronic mail, bank accounts, and even their habits of book borrowing from libraries. But by these and other means they breach the civil liberties of their people; and they do it to everyone in order to catch the few bad people who threaten to commit terrorism. Critics of what democratic governments are doing to their own countries' civil liberties point out that the bad people they aim to catch are indeed very few: two, or two dozen, or two hundred; even if it were two thousand the price, they argue, of limiting the hard-won liberties of millions is too high.

If the terrorists were so ambitious as to wish to take over the targeted society and introduce their own brand of religious hegemony – a stated aim of certain Islamists in the United Kingdom, for example – one of the first casualties would be civil liberties, especially those of women. If the governments of liberal democracies incrementally reduce the liberties of their people, they will thereby achieve on the terrorists' behalf what the terrorists wish, which is to harm the targeted society and undermine its institutions and traditions. Thus in limiting freedoms and giving up aspects of civil liberties, the governments of those countries are doing the terrorists' work for them.

In some cases this retrograde effect happens with terrorism as the excuse, rather than the legitimate reason, for scaling back liberties, because doing so makes life easier for government and security services, for whom civil liberties are a standing hindrance. A classic case in point is the British government decision to introduce biometric identity cards linked to a 'National Identity Register'. The real reason for their introduction is to make all policing activities easier, both for the regular police and for the immigration services, because the effect of an identity card is to give each individual a number, like the vehicle registration number on a car, by which each individual can be tracked. Identity cards are surveillance devices, leaving a trail through the individual's encounters with public agencies at very least, and doubtless such private ones as banks and airlines, car purchase and use, and more.

The British government's ostensible reasons given for introducing identity cards were many and various, changing as the claims for their necessity were challenged. They began as 'entitlement cards' to catch illegal immigrants. Then they became safeguards against identity fraud. Then they were said to be bulwarks against terrorism, though this claim was very soon dropped; the mass murderers who perpetrated the atrocity of 7 July 2005 in London were British citizens, Muslims all but one of whom were of Pakistani descent, who would have ensured that their identity cards were prominently on their persons when they killed themselves and dozens of others, so that they could get the credit for what they imagined was their heroism. At the time identity cards were said to be for use against serious crime such as the trafficking of drugs and human beings. Occasionally a bold government minister claims that they are for two of these things simultaneously.[8]

Expert opinion from every quarter has pointed out that identity cards will not be effective for any of the various purposes stated, and will add a raft of difficulties of their own.[9] Civil liberties organisations attack them on the ground that they change the relationship between the citizen and the state in a deeply negative way. Until people begin to think of their implications, they assume that since they already have credit cards, store cards and library cards, a passport and a driving licence, one more card will make no difference. But all these are voluntary cards, and they establish a link between their possessor and a single organisation which issues the card for a specific purpose. A national identity card is intended to be compulsory, and is linked to a central government computer on which the holder's personal data are stored, so that a police card-reader can summon complete information about individuals whether or not they are suspected of a crime; and the information can inform the police, or any other agency with access to the central information source, what that individual has lately been doing.

To make the scheme acceptable, the government assures the public that it will not be compulsory to carry the card at all times – how long will this polite arrangement last? – and people will not be stopped in the street and asked to show the card to a policeman or an official (in old films the Gestapo stop the dashing hero and ask for his 'papers': to its critics, a biometric identity card is no different from 'papers'). The least of the harms this does to civil liberties is that it is an invasion of privacy; the fundamental objection is that it makes citizens public conscripts as opposed to private members of their own society.

That is just one example of the assault on civil liberties that is now under way. For their defenders, the list of things that the governments of the United States and the United Kingdom are doing which compromise civil liberties, at the end of five centuries of struggle to attain them, is a much longer one.

In the United States the effect of the Patriot Act and other measures has been to increase government secrecy, to break down the distinction between collecting foreign intelligence and conducting criminal enquiries at home, and to erode safeguards on citizens' privacy.[10]

An important feature of a liberal democracy is that government should be transparent, because it is accountable to the people; the people cannot hold it to account unless they can see what it is doing. Government in the United States has been far more open and transparent than in the United Kingdom where, despite a notional Freedom of Information Act, most of what happens behind the doors of Whitehall and Downing Street is kept well away from public scrutiny.[11] But in Washington since 9/11[12] the administration has been drawing veils over its activities in deeply troubling ways. For a prime example, it refuses to inform the public about hundreds of detainees held in federal prisons on suspicion of alleged terrorist activity. For another it keeps secret the use it makes of information it has gathered about individuals, and what it has done with that information – for example, who it has shared the information with. At least some, if not most, of these individuals are likely to be innocent of any criminal or terrorist activity, and their rights are accordingly in serious jeopardy. This situation has arisen because the Patriot Act reverses privacy laws that formerly required the government to inform people if any of their personal data had been accessed in the course of an enquiry; data such as bank details, student records, credit standing, and the like.

The US government has passed laws allowing people's homes to be searched without their knowledge. It has removed the competence of the courts to review actions that the government claims have been taken in the interests of national security. The security services have increased powers of arrest and detention in immigration cases. The standards required for issuing warrants for searching premises and seizing items found there have been lowered. Wiretapping and mail interception powers have been greatly extended, and placed under the cloak of permanent secrecy.[13]

Among the most significant developments, the US government has established military tribunals to try terrorist suspects that are outside the regular judicial system; these have no jury, nor do they have the public surveillance that a system of justice requires (in breach of the long-standing principle that 'justice must be seen to be done'). It has even permitted itself the use of coercive means – torture – in the interrogation of terrorist suspects.[14]

The establishment of military tribunals is a mark of how the US government has sought to sideline the judiciary in the so-called 'war on terror', finding due process of law a hindrance to what it deems necessary for public safety. But it thereby does precisely the wrong thing: for the hindrance that independent judges represent constitutes the most powerful protection of civil liberties that a society can have. Judges are there to protect the individual against overweening authority, to ensure that due process is observed, to give accused persons every chance to defend themselves, to advise and assist juries, to monitor the conduct of prosecution and defence teams, and in all these ways to ensure that cases are fairly and properly tried. Their independence is one of the pillars of the Constitution; Montesquieu and James Madison would be shocked by the way that the US administration has weakened one of the fundamental balances of the Constitution.

The American Civil Liberties Union has focused attention on the fact that the US government has reintroduced practices which were the cause of outrage during the Civil Rights and anti-Vietnam War campaigns, when the FBI acted inside America as the CIA acted outside it, spying on activists and harassing them. The result was that measures were taken to protect the American public from a repetition of that behaviour. The US administration has reintroduced them, and in an exacerbated climate of civil liberties limitations it can act with impunity in several ways, not least by never having to disclose its use of secretly obtained warrants to gather information (nor does it have to prove to the secret warrant-issuing authority that it legitimately requires them).

And the president has suggested that his government might change the posse comitatus law, introduced after the Civil War, that forbids the use of troops as police. Some of the more anxious voices in the United States ask how this, if accompanied by the legalisation of torture and the building of internment camps for suspect persons – both hinted at by the Attorney General – can possibly add up to a desirable picture.[15]

The United States has always prided itself on being the home of justice and liberty, even though in the past it has lapsed at times – usually at difficult times, which are precisely when threats to liberties usually arise: for example habeas corpus was suspended in the Civil War; opposition to entry to the First World War was suppressed with a heavy hand; one hundred and twenty thousand Japanese-Americans were interned in the Second World War; the FBI acted almost as a political hit squad in the 1960s – and the record of the CIA in various quarters of the world has invited sharp criticism. The Patriot Act and other measures taken by the US government in the wake of 9/11 are chapters in this less happy part of the American story, which in so many other ways has been a glorious one. What this less happy aspect of the story involves is antithetical to ideals of justice and liberty; it makes the freest country in the world do things that only stereotypical police states do.

Pro-US government voices accuse those who contest the measures taken as unpatriotic. On the contrary, say the defenders of civil liberties, true patriotism lies in resisting the extension of the executive's power, its restriction of Bill of Rights freedoms, and its secret spying on citizens. It amounts to what the American Civil Liberties Union calls 'the worst civil liberties crisis our country has ever seen', and it is being done in the name of an entirely false promise: increased security.[16]

In the United Kingdom the government has profited from the unease prompted by terrorism – an unease it periodically keeps at a certain pitch by announcing the imminence of threats and the seriousness of the situation. This has enabled it not only to introduce a raft of 'anti-terrorism' laws, but also to widen its large and continuous programme of civil-liberties-reducing legislation to other matters: to what it also chooses to call a 'war on crime', to civil disobedience, and to a variety of social problems (such as those caused by rowdy youngsters on Saturday nights). In the US the claim could be that the new illiberal measures are directed at terrorism. The situation is being used as an excuse for attaining a much broader aim in the UK, where the general reduction of civil liberties is designed to introduce many conveniences for the authorities into their management of society.

For example, a proposal to seize the assets of drug traffickers has the implication that anyone found with more than £1,000 on their person will have the money confiscated until he can prove that he is carrying it for legitimate purposes.

For another, persons suspected (but not proved or found guilty) of involvement in drug crime or human trafficking can be banned from certain places or from meeting certain other persons, when a new breed of 'civil banning orders' has been introduced. These would be issued, note, on suspicion only: this is an arbitrary power of the kind that policemen in China and other totalitarian regimes possess.

The new restriction of 'Anti-Social Banning Orders' already in place can be applied to individuals by the police without needing the authority of a magistrate.

Yet these restrictions on civil liberties, standing outside the domain of the courts because they consist in summary police powers, are minor in comparison to the identity card law, to longer periods of detention without trial for terror suspects, and to stricter immigration controls and other police powers alleged to be necessitated by the terrorist threat. Britain has more closed-circuit television cameras constantly monitoring public space than any other country in the world; individuals are filmed a number of times a day going about their ordinary private business, and the film is held for an unspecified length of time in case crime or terrorism requires re-examination of the footage.

No one knows how much monitoring of mail, email and telephone communications occurs, or what use it is put to. That it happens is not in doubt; discussion on the use of it as evidence in court continues. As with America the degree of government secrecy, already an ingrained habit, has increased, and a stridently authoritarian tone has taken over government rhetoric.[17]

In its defence the British government, in line with several other European governments, claims that its highest duty is the security of the public.[18] This is false. The security of the public is certainly a high duty of government; but it is not the highest one. Its highest duty is the protection of individual liberties. Yet these the government has chosen to attack, instead of resisting the seductive voices of police and security services, and of the commercial biometric data companies which stand to make billions of pounds out of the identity card scheme, all selling the government – which is itself anyway eager to hear the sales talk – the false promise that the country can be made more secure if it lessens the liberty of its people.

The terrorist threat and the turn to authoritarianism in some Western governments are not the only threats either to human rights or civil liberties. There are many other pressures in the world whose tendency is to restrict and circumscribe the freedom and privacy of individuals. More assertive religious organisations impose limitations on the free speech of others by claiming to be 'offended' by criticisms of them or 'insults' to aspects of their faith. In response, and with a desire generally to be concessive and polite, people impose censorship on themselves. The demand for 'PC' attitudes and behaviour has been a threat to free speech for some time now, having started on campuses in America and spread to other countries and other areas of social life. The motives behind it – the desire to see equality and respect reign – are good; some of the effects are bad.

The technology of our age is itself a threat to freedoms. The British government, in choosing to go down the route of biometric data identity cards, has accepted the fallacious argument that because one *can* do a thing, one *must* do it. Its use of surveillance cameras and electronic monitoring of internet traffic has already made true the prediction that technology will allow for the constant unobtrusive policing of individuals, not just for detecting crime and terror, but for controlling and managing, for keeping watch even over the innocent and the private. Technology is the instrument for the realisation of that bureaucratic despotism against which Max Weber long ago warned.[19]

It is not a large step from surveillance and control of the actions of persons in public space to surveillance and control of the opinions of persons in private space. In part the latter is already happening; personal emails and telephone conversations are being monitored. Circumstances in which opinions, beliefs and attitudes were unacceptable to the authorities abounded in the past, and a number have been surveyed in the foregoing pages as a reason why liberties and rights had to be fought for. It still happens; in strict Muslim countries not only do the Religious Police strike women with their whips for showing an ankle, but also the entire society is geared to preventing unorthodox thought or opinion – the society is itself an agent of policing, forcing conformity. There is no guarantee that what happened in the past in Western countries, and what happens in these strict religious countries now, will not happen again in our societies. And this dismal thought occurs even though we believed our rights and liberties were guaranteed by our human rights conventions and our civil liberties. They are fraying before our eyes; and we have to ask at what point the fraying will stop.

The world has international conventions on human rights – they are far from fully effective but they make a difference at times – and a nascent International Criminal Court as a step towards enforcement of them. In national polities the rights and freedoms of citizens – their civil liberties – are not an exact mirror of human rights, though there is a large overlap. One main reason why a given country's civil liberties regime is not a straightforward download (so to put it) of one or another standard human rights convention is the margin of discretion taken by states in matters of interpretation. Genuine differences of opinion can exist over what counts as an invasion of privacy, or what comes too close to being a cruel punishment (capital punishment?), or where the limits of free speech lie, and what sorts of expression count as speech at all (is pornography speech? Should it be protected by free speech provisions?). Nuances of policing practice, the handling of race and sex discrimination cases, the degree to which religious observance is present in the public sphere, all involve civil liberties considerations too, and societies are in a constant state of negotiation with themselves about them.

There is nevertheless a consensus in Western liberal democracies over what count as the core civil liberties, and since the atrocities of 9/11 these, as we see, are being subjected to persistent and mounting threat under the guise, partly spurious and partly self-deceiving, that their erosion is a price worth paying for security.

Such a process is hard to stop, and whereas it is easy to pass a hasty law limiting or abolishing a liberty, it is far harder to get that liberty back. Interference with any liberty that a people has should only be allowed after a thorough examination of how long it took to get, and at what cost, and why it was needed in the first place. As the foregoing chapters here show, the liberties and rights of modern Western people were bought with such blood, tears and sweat, and their possession is so precious, that their abrogation is a scandal, and worse: a crime.

If there is one thing these pages might do, therefore, it is to remind us of the reasons why we struggled for our liberties, how much it cost our forebears to get them, and therefore why it matters so much that we should fight to keep them, now that we are actually in process of losing them. Let us fight, and fight again, to keep them, remembering the much-quoted adjuration of Churchill: 'Never give in, never, never, never, never, in nothing great or small, large or petty, never give in except to convictions of honour and good sense. Never yield to force, never yield to the apparently overwhelming might of the enemy.'[20] They were words spoken in the darkest hour of war, in 1941, when his country stood alone against Nazi Germany, and help had not yet come. For us now the adaptation has to be: never give in to the thieves of our liberties, for possessing them and protecting them is the duty that our rights impose. It is what we owe the dead who bought them for us with their lives, it is what we owe ourselves in our aspiration for good lives, and it is what we owe those whose lives are to come: the inestimable gift of liberty, and the security of inalienable rights.

APPENDICES

LANDMARKS ON THE ROAD TO FREEDOM

Appendix 1

The Bill of Rights 1689

An Act Declareing the Rights and Liberties of the Subject and Settling the Succession of the Crowne

Whereas the Lords Spirituall and Temporall and Commons assembled at Westminster lawfully fully and freely representing all the Estates of the People of this Realme did upon the thirteenth day of February in the yeare of our Lord one thousand six hundred eighty eight present unto their Majesties then called and known by the Names and Stile of William and Mary Prince and Princesse of Orange being present in their proper Persons a certaine Declaration in Writeing made by the said Lords and Commons in the Words following viz

Whereas the late King James the Second by the Assistance of diverse evill Counsellors Judges and Ministers imployed by him did endeavour to subvert and extirpate the Protestant Religion and the Lawes and Liberties of this Kingdome

1. By Assumeing and Exerciseing a Power of Dispensing with and Suspending of Lawes and the Execution of Lawes without consent of Parlyament.

2. By Committing and Prosecuting diverse Worthy Prelates for humbly Petitioning to be excused from Concurring to the said Assumed Power.

3. By issueing and causeing to be executed a Commission under the Great Seale for Erecting a Court called The Court of Commissioners for Ecclesiasticall Causes.

4. By Levying Money for and to the Use of the Crown by pretence of Prerogative for other time and in other manner than the same was granted by Parlyament.

5. By raising and keeping a Standing Army within this Kingdome in time of Peace without Consent of Parlyament and Quartering Soldiers contrary to Law.

6. By causing several good Subjects being Protestants to be disarmed at the same time when Papists were both Armed and Imployed contrary to Law.

7. By Violating the Freedome of Election of Members to serve in Parlyament.

8. By Prosecutions in the Court of Kings Bench for Matters and Causes cognizable onely in Parlyament and by diverse other Arbitrary and Illegal Courses.

9. And whereas of late years Partial Corrupt and Unqualifyed Persons have been returned and served on Juryes in Tryalls and particularly diverse Jurors in Tryalls for High Treason which were not Freeholders.

10. And excessive Baile hath beene required of Persons committed in Criminall Cases to elude the Benefitt of the Lawes made for the Liberty of the Subjects.

11. And excessive Fines have been imposed.

12. And illegall and cruell Punishments inflicted.

13. And severall Grants and Promises made of Fines and Forfeitures before any Conviction or Judgement against the Persons upon whome the same were to be levied.

All which are utterly and directly contrary to the known Lawes and Statutes and Freedom of this Realme.

And whereas the said late King James the Second haveing Abdicated the Government and the Throne being thereby Vacant, his [Highnesse] the Prince of Orange (whome it hath pleased Almighty God to make the glorious Instrument of Delivering this Kingdome from Popery and Arbitrary Power) did (by the advice of the Lords Spirituall and Temporall and diverse principall Persons of the Commons) cause

Letters to be written to the Lords Spirituall and Temporall being Protestants and other Letters to the severall Countyes Cityes Universities Burroughs and Cinque Ports for the Choosing of such Persons to represent them as were of right to be sent to Parlyament at Westminster upon the two and twentyeth day of January in this Yeare one thousand six hundred eighty and eight in order to such an Establishment as that their Religion Lawes and Liberties might not againe be in danger of being Subverted, Upon which Letters Elections haveing beene accordingly made.

And thereupon the said Lords Spirituall and Temporall and Commons pursuant to their respective Letters and Elections being now assembled in a full and free Representative of this nation takeing into their most serious Consideration the best meanes for attaining the Ends aforesaid Doe in the first place (as their Auncestors in like Case have usually done) for the Vindicating and Asserting their auntient Rights and Liberties, Declare;

1. That the pretended Power of Suspending of Lawes or the Execution of Lawes by Regall Authority without Consent of Parlyament is illegall.

2. That the pretended Power of Dispensing with Lawes or the Execution of Lawes by Regal Authoritie as it hath beene assumed and exercised of late is illegall.

3. That the Commission for erecting the late Court of Commissioners for Ecclesiasticall Causes and all other Commissions and Courts of like nature are Illegall and Pernicious.

4. That levying Money for or to the Use of the Crowne by pretence of Prerogative without Grant of Parlyament for longer time or in other manner than the same is or shall be granted is Illegall.

5. That it is the Right of the Subjects to petition the King and all Commitments and Prosecutions for such Petitioning are Illegall.

6. That the raising or keeping a standing Army within the Kingdome in time of Peace unlesse it be with Consent of Parlyament is against Law.

7. That the Subjects which are Protestants may have Arms for their Defence suitable to their Conditions and as allowed by Law.

8. That Election of Members of Parlyament ought to be free.

9. That the Freedome of Speech and Debates or Proceedings in Parlyament ought not to be impeached or questioned in any Court or Place out of Parlyament.

10. That excessive Baile ought not to be required nor excessive Fines imposed nor cruell and unusuall Punishments inflicted.

11. That Jurors ought to be duely impannelled and returned and Jurors which passe upon Men in Trialls for High Treason ought to be Freeholders.

12. That all Grants and Promises of Fines and Forfeitures of particular persons before Conviction are illegall and void.

13. And that for Redresse of all Grievances and for the amending strengthening and preserveing of the Lawes Parlyaments ought to be held frequently.

And they do Claime Demand and Insist upon all and singular the Premises as their undoubted Rights and Liberties and that noe Declarations Judgments Doeings or Proceedings to the Prejudice of the People in any of the said Premisses ought in any wise to be drawne hereafter into Consequence or Example.

To which Demand of their Rights they are particularly encouraged by the Declaration of his Highnesse the Prince of Orange as being the onley means for obtaining a full Redresse and Remedy therein. Haveing therefore an entire Confidence That his said Highenesse the Prince of Orange will perfect the Deliverance so far advanced by him and will still preserve them from the Violation of their Rights which they have here asserted and from all other Attempts upon their Religion Rights and Liberties. The said Lords Spiritual and Temporal and Commons assembled at Westminster do Resolve that William and Mary Prince and Princesse of Orange be and be declared King and Queen of England France and Ireland . . .

Appendix 2

The United States Bill of Rights 1791

*Amendments 1–10 of the Constitution
of the United States of America*

The Conventions of a number of the States having, at the time of adopting the Constitution, expressed a desire, in order to prevent misconstruction or abuse of its powers, that further declaratory and restrictive clauses should be added, and as extending the ground of public confidence in the Government will best insure the beneficent ends of its institution;

Resolved, by the Senate and House of Representatives of the United States of America, in Congress assembled, two-thirds of both Houses concurring, that the following articles be proposed to the Legislatures of the several States, as amendments to the Constitution of the United States; all or any of which articles, when ratified by three-fourths of the said Legislatures, to be valid to all intents and purposes as part of the said Constitution, namely:

Amendment I
Congress shall make no law respecting an establishment of religion, or prohibiting the free exercise thereof; or abridging the freedom of speech, or of the press; or the right of the people peaceably to assemble, and to petition the government for a redress of grievances.

Amendment II

A well regulated militia, being necessary to the security of a free state, the right of the people to keep and bear arms, shall not be infringed.

Amendment III

No soldier shall, in time of peace be quartered in any house, without the consent of the owner, nor in time of war, but in a manner to be prescribed by law.

Amendment IV

The right of the people to be secure in their persons, houses, papers, and effects, against unreasonable searches and seizures, shall not be violated, and no warrants shall issue, but upon probable cause, supported by oath or affirmation, and particularly describing the place to be searched, and the persons or things to be seized.

Amendment V

No person shall be held to answer for a capital, or otherwise infamous crime, unless on a presentment or indictment of a grand jury, except in cases arising in the land or naval forces, or in the militia, when in actual service in time of war or public danger; nor shall any person be subject for the same offence to be twice put in jeopardy of life or limb; nor shall be compelled in any criminal case to be a witness against himself, nor be deprived of life, liberty, or property, without due process of law; nor shall private property be taken for public use, without just compensation.

Amendment VI

In all criminal prosecutions, the accused shall enjoy the right to a speedy and public trial, by an impartial jury of the state and district wherein the crime shall have been committed, which district shall have been previously ascertained by law, and to be informed of the nature and cause of the accusation; to be confronted with the witnesses against him; to have compulsory process for obtaining witnesses in his favour, and to have the assistance of counsel for his defence.

Amendment VII

In suits at common law, where the value in controversy shall exceed twenty dollars, the right of trial by jury shall be preserved, and no fact tried by a jury, shall be otherwise re-examined in any court of the United States, than according to the rules of the common law.

Amendment VIII

Excessive bail shall not be required, nor excessive fines imposed, nor cruel and unusual punishments inflicted.

Amendment IX

The enumeration in the Constitution, of certain rights, shall not be construed to deny or disparage others retained by the people.

Amendment X

The powers not delegated to the United States by the Constitution, nor prohibited by it to the states, are reserved to the states respectively, or to the people.

Appendix 3

Declaration of the Rights of Man and of the Citizen

Approved by the National Assembly of France, 26 August, 1789

The representatives of the French people, organised as a National Assembly, believing that the ignorance, neglect, or contempt of the rights of man are the sole cause of public calamities and of the corruption of governments, have determined to set forth in a solemn declaration the natural, unalienable, and sacred rights of man, in order that this declaration, being constantly before all the members of the Social body, shall remind them continually of their rights and duties; in order that the acts of the legislative power, as well as those of the executive power, may be compared at any moment with the objects and purposes of all political institutions and may thus be more respected, and, lastly, in order that the grievances of the citizens, based hereafter upon simple and incontestable principles, shall tend to the maintenance of the constitution and redound to the happiness of all. Therefore the National Assembly recognises and proclaims, in the presence and under the auspices of the Supreme Being, the following rights of man and of the citizen:

Articles:

1. Men are born and remain free and equal in rights. Social distinctions may be founded only upon the general good.

2. The aim of all political association is the preservation of the natural and imprescriptible rights of man. These rights are liberty, property, security, and resistance to oppression.

3. The principle of all sovereignty resides essentially in the nation. No body nor individual may exercise any authority which does not proceed directly from the nation.

4. Liberty consists in the freedom to do everything which injures no one else; hence the exercise of the natural rights of each man has no limits except those which assure to the other members of the society the enjoyment of the same rights. These limits can only be determined by law.

5. Law can only prohibit such actions as are hurtful to society. Nothing may be prevented which is not forbidden by law, and no one may be forced to do anything not provided for by law.

6. Law is the expression of the general will. Every citizen has a right to participate personally, or through his representative, in its foundation. It must be the same for all, whether it protects or punishes. All citizens, being equal in the eyes of the law, are equally eligible to all dignities and to all public positions and occupations, according to their abilities, and without distinction except that of their virtues and talents.

7. No person shall be accused, arrested, or imprisoned except in the cases and according to the forms prescribed by law. Any one soliciting, transmitting, executing, or causing to be executed, any arbitrary order, shall be punished. But any citizen summoned or arrested in virtue of the law shall submit without delay, as resistance constitutes an offence.

8. The law shall provide for such punishments only as are strictly and obviously necessary, and no one shall suffer punishment except it

be legally inflicted in virtue of a law passed and promulgated before the commission of the offence.

9. As all persons are held innocent until they shall have been declared guilty, if arrest shall be deemed indispensable, all harshness not essential to the securing of the prisoner's person shall be severely repressed by law.

10. No one shall be disquieted on account of his opinions, including his religious views, provided their manifestation does not disturb the public order established by law.

11. The free communication of ideas and opinions is one of the most precious of the rights of man. Every citizen may, accordingly, speak, write, and print with freedom, but shall be responsible for such abuses of this freedom as shall be defined by law.

12. The security of the rights of man and of the citizen requires public military forces. These forces are, therefore, established for the good of all and not for the personal advantage of those to whom they shall be intrusted.

13. A common contribution is essential for the maintenance of the public forces and for the cost of administration. This should be equitably distributed among all the citizens in proportion to their means.

14. All the citizens have a right to decide, either personally or by their representatives, as to the necessity of the public contribution; to grant this freely; to know to what uses it is put; and to fix the proportion, the mode of assessment and of collection and the duration of the taxes.

15. Society has the right to require of every public agent an account of his administration.

16. A society in which the observance of the law is not assured, nor the separation of powers defined, has no constitution at all.

17. Since property is an inviolable and sacred right, no one shall be deprived thereof except where public necessity, legally determined, shall clearly demand it, and then only on condition that the owner shall have been previously and equitably indemnified.

Appendix 4

The Chartists' 'Six Points' and Petition

The six points of the People's Charter

1. A VOTE for every man twenty one years of age, of sound mind, and not undergoing punishment for crime.

2. THE BALLOT. To protect the elector in the exercise of his vote.

3. NO PROPERTY QUALIFICATION for members of Parliament – thus enabling the constituencies to return the man of their choice, be he rich or poor.

4. PAYMENT OF MEMBERS, thus enabling an honest tradesman, working man, or other person, to serve a constituency, when taken from his business to attend to the interests of the country.

5. EQUAL CONSTITUENCIES, securing the same amount of representation for the same number of electors, – instead of allowing small constituencies to swamp the votes of larger ones.

6. ANNUAL PARLIAMENTS, thus presenting the most effectual check to bribery and intimidation, since though a constituency might be bought once in seven years (even with the ballot), no purse could buy a constituency (under a system of universal

suffrage) in each ensuing twelvemonth; and since members, when elected for a year only, would not be able to defy and betray their constituents as now.

Subjoined are the names of the gentlemen who embodied these principles into the document called the 'People's Charter' at an influential meeting held at the British Coffee House, London, on the 7th of June, 1837:
Daniel O'Connell, Esq., M.P.
Mr Henry Hetherington.
John Arthur Roebuck, Esq., M.P.
Mr John Cleave.
John Temple Leader, Esq., M.P.
Mr James Watson.
Charles Hindley, Esq., M.P.
Mr Richard Moore.
Thomas Perronet Thompson, Esq., M.P.
Mr William Lovett.
William Sharman Crawford, Esq., M.P.
Mr Henry Vincent.

The 1838 Chartists' Petition

Unto the Honourable the Commons of the United Kingdom of Great Britain and Ireland in Parliament assembled, the Petition of the undersigned, their suffering countrymen,

HUMBLY SHEWETH,

That we, your petitioners, dwell in a land where merchants are noted for enterprise, whose manufacturers are very skilful, and whose workmen are proverbial for their industry.

The land itself is goodly, the soil rich, and the temperature wholesome; it is abundantly furnished with the materials of commerce and trade; it has numerous and convenient harbours; in facility of internal communication it exceeds all others.

For three-and-twenty years we have enjoyed a profound peace. Yet with all these elements of national prosperity, and with every disposition and capacity to take advantage of them, we find ourselves over-whelmed with public and private suffering.

We are bowed down under a load of taxes; which, notwithstanding, fall greatly short of the wants of our rulers; our traders are trembling on the verge of bankruptcy; our workmen are starving; capital brings no profit and labour no remuneration; the home of the artificer is desolate, and the warehouse of the pawnbroker is full; the workhouse is crowded and the manufactory is deserted.

We have looked upon every side, we have searched diligently in order to find out the causes of a distress so sore and so long continued.

We can discover none, in nature, or in providence.

Heaven has dealt graciously by the people; but the foolishness of our rulers has made the goodness of God of none effect.

The energies of a mighty kingdom have been wasted in building up the power of selfish and ignorant men, and its resources squandered for their aggrandisement.

The good of a party has been advanced to the sacrifice of the good of the nation; the few have governed for the interest of the few, while the interest of the many has been neglected, or insolently and tyrannously trampled upon.

It was the fond expectation of the people that a remedy for the greater part, if not for the whole, of their grievances, would be found in the Reform Act of 1832.

They were taught to regard that Act as a wise means to a worthy end; as the machinery of an improved legislation, when the will of the masses would be at length potential.

They have been bitterly and basely deceived.

The fruit which looked so fair to the eye has turned to dust and ashes when gathered.

The Reform Act has effected a transfer of power from one dom-ineering faction to another, and left the people as helpless as before.

Our slavery has been exchanged for an apprenticeship to liberty, which has aggravated the painful feeling of our social degradation, by adding to it the sickening of still deferred hope.

We come before your Honourable House to tell you, with all

humility, that this state of things must not be permitted to continue; that it cannot long continue without very seriously endangering the stability of the throne and the peace of the kingdom; and that if by God's help and all lawful and constitutional appliances an end can be put to it, we are fully resolved that it shall speedily come to an end.

We tell your Honourable House that the capital of the master must no longer be deprived of its due reward; that the laws which make food dear, and those which, by making money scarce, make labour cheap, must be abolished; that taxation must be made to fall on property, not on industry; that the good of the many, as it is the only legitimate end, so must it be the sole study of the Government.

As a preliminary essential to these and other requisite changes; as means by which alone the interests of the people can be effectually vindicated and secured, we demand that those interests be confided to the keeping of the people.

When the State calls for defenders, when it calls for money, no consideration of poverty or ignorance can be pleaded, in refusal or delay of the call. Required, as we are universally, to support and obey the laws, nature and reason entitle us to demand that in the making of the laws, the universal voice shall be implicitly listened to. We perform the duties of freemen; we must have the privileges of freemen. Therefore, we demand universal suffrage. The suffrage, to be exempt from the corruption of the wealthy and the violence of the powerful, must be secret.

Appendix 5

United Nations Universal Declaration of Human Rights

Adopted and proclaimed by General Assembly of the United Nations resolution 217 A (III) of 10 December 1948

On December 10, 1948 the General Assembly of the United Nations adopted and proclaimed the Universal Declaration of Human Rights the full text of which appears in the following pages. Following this historic act the Assembly called upon all Member countries to publicise the text of the Declaration and 'to cause it to be disseminated, displayed, read and expounded principally in schools and other educational institutions, without distinction based on the political status of countries or territories.'

PREAMBLE

Whereas recognition of the inherent dignity and of the equal and inalienable rights of all members of the human family is the foundation of freedom, justice and peace in the world,

Whereas disregard and contempt for human rights have resulted in barbarous acts which have outraged the conscience of mankind, and the advent of a world in which human beings shall enjoy freedom of speech and belief and freedom from fear and want has been proclaimed as the highest aspiration of the common people,

Whereas it is essential, if man is not to be compelled to have recourse, as a last resort, to rebellion against tyranny and oppression, that human rights should be protected by the rule of law,

Whereas it is essential to promote the development of friendly relations between nations,

Whereas the peoples of the United Nations have in the Charter reaffirmed their faith in fundamental human rights, in the dignity and worth of the human person and in the equal rights of men and women and have determined to promote social progress and better standards of life in larger freedom,

Whereas Member States have pledged themselves to achieve, in co-operation with the United Nations, the promotion of universal respect for and observance of human rights and fundamental freedoms,

Whereas a common understanding of these rights and freedoms is of the greatest importance for the full realisation of this pledge,

Now, Therefore THE GENERAL ASSEMBLY proclaims THIS UNIVERSAL DECLARATION OF HUMAN RIGHTS as a common standard of achievement for all peoples and all nations, to the end that every individual and every organ of society, keeping this Declaration constantly in mind, shall strive by teaching and education to promote respect for these rights and freedoms and by progressive measures, national and international, to secure their universal and effective recognition and observance, both among the peoples of Member States themselves and among the peoples of territories under their jurisdiction.

Article 1
All human beings are born free and equal in dignity and rights. They are endowed with reason and conscience and should act towards one another in a spirit of brotherhood.

Article 2

Everyone is entitled to all the rights and freedoms set forth in this Declaration, without distinction of any kind, such as race, colour, sex, language, religion, political or other opinion, national or social origin, property, birth or other status. Furthermore, no distinction shall be made on the basis of the political, jurisdictional or international status of the country or territory to which a person belongs, whether it be independent, trust, non-self-governing or under any other limitation of sovereignty.

Article 3

Everyone has the right to life, liberty and security of person.

Article 4

No one shall be held in slavery or servitude; slavery and the slave trade shall be prohibited in all their forms.

Article 5

No one shall be subjected to torture or to cruel, inhuman or degrading treatment or punishment.

Article 6

Everyone has the right to recognition everywhere as a person before the law.

Article 7

All are equal before the law and are entitled without any discrimination to equal protection of the law. All are entitled to equal protection against any discrimination in violation of this Declaration and against any incitement to such discrimination.

Article 8

Everyone has the right to an effective remedy by the competent national tribunals for acts violating the fundamental rights granted him by the constitution or by law.

Article 9
No one shall be subjected to arbitrary arrest, detention or exile.

Article 10
Everyone is entitled in full equality to a fair and public hearing by an independent and impartial tribunal, in the determination of his rights and obligations and of any criminal charge against him.

Article 11
1. Everyone charged with a penal offence has the right to be presumed innocent until proved guilty according to law in a public trial at which he has had all the guarantees necessary for his defence.
2. No one shall be held guilty of any penal offence on account of any act or omission which did not constitute a penal offence, under national or international law, at the time when it was committed. Nor shall a heavier penalty be imposed than the one that was applicable at the time the penal offence was committed.

Article 12
No one shall be subjected to arbitrary interference with his privacy, family, home or correspondence, nor to attacks upon his honour and reputation. Everyone has the right to the protection of the law against such interference or attacks.

Article 13
1. Everyone has the right to freedom of movement and residence within the borders of each state.
2. Everyone has the right to leave any country, including his own, and to return to his country.

Article 14
1. Everyone has the right to seek and to enjoy in other countries asylum from persecution.

2. This right may not be invoked in the case of prosecutions genuinely arising from non-political crimes or from acts contrary to the purposes and principles of the United Nations.

Article 15

1. Everyone has the right to a nationality.
2. No one shall be arbitrarily deprived of his nationality nor denied the right to change his nationality.

Article 16

1. Men and women of full age, without any limitation due to race, nationality or religion, have the right to marry and to found a family. They are entitled to equal rights as to marriage, during marriage and at its dissolution.
2. Marriage shall be entered into only with the free and full consent of the intending spouses.
3. The family is the natural and fundamental group unit of society and is entitled to protection by society and the State.

Article 17

1. Everyone has the right to own property alone as well as in association with others.
2. No one shall be arbitrarily deprived of his property.

Article 18

Everyone has the right to freedom of thought, conscience and religion; this right includes freedom to change his religion or belief, and freedom, either alone or in community with others and in public or private, to manifest his religion or belief in teaching, practice, worship and observance.

Article 19

Everyone has the right to freedom of opinion and expression; this right includes freedom to hold opinions without interference and to seek, receive and impart information and ideas through any media and regardless of frontiers.

Article 20

1. Everyone has the right to freedom of peaceful assembly and association.
2. No one may be compelled to belong to an association.

Article 21

1. Everyone has the right to take part in the government of his country, directly or through freely chosen representatives.
2. Everyone has the right of equal access to public service in his country.
3. The will of the people shall be the basis of the authority of government; this will shall be expressed in periodic and genuine elections which shall be by universal and equal suffrage and shall be held by secret vote or by equivalent free voting procedures.

Article 22

Everyone, as a member of society, has the right to social security and is entitled to realisation, through national effort and international co-operation and in accordance with the organisation and resources of each State, of the economic, social and cultural rights indispensable for his dignity and the free development of his personality.

Article 23

1. Everyone has the right to work, to free choice of employment, to just and favourable conditions of work and to protection against unemployment.
2. Everyone, without any discrimination, has the right to equal pay for equal work.
3. Everyone who works has the right to just and favourable remuneration ensuring for himself and his family an existence worthy of human dignity, and supplemented, if necessary, by other means of social protection.
4. Everyone has the right to form and to join trade unions for the protection of his interests.

Article 24

Everyone has the right to rest and leisure, including reasonable limitation of working hours and periodic holidays with pay.

Article 25

1. Everyone has the right to a standard of living adequate for the health and well-being of himself and of his family, including food, clothing, housing and medical care and necessary social services, and the right to security in the event of unemployment, sickness, disability, widowhood, old age or other lack of livelihood in circumstances beyond his control.
2. Motherhood and childhood are entitled to special care and assistance. All children, whether born in or out of wedlock, shall enjoy the same social protection.

Article 26

1. Everyone has the right to education. Education shall be free, at least in the elementary and fundamental stages. Elementary education shall be compulsory. Technical and professional education shall be made generally available and higher education shall be equally accessible to all on the basis of merit.
2. Education shall be directed to the full development of the human personality and to the strengthening of respect for human rights and fundamental freedoms. It shall promote understanding, tolerance and friendship among all nations, racial or religious groups, and shall further the activities of the United Nations for the maintenance of peace.
3. Parents have a prior right to choose the kind of education that shall be given to their children.

Article 27

1. Everyone has the right freely to participate in the cultural life of the community, to enjoy the arts and to share in scientific advancement and its benefits.
2. Everyone has the right to the protection of the moral and material interests resulting from any scientific, literary or artistic production of which he is the author.

Article 28
Everyone is entitled to a social and international order in which the rights and freedoms set forth in this Declaration can be fully realised.

Article 29
1. Everyone has duties to the community in which alone the free and full development of his personality is possible.
2. In the exercise of his rights and freedoms, everyone shall be subject only to such limitations as are determined by law solely for the purpose of securing due recognition and respect for the rights and freedoms of others and of meeting the just requirements of morality, public order and the general welfare in a democratic society.
3. These rights and freedoms may in no case be exercised contrary to the purposes and principles of the United Nations.

Article 30
Nothing in this Declaration may be interpreted as implying for any State, group or person any right to engage in any activity or to perform any act aimed at the destruction of any of the rights and freedoms set forth herein.

Notes

1. Setting the Scene

1 From a military point of view the Soviet Union might have been the largest single factor in the final defeat of Nazism, but it was vastly aided by the economic power of the United States and the existence of the other fronts – in North Africa, Italy and finally Western Europe after D-Day – which were endeavours of the Western Allies. Put these facts together with the Cold War defeat of the Soviet Union, and the claim here is made.

2. The Reformation and the Beginning of Modern Liberty

1 For Acton the Church's main contribution to liberty was its late medieval resistance to attempts by temporal powers to control it. See pp. 29 et seq. and Lord Acton (ed. J. Rufus Fears), *Essays in the History of Liberty: Selected Writings of Lord Acton* (Indianopolis, IN, 1985).
2 See Plato's *Apology*.
3 Grayling, A. C., *What Is Good?* (London, 2003), ch. 1, *passim*.
4 This point has become controversial in recent times but once meant what it said; see the unequivocal nature of the Church Fathers' opinions, in Ignatius of Antioch (*Letter to the Philadelphians* 3:3–4:1 [AD 110]); Justin Martyr (*First Apology* 46 [AD 151]); Irenaeus (*Against Heresies* 3:24:1 [AD 189]); Clement of Alexandria (*Miscellanies* 1:5 [AD 208]); Origen (*Against Celsus* 4:7 [AD 248]); Cyprian of Carthage (*Treatise on Rebaptism* 10 [AD 256]) – and so on through Lactantius, Jerome, Augustine (for this latter see *Faith and the Creed* 10:21 [AD 393], *On Baptism, Against the Donatists* 4:4[6] [AD 400], *Letters* 43:1 [AD 412], etc.). Writings of the Early Church Fathers, 38 vols, available online at www.ccel.org/fathers.
5 Nicholas Barker 'Textual Forgery' and David Lowenthal 'Forging the Past' in *Fake? The Art of Deception*, edited by Mark Jones, with Paul Craddock and Nicholas Barker (London, 1990). See e.g. the controversies over the Donation of Constantine, the Decretals of Isidore, the Gratian Decretum, spurious saints' lives, faked relics, etc.
6 Erasmus, *The Praise of Folly and Other Writings* (New York, NY, 1989); see J. Huizinga, 'The Erasmus Mind' in the Critical Commentary to this edition, *passim*.

7 See works on Torquemada in the bibliography for an account of his life, e.g. Sabatini, *Torquemada and the Spanish Inquisition* (New York, NY, 1924), and references to the Inquisition for a general account of the Spanish Inquisition, esp. H. Kamen, *The Spanish Inquisition* (London, 1997).

8 This might be a moot point: the Egyptian and Babylonian captivities might have caused conversions, and the various Old Testament episodes in which gods other than Yahweh are worshipped, severely visited by the deity, are possible examples too.

9 See E. Burman, *The Inquisition: The Hammer of Heresy* (Wellingborough, 1984), and Kamen, *The Spanish Inquisition.*

10 For the history of the early Church see Justo L. González, *The Story of Christianity, Vol. 1: The Early Church to the Reformation* (San Francisco, CA, 1985); Kenneth Scott Latorette, *A History of Christianity, Volume 1: Beginnings to 1500* (San Francisco, CA, 1975 revised).

11 Deuteronomy ch. 13 verse 6. It is said that Deuteronomy is a forgery, conveniently 'found' in the Temple during its rebuilding by one of the bitterly competing parties in the politics of Israel, which it greatly helped in getting the upper hand. See Paul M. Johnson, *A History of the Jews* (London, 1988).

12 See W.H.C. Friend, *Martyrdom and Persecution in the Early Church* (London, 1965).

13 See Ronald Christenson, 'The Political Theory of Persecution: Augustine and Hobbes', in *Midwest Journal of Political Science,* vol. 12, no. 3 (August 1968), p. 419.

14 For a biography of Bernard of Clairvaux see W. Williams, *Saint Bernard of Clairvaux* (London, 1952).

15 Michael T. Ott, 'Gregory IX', in C. G. Herbermann et al. (eds), *The Catholic Encyclopaedia* (New York, NY, 1907–14), vol. VI, 1909.

16 See C. Roth, *The Spanish Inquisition* (New York, NY, 1964).

17 See H. Kamen, *Spain 1469–1714: A Society of Conflict (3rd edition)* (London and New York, 2005).

18 The methods of the inquisitors are very close to those of Communist Party appointees in Maoist China who spied on their neighbours, ferreted for signs and indications of disloyalty, snooped and informed, and created a climate of mutual suspicion where everyone was informing on everyone else. This is a characteristic of totalitarian polities; it happened in Soviet Russia and in Nazi Germany, and is one of the main sources of power and control in such regimes.

19 See Kamen, *The Spanish Inquisition,* p. 145.

20 See Sabatini, *Torquemada and the Spanish Inquisition,* p. 83.

21 It is a remarkable fact that within a generation of Luther's first act of rebellion, the states of north Germany, Scandinavia, England, Scotland, the northern provinces of the Netherlands and most of the cantons of Switzerland had seceded permanently from papal authority. In the next century Poland and Bohemia were to secede and return (the latter under brutal force following the Battle of the White Mountain in 1620), and France was to be permanently semi-detached in political terms though still Catholic. If one example can illuminate the motivation additional to questions of right piety, it is the complaint in the English Parliament long beforehand – as long before as 1376 – that the pope was receiving tax revenues from England five times greater than the king was. When temporal rulers saw their chance to get their hands on money streaming towards Vatican coffers, they were not loth to find in their hearts a desire to embrace a more biblical version of the faith.

22 See James Atkinson, *The Great Light: Luther and the Reformation* (Grand Rapids, MI, 1968) and Bernhard Lohse, *Martin Luther: An Introduction to His Life and Work* (Edinburgh, 1986) for Luther's biography.

23 See W. P. Stephens, *The Theology of Huldrych Zwingli* (Oxford, 1984) for an account of Zwingli's life and teachings.

24 James M. Stayer, *Anabaptists and the Sword* (London, 1972).

25 The revival of Roman law in late medieval and Reformation Europe is described in J.A.C. Thomas, *Textbook of Roman Law* (Amsterdam and Oxford, 1976).
26 For the Peasants' War see the papers collected in R. Scribner and G. Benecke, *The German Peasant War* (London, 1979).
27 Götz von Berlichingen was to become the eponymous subject of one of Goethe's most famous tragedies.
28 See William J. Bouwsma, *John Calvin: A Sixteenth Century Portrait* (Oxford, 1988) for the life of Calvin.
29 The text of Calvin's *Sermons on Deuteronomy* is available online.
30 See R. H. Bainton, *Hunted Heretic: The Life and Death of Michael Servetus 1511–1553* (London, 1953). Bainton is the outstanding authority on Servetus and Castellio (see below) and the following account draws on his scholarly rescue of both figures from the margins of history.
31 See Justo L. González, *The Story of Christianity*, on this aspect of the history of the Church.
32 See R. H. Bainton, *Hunted Heretic: The Life and Death of Michael Servetus, 1511–1553* (Boston, MA, 1953), p. 103.
33 Quoted in R. H. Bainton, *The Travail of Religious Liberty* (London, 1953), pp. 91–2.
34 *Ibid.*, pp. 93 *et seq.*
35 Quoted in *ibid.*, p. 110.
36 *Ibid.*, p. 111.
37 *Ibid.*
38 *Ibid.*, p. 116.

3. Freeing the Mind

1 See J. Yolton (ed.), *Philosophy, Religion and Science in the Seventeenth and Eighteenth Centuries* (New York, NY, 1990), Introduction.
2 See B. J. Kidd, *The Counter Reformation 1550–1600* (London, 1993), pp. 2–3.
3 The Peace of Augsburg was a treaty signed between Emperor Charles V and the Schmalkaldic League in September 1555, ending the Schmalkaldic Wars and allowing German princes to choose between Catholicism and Lutheranism.
4 See A. J. Grant, *The Huguenots* (London, 1934); Euan Cameron, *The European Reformation* (Oxford, 1991).
5 See González, *The Story of Christianity*, vol. 2, *passim*.
6 This sketch of two centuries of religious strife covers an enormously complex and difficult period. Among good narrative surveys are Euan Cameron, *The European Reformation* (Oxford, 1991) and González, *The Story Of Christianity*.
7 The case of Giordano Bruno is well known. For Cesare Vanini see A. C. Grayling, *Descartes*, p. 113.
8 For lives of Milton and Locke see William Riley Parker, *Milton: A Biography, Volume 1: The Life* (Oxford, 1968; 2nd edition revised by Gordon Campbell, 1996); A. N. Wilson, *The Life of John Milton* (Oxford, 1984); Maurice Cranston, *John Locke, A Biography* (Oxford, 1957; reprinted 1985); R. S. Woolhouse, *Locke: A Biography* (Cambridge, 2007).
9 'Premalic' – I coin a phrase to denote 'before the apple', as useful to anyone who thinks that eating it was not a Fall, and hence as an alternative to 'prelapsarian'. Incidentally, it has been suggested that in Rome his sexual interests had not been limited to heterosexuality. In fact there is an imputation in later attacks on him that he had been a 'rent boy' there, a fact not mentioned in subsequent apotheoses of him as the second great poet of the tongue.
10 Milton's masque *Comus* was performed before the king at Ludlow Castle, 1634, before the Earl of Bridgewater, then president of Wales, and others including the Lord Bracly, Mr Thomas Egerton and the Lady Alice Egerton.

11 For the early Stuarts see Godfrey Davies, *The Early Stuarts 1603–1660* (Oxford, 1937; 2nd edition 1963).

12 John Milton, 'The Reason of Church Government' Book 1 (1642), in Ernest Sirluck (ed.), *The Complete Prose Works of John Milton, Vol. 1* (New Haven, CT, and London, 1959).

13 Godfrey Davies, *The Early Stuarts 1603–1660* (Oxford 1937 and 1963).

14 John Milton, *The Doctrine and Discipline of Divorce* (1643; first published 1644), *The Judgement of Martin Bucer* (1644), *Colasterion* (1645), *Tetrachordon* (1645). All in *The Complete Prose Works of John Milton, vol. 2*.

15 *Ibid.*

16 John Milton, *Areopagitica* (1644), in *The Complete Prose Works of John Milton, vol. 2*.

17 All quotations here are from *Areopagitica*.

18 See Christopher Hill, *Intellectual Origins of the English Revolution* (Oxford, 1965; revised edition 2001).

19 See J. W. Johnson, *A Profane Wit: The Life of John Wilmot, Earl of Rochester* (New York, NY, 2004).

20 Godfrey Davies, *Essays on the Later Stuarts* (London, 1976).

21 González, *The Story of Christianity.*

22 For more on Bunyan, see Christopher Hill, *Turbulent, Seditious and Factious People: John Bunyan and His Church, 1628–88* (Oxford, 1989).

23 Davies, *The Early Stuarts.*

24 J. Israel, *Radical Enlightenment* (London, 2001) treats in detail of the profound influence of Spinoza's thought on the eighteenth-century Enlightenment.

25 See also John Locke, *An Essay on Toleration* (1667), in Mark Goldie (ed.), *John Locke: Political Essays* (Cambridge, 1997): 'could persecution . . . at once drive all dissenters within the pale of the church, it would not thereby secure, but more threaten, the government, and make the danger as much greater as it is to have a false, secret, but exasperated enemy, rather than a fair, open adversary' (p. 155); 'if [fear of power] be the chain that ties them to you, it would certainly hold surer were they open dissenters than secret malcontents' (p. 156).

26 John Locke, 'A Letter Concerning Toleration' (1685), in David Wootton (ed.), *John Locke: Political Writings* (London, 1993), p. 396.

27 *Ibid.*, p. 397.

28 J.C.H. Aveling, *The Handle and the Axe: The Catholic Recusants in England from Reformation to Emancipation* (London, 1976).

29 John Locke, *An Essay Concerning Human Understanding* (1689), Roger Woolhouse (ed.) (London, 1998), Book I, ch. 1, p. 57.

30 Maurice Cranston, *John Locke: A Biography* (London, 1957), p. 231.

31 Pierre Bayle, *Historical and Critical Dictionary* (1697), various entries, e.g. 'Paulicians'. Reprinted in Richard H. Popkin (trans. and ed.), *Pierre Bayle Historical and Critical Dictionary: Selections* (Indianapolis, IN, 1991), pp. 166–193.

32 *Ibid.*

33 Voltaire made so much of a point of attacking clerical influence in French society that his slogan '*écrasez l'infâme*' is practically one of the mottoes of the Enlightenment. See some of the relevant entries in his *Philosophical Dictionary* (1764), trans. P. Besterman (London, 1979), for a flavour of the assault.

34 Saint Thomas Aquinas, ed. Robert Maynard Hutchins, *Summa Theologica*, Encyclopaedia Britannica (London, 1952).

35 Discussion of philosophical theology's arguments for the existence of supernatural agencies abound; see for example the 'Dialectic' in I. Kant, *Critique of Pure Reason* (1781), for a classic statement and analysis of the arguments.

36 For the world view current prior to the scientific revolution see W. Cook and R. Herzman, *The Medieval World View*, 2nd edition (Oxford, 2004).

37 For Jesuits on education see A. C. Grayling, *The Heart of Things* (London, 2005), p. 26.

38 Nicolaus Copernicus, ed. Stephen Hawking, *De revolutionibus orbium coelestium (On the Revolving Heavenly Spheres)*, (1530) (Philadelphia, PA, 2005).

39 See John Gribbin, *Science: A History 1543–2001* (London, 2002). There is no good reason for anyone not to know in outline what contemporary science has to say about the world; many excellent popular introductions exist by leaders in their fields, and almost all of them discuss scientific method and outlook.

40 On string theory see L. Smolin, *The Trouble with Physics* (London, 2007).

41 Martin Rees, *Before the Beginning: Our Universe and Others* (Reading, MA, 1997).

42 R. Dawkins, *The Selfish Gene* (Oxford, 1976).

43 The reference here is to the work of Trofim Denisovich Lysenko, a biologist in the Soviet Union who claimed that he had achieved evolution of grains in a single generation by application of Lamarckian principles. He was Director of Genetics at the USSR Academy of Sciences.

44 Michael Sharratt, *Galileo: Decisive Innovator* (Cambridge, 2006).

45 On Copernicus see O. Gingerich, *The Book Nobody Read* (London, 2004). The following account draws on this and on Gribbin, *Science: A History* (London, 2002).

46 It was common practice of scholars and writers of the time to Latinise their names. In this instance Johannes Mueller came from Konigsberg, German for 'King's Mountain', so he Latinised it as Regiomontanus which in straight translation means King Mountain.

47 Bellarmine's letter is printed in Maurice A. Finocchiaro (trans. and ed.), *The Galileo Affair: A Documentary History* (Berkeley, CA, 1989), pp. 67–9.

48 Galileo Galilei, 'Letter to the Grand Duchess Christina of Tuscany' (1615), *ibid.*, p. 89.

48 Consultant's Report on Copernicanism (1616), *ibid.*, p. 146.

49 *Ibid.*

50 The hypothesised Bellarmine ruse regarding Galileo is recounted in Gribbin, *Science: A History*.

51 For the Thirty Years War see the unparalleled *Cambridge Modern History*, vol. IV, ed. A. W. Ward, G. W. Prothero, and S. Leathes (Cambridge, 1970).

52 See Sharratt, *Galileo: Decisive Innovator*, ch. 7, pp. 132–152.

53 *Ibid.*

54 See A. C. Grayling, *Descartes: The Life of René Descartes and its Place in his Times* (London, 2005); Lisa Jardine and Alan Stewart, *Hostage to Fortune: the Troubled Life of Francis Bacon* (New York, NY, 2000).

55 See T. Crane and S. Patterson, *History of the Mind–Body Problem* (Oxford, 2006).

56 Isaac Newton, *The Principia: The Mathematical Principles of Natural Philosophy*, trans. Bernard Cohen, Anne Whitman and Julia Buden (Berkeley, CA, 1999); Nora Barlow (ed.), *The Autobiography of Charles Darwin 1809–1882* (London, 1958).

57 Francis Bacon, *Novum Organum* (1620), in Jardine and Silverthorne (eds), *The New Organon* (Cambridge, 2002), Aphorism 89.

58 Francis Bacon, *Of Atheism* (1607), in Michael Kiernan (ed.), *The Oxford Francis Bacon XV: The Essayes or Counsels, Civil and Morall* (Oxford, 2000).

59 David Hume, 'Whether the British Government Inclines More to Absolute Monarchy, or to a Republic', in Eugene F. Miller (ed.), *David Hume: Essays, Moral, Political, and Literary*, Part I, Essay VII (LVII.5) (Indianapolis, IN, 1995).

4. The Fight Against Absolutism

1 For a biography of Louis XIV see Vincent Cronin, *Louis XIV* (London, 1964; 1996); Richard Wilkinson, *Routledge Historical Biographies: Louis XIV* (Oxford, 2007); A.H.T. Levi, *Louis XIV* (London, 2004); Ian Dunlop, *Louis XIV* (London, 2001).

2 Jonathon Scott, *England's Troubles: Seventeenth-Century English History in European Perspective* (Cambridge, 2000).

3 Jeffrey R. Collins, *The Allegiance of Thomas Hobbes* (Oxford, 2005); Maurice Cranston, *John Locke: A Biography*; R. S. Woolhouse, *Locke: A Biography* (Cambridge, 2007).

3 Christopher Hill on English Civil War, *Intellectual Origins of the English Revolution*, p. 286.

4 *Ibid.*

5 Orest Ranum, *The Fronde: A French Revolution* (New York, NY, 1993).

6 John C. Rule (ed.), *Louis XIV and the Craft of Kingship* (Columbus, OH, 1969), pp. 20–24.

7 John Miller, *Bourbon and Stuart: Kings and Kingship in France and England in the Seventeenth Century* (London, 1987), pp. 15–55.

8 Jacques Bossuet, ed. Patrick Riley, *Politics Drawn from the Very Words of Holy Scripture* (Cambridge, 1990; 1999).

9 *Ibid.*

10 Louis XIV, trans. P. Sonnino, *Memoirs for the Instruction of the Dauphin* (New York, NY, 1970).

11 William Beik, *Louis XIV and Absolutism: A Brief Study with Documents* (Boston, MA, 2000).

12 Andrew Lossky, *Louis XIV and the French Monarchy* (New Brunswick, NJ, 1994), pp. 149–150.

13 Roger Mettam, *Power and Faction in Louis XIV's France* (Oxford, 1988), pp. 197–202.

14 Pierre Jurieu, *Les soupirs de la France esclave, qui aspire après la liberté* (1689).

15 One consequence of George III's anti-democratic instincts was the loss of the American colonies. Their rebellion against his rule was in its own turn a consequence of the principles, enunciated by Locke, that had placed George III's forebears on the throne of England.

16 Andrew Sharp (ed.), *The English Levellers* (Cambridge, 1998).

17 See for example Christopher Hill, *The World Turned Upside Down: Radical Ideas During the English Revolution* (London, 1991).

18 Thomas Hobbes, ed. Richard Tuck, *Leviathan* (1651) (Cambridge, 1996), ch. XVII, p. 118.

19 *Ibid.*, ch. XVII, p. 121.

20 *Ibid.*, ch. XVIII, p. 124.

21 *Ibid.*, ch. XVIII, p. 127.

22 *Ibid.*, ch. XXX, p. 231.

23 John Locke, ed. Peter Laslett, *Two Treatises of Government* (1689), Second Treatise, ch. 2, Section 4, p. 269 (Cambridge, 1988).

24 *Ibid.*, ch. 5, Section 49, p. 301.

25 *Ibid.*, ch. 4, Section 23, p. 284.

26 *Ibid.*, ch. 11, Section 135, p. 357.

27 *Ibid.*, ch. 19, Section 240, p. 427.

28 *Ibid.*, ch. 12, Section 143, p. 364.

29 *Ibid.*, ch. 19, esp. Sections 214–221, pp. 408–412.

30 Thomas Hobbes, ed. Ferdinand Tönnies, *Behemoth; or, the Long Parliament* (1668) (Chicago, IL, 1990).

31 Benedict de Spinoza, trans. R.H.M. Elwes, *A Theological–Political Treatise* (1670) (Toronto, 1951), ch. 16, p. 207.

32 Peter Gay, *The Enlightenment: An Interpretation* (1966 and 1969), 2 vols (New York, NY, 1995 and 1996).

33 Denis Diderot, *Philosophic Thoughts* (1746), ch. 3, reprinted in Denis Diderot, ed. Lester G. Crocker, *Selected Writings* (London, 1966).

34 Marquis de Condorcet, ed. Stuart Hampshire, trans. June Barraclough, *Sketch for a Historical Picture of the Progress of the Human Mind* (1795) (London, 1955), p. 72.

35 David Hume, ed. Tom L. Beauchamp, *An Enquiry Concerning Human Understanding* (1748), ch. 10 'On Miracles', (Oxford, 1999).

36 Voltaire, *A Treatise on Toleration* (1764), ch. 20, pp. 243–244 (Cambridge, 2000).

37 Edward Gibbon, ed. J. B. Bury, *The Decline and Fall of the Roman Empire* (1776–1788), ch. 28 (New York, NY, 1977).

38 *Ibid.*, chapter 40.

39 Voltaire, *Philosophical Letters* (1733), 'The English Parliament', reprinted in Morley, Smollett and Fleming, *The Works of Voltaire, A Contemporary Version* (New York, NY, 1901), vol. 19, p. 5.

40 Denis Diderot, *Encyclopaedia* (1751–1766) (New York, NY, 1969).

41 'Conversation between d'Alembert and Diderot', 1769, trans. J. Stewart and J. Kemp (New York, NY, 1943).

42 Immanuel Kant in his 1784 essay 'What Is Enlightenment?', in Mary J. Gregor (ed.), *Immanuel Kant: Practical Philosophy* (Cambridge, 1999), p. 17.

43 *Ibid.*, p. 18.

44 *Ibid.*

45 As already noted, this expression appears frequently in Voltaire's works, especially his private letters.

46 Denis Diderot, *Encyclopaedia* (1751–1766).

47 Jeremy Bentham, ed. J. H. Burns and H.L.A. Hart, *A Fragment on Government* (1776) (Cambridge, 1988), p. 3.

48 Jean le Rond d'Alembert, 'Essay on the Elements of Philosophy' (1779), p. 1.

49 James Madison, *Writings 1772–1836* (New York, NY, 1999).

50 Robert Shackleton, *Montesquieu: A Critical Biography* (New York, NY, 1961).

51 Baron de Montesquieu, trans. Thomas Nugent, *The Spirit of the Laws* (1748), Book 11, ch. 6 (New York, NY, 1949).

52 Thomas Paine, ed. Isaac Cramnick, *Common Sense* (1776), ch. 1 'Of the Origin and Design of Government in General. With concise Remarks on the English Constitution' (London, 1976).

53 Alexander Hamilton et al., ed. Jacob E. Cooke, *The Federalist* (Middletown, CT, 1961), p. 3.

54 *Ibid.*, p. 579.

55 See Appendix 3.

56 Simon Schama, *Citizens: A Chronicle of the French Revolution* (London, 2004).

57 Hamilton, *The Federalist.*

58 Edmund Burke, *Reflections on the Revolution in France* (1790) (Oxford, 1999), p. 246 and p. 168.

59 *Ibid.*, p. 93.

60 W. Godwin, *Enquiry Concerning Political Justice* (London, 1793).

61 Not to be confused with the Manchester radical of the same name.

62 Elie Halévy, *A History of the English People (in the nineteenth century)* (1947) (London, 1968); E. P. Thompson, *The Making of the English Working Class* (London, 1991).

63 I tell the story of this trial in my book, *Quarrel of the Age: The Life and Times of William Hazlitt* (London, 2001).

64 Marilyn Butler, *Burke, Paine, Godwin and the Revolution Controversy* (Cambridge, 1984), p. 176.

65 See A. C. Grayling, *The Meaning of Things* (London, 2001).

66 Thomas Holcroft, *The Life of Thomas Holcroft* (North Stratford, NH, 1968).

67 A. R. Waller and A. Glover (eds), *The Collected Works of William Hazlitt* (London, 1902), vol. II, p. 156.

68 Reported in Conway Moncure, *The Life of Thomas Paine*, 2 vols, (London, 1908).

5. Slaves, Workers, Women and the Struggle for Liberty

1 For details of the life of Benezet see George Brookes, *Friend Anthony Benezet* (1817) (Philadelphia, PA, 1937); Wilson Armistead *Anthony Benezet. From the original memoir [by Roberts Vaux]: revised, with additions* (London, 1859).

2 Anthony Benezet, 'Caution and a Warning', reprinted in John Wesley, *Views of American Slavery, Taken a Century ago* (1858) (New York, NY, 1969), p. 25.

3 For Quakers and slavery see Jean R. Soderland, *Quakers and Slavery: A Divided Spirit* (Princeton, NJ, 1989). For the history of abolition see David Brion Davis, *Inhuman Bondage: The Rise and Fall of Slavery in the New World* (New York, NY, 2006); Adam Hochschild, *Bury the Chains, The British Struggle to Abolish Slavery* (London, 2005).

4 John Locke, ed. Peter Laslett, *Two Treatises of Government* (1689), Second Treatise (Cambridge, 1988).

5 Anthony Benezet, *Some Historical Account of Guinea, its Situation, Produce, and the General Disposition of its Inhabitants* (1771) (Kila, MT, 2004), Introduction.

6 See Hugh Brogan's 'Thomas Clarkson' entry in *Oxford Dictionary of National Biography* (Oxford, 2005).

7 Sharp and the Committee for the Abolition of the Slave Trade are discussed in Hochschild, *Bury the Chains.*

8 See John Pollock, *Wilberforce* (New York, NY, 1978).

9 Reprinted in Peter Kitson et al. (eds), *Slavery, Abolition and Emancipation: Writings in the British Romantic Period,* 8 vols (London, 1999), vol. 2, pp. 135–151.

10 For the Haiti rebellion see C.L.R. James, *The Black Jacobins: Toussaint L'Ouverture and the San Domingo Revolution* (London, 1989).

11 Steven M. Wise, *Though the Heavens May Fall: The Landmark Trial That Led to the End of Human Slavery* (Cambridge, MA, 2006).

12 See James Walvin, *Slavery and the Slave Trade: A Short Illustrated History* (Jackson, MS, 1983).

13 Printed in Foot and Kramnick (eds), *The Thomas Paine Reader* (London, 1987), pp. 52–56.

14 Walvin, *Slavery and the Slave Trade.*

15 For the history of civil rights in America see J. R. Pole, *The Pursuit of Equality in American History* (Berkeley, CA, 1978).

16 Josh. 9:21–27; Num. 31:26–47.

17 Christian Abayomi Cassell, *Liberia: History of the First African Republic* (New York, NY, 1970).

18 Rousseau on the 'noble savage' is to be found in *The Social Contract* and applied in *Emile.*

19 A. C. Grayling, *The Quarrel of the Age: The Life and Times of William Hazlitt.*

20 Richard Oastler's letter on slavery in Yorkshire appeared in the *Leeds Mercury* on 29 September 1830.

21 Among the many general histories of the industrial revolution are F. C. Dietz, *The Industrial Revolution* (London, 1973); W. O. Henderson, *The Industrialization of Europe, 1780–1914* (London, 1969); R. M. Hartwell, *The Industrial Revolution and Economic Growth* (London, 1971).

22 For the agricultural rebellion of 1830 see J. L. and Barbara Hammond, *The Village Labourer, 1760–1832* (London, 1911; 1920), p. 151.

23 *Ibid.*, p. 173.

24 For a life of Cobbett see George Spater, *William Cobbett: The Poor Man's Friend,* 2 vols (Cambridge, 1982).

25 Robert Owen's life is described in Frank Podmore, *Robert Owen: A Biography* (1907) (Honolulu, HI, 2004).

26 'The Select Committee to Enquire into the State of Children employed in the Manu-

factories of the United Kingdom', Parliamentary Papers, iii, 20, published in A. Cooke et al. (eds), *Modern Scottish History*, vol. 5 (East Linton, 1998).

27 Thompson, *The Making of the English Working Class*, pp. 411–40, pp. 460–1.

28 Sir Samuel Romilly's remark is recorded in Paul Smith (ed.), *Bagehot: The English Constitution* (Cambridge, 2001).

29 For the history of parliamentary reform see Sir Llewellyn Woodward, *The Age of Reform, 1815–70* (Oxford, 1938), pp. 52–77.

30 *Ibid.*, pp. 77–86.

31 To this day Bristol remains acutely aware of its past and its place in the turbulent history of the island's commerce – not least in relation to the slave trade. Its part in endeavours to improve the lot of the working man and to secure parliamentary reform is a noble one.

32 This remark applies chiefly to the United Kingdom, despite – as the sequel shows – agitation and revolutionary talk at certain crucial moments; but it also applies to the Western world at large, also despite the European and especially French experience of the subsequent period, not least 1848. The point is not that dramatic change occurred, but the *norm of expectation* is that the right way to bring it about is by constitutional means. In the sense that war is not the expected norm of affairs, yet again despite its too frequent occurrence, the dramatic changes wrought in Europe by the two World Wars constitute a major exception. Unification of Germany under Bismarck differed from unification of Italy in that the latter involved warfare. Since 1945 the norm of expectation has become something more in the West; it has become the norm.

33 For the events of 1848 see J. Sperber, *The European Revolutions 1848–1851*, 2nd edition (Cambridge, 2007).

34 For the Poor Law see A. Brundage, *The Making of the New Poor Law: The Politics of Inquiry, Enactment and Implementation 1832–9* (London, 1978).

35 For the anti-combination laws see e. g. Mark Curthoys, *Governments, Labour and the Law in mid-Victorian Britain* (Oxford, 2004).

36 For trade union history see Alastair J. Reid, *United We Stand: A History of Britain's Trade Unions* (London, 2005).

37 Podmore, *Robert Owen: A Biography*.

38 For a comprehensive history of economics see R. Backhouse, *The Ordinary Business of Life* (Princeton, NJ, 2004).

39 David Ricardo, *On the Principles of Political Economy and Taxation* (London, 1819).

40 P. Colquhoun, *Treatise on the Wealth, Power, and Resources of the British Empire* (London, 1814).

41 A classic document on the co-operative movement is G.D.H. Cole, *The British Co-Operative Movement in a Socialist Society* (London, 1951).

42 The quotations are taken from the works cited.

43 A striking feature of these views is that they demonstrate the indivisibility of the good. It would not have been possible for some of these imaginative practices, far ahead of their time, to be introduced without all of them being so; and Owen, who saw consequences clearly, did not hesitate to do the thing that was both logical and right.

44 Joyce Marlow, *The Tolpuddle Martyrs* (London, 1971 and 1985).

45 For Lovett see David Goodway, 'Lovett, William (1800–1877)', *Oxford Dictionary of National Biography* (Oxford, 2004).

46 See Appendix 4 for the Charter. For Chartism see Gregory Clayes (ed.), *The Chartist Movement in Britain, 1838–1856*, 6 vols (London, 2000), Introduction.

47 For Napier see *Oxford Dictionary of National Biography*.

48 Debate in the House of Commons on the Chartist Petition of 1842. Recorded in *Hansard*, 3rd Series, vol. Lxiii, p. 46.

49 One of the great achievements of reform instigated by trades unions is the comprehensive

administration of health and safety measures that now exists in advanced industrial societies.

50 See references to trade union history above.

51 In Britain the laws curbing effectiveness of union activism by outlawing certain forms of picketing, co-operative action from other unions, strikes on a mere show of hands, wildcat strikes and the like, were the work of the government of Mrs Margaret Thatcher, and were bitterly opposed by the unions; the great showdown came in the miners' strikes of the early 1980s. The government, as was inevitable, won.

52 There is good evidence that in certain quarters – the Mosleyites, and some of the aristocracy – there was sympathy for Hitler prior to the war. See R. Thurlow, *Fascism in Britain* (Oxford, 1987).

53 The history of women's rights is recent in both the senses that it is only in the last two centuries that the question has been salient, and that it has been written about historically as well as polemically. Its history in the first sense is still at an early stage.

54 See Elizabeth Cady Stanton et al. (1881), *History of Woman Suffrage* (New York, NY, 1881), ch. 3.

55 Mary Wollstonecraft, ed. Carol H. Poston, *A Vindication of the Rights of Women* (1792) (Toronto, 1975).

56 *Ibid.*, p. 4.

57 *Ibid.*, p. 35.

58 Margaret Brent's request is documented in the *Archives of Maryland*, vol. 1, quoted in W. B. Chilton, *The Brent Family* (Alexandria, VA, 1981), p. 215.

59 This is shown by the mutual annexation of the two questions by Elizabeth Stanton Cady and her colleagues.

60 Robert Owen, *The Book of the New Moral World* (1841), Part 6 (London, 1970).

61 Mill's feminist credentials are secured by his efforts as a Member of Parliament to further the cause of women's suffrage.

62 Ray Monk, *Bertrand Russell: 1872–1921* (London, 1996), pp. 189–90.

63 Queen Victoria (March, 1870). See e.g. Lytton Strachey, *Queen Victoria* (London, 2000), p. 409.

64 Principally written by Elizabeth Cady Stanton, the Seneca Falls *Declaration of Sentiments* was signed in 1848 by sixty-eight women and thirty-two men.

65 This occurs in a conversational book on the history of the colleges of Oxford University, by Christopher Hobhouse (Oxford, 1939), unfortunately spoiled by its misogyny.

66 Eleanor Roosevelt, ed. Allida M. Black, *Courage in a Dangerous World: The Political Writings of Eleanor Roosevelt* (New York, NY, 2000), pp. 180–86. For more on Eleanor Roosevelt see *The Autobiography of Eleanor Roosevelt* (New York, NY, 1992).

6. The Liberty Century

1 See A. C. Grayling, *The Quarrel of the Age: The Life and Times of William Hazlitt* (London, 2000), p. 193.

2 *Ibid.*, p. 340.

3 Santo Correnti, *A Short History of Sicily* (Montreal, 2002).

4 See A. Janik and S. Toulmin, *Wittgenstein's Vienna* (London, 1973).

5 Dieter Dowe, trans. David Higgins, *Europe in 1848: Revolution and Reform* (New York, NY, and Oxford, 2001), pp. 325–6.

6 *Ibid.*, p. 405.

7 David Goodway, *London Chartism 1838–1848* (Cambridge, 2002), pp. 129–152.

8 See Dowe, *Europe in 1848: Revolution and Reform*, p. 920.

9 Andrew C. Gould, *Origins of Liberal Dominance* (Ann Arbor, MI, 1999), p. 107.

10 Karl Marx and Friedrich Engels, *The Communist Manifesto* (1848) (London, 1998), p. 33.

11 Nationalism has a propensity to lead to war, and war is a standing threat to liberty; one of the arguments used in nationalist movements was that they would free 'the people' from the tyranny or at least hegemony of foreign powers; but by the chemistry of differences thus deepened, a different and in many ways worse 'unfreedom' followed.

12 Adolf Hitler, *Mein Kampf* (1925) (Reedy, WV, 2004).

13 See my comment above on nationalism.

14 Elias Canetti, *The Memoirs of Elias Canetti: The Tongue Set Free, the Torch in My Ear, the Play of the Eyes* (New York, NY, 1999), p. 230.

15 Effects of nationalist movements on international relations within Europe in the century after 1850 are common knowledge.

16 This thought alludes to the pre-Westphalian arrangement by which a constantly reassembling Europe governed by an extended royal family – the major contrasts being England and France on the Western margin, which formed as internally coherent empires relatively early – had its different advantages and disadvantages.

17 This point does not touch on a different argument, about the idea of the state. Somewhere ambiguously between the concepts needed to make sense of nationalism and the assumptions that lie behind the idea of the 'nation-state', the state as a self-governing entity might be made up of many nations; the multinational state is in fact a commonplace of European history and of the United Kingdom itself. The *federal* state, as the USA is, deals with the pluralism and diversity problem in a different way, each state within the state having its own attitude to diversity.

18 See Andre Jardin, trans. Lydia Davis with Robert Hemingway, *Tocqueville: A Biography* (Baltimore, MD, and London, 1998), p. 117.

19 *Ibid.*, p. 1.

20 *Ibid.*, p. 10.

21 *Ibid.*

22 'Jacksonian America' is the America of the period between 1824 and 1854.

23 For Andrew Jackson and his period see Robert V. Remini, *Andrew Jackson and the Course of American Empire, 1767–1821* (New York, NY, 1977) and Robert V. Remini, *Andrew Jackson and the Course of American Freedom, 1822–1832* (New York, NY, 1981).

24 John Stuart Mill, *On Liberty* (1859) (London, 1982), e.g. p. 63.

25 John Stuart Mill, *Considerations on Representative Government* (1861) (Whitefish, MT, 2004).

26 *Ibid.*, p. 131.

27 *Ibid.*, p. 94.

28 This was Mill's chief anxiety about the effects of democracy, which at worst he thought might constitute a tyranny over minorities and individuals.

29 J. S. Mill, *On Liberty.*

30 See A. C. Grayling, *The Reason of Things* (London, 2002), ch. 2 *passim* and pp. 157–8.

31 John Emerich Edward Dalberg Acton, 'The History of Freedom in Antiquity', in J. R. Fears (ed.), *Essays in the History of Liberty* (1877) (Indianapolis, IN, 1985), p. 22.

32 *Proclamation of Papal Infallibility* (1870).

33 Acton, *Essays in the History of Liberty*, p. 7.

34 John Emerich Edward Dalberg Acton, 'Inaugural Lecture on the Study of History', in his *Lectures on Modern History* (London, 1906), p. 28.

35 Acton, *Essays in the History of Liberty*, pp. 29–53.

36 *Ibid.*, pp. 32–33.

37 'Letter on Self-Government and State-Absolutism', in John Emerich Edward Dalberg Acton, ed. Abbot Gasquet, *Lord Acton and his Circle* (1906) (New York, NY, 1968), p. 255.

38 *Ibid.*, p. 50.

7. Rights out of Wrongs

1 It should come as no surprise that this powerful remark emanated from a soldier; who better to grasp the truth of these things than one who had seen the harshest truths in action.

2 The argument of Fukuyama's *The End of History* is that the end of the Cold War and the fall of the Berlin Wall proved that free markets and liberal democracy had won, and the tumults and changes of history were coming to an end as a result. He had not seen the next earthquake, coming from the direction of Mecca.

3 See A. C. Grayling, *Among the Dead Cities* (London, 2006), *passim.*

4 See e.g. C. Douzinas, *The End of Human Rights* (London, 2000).

5 Thucidydes, *The Peloponnesian War.*

6 Such is the lesson of Machiavelli's *The Prince.*

7 See J. E. Persico, *Nuremberg: Infamy on Trial* (London, 1994).

8 See the text of the indictment reprinted in *ibid.*

9 The author was a member, and for a time chairman, of a human rights group called June Fourth, which joined with NGOs lobbying at the UN Commission on Human Rights at Geneva on the question of human rights violations in the People's Republic of China. For a number of years from the early 1990s he attended the annual meetings of the Commission and of the Sub-Commission in connection with this matter, and was an interested witness to the vigorous and expensive endeavours made by the Chinese government to avert condemnation for its record.

10 Human Rights Watch maintains information on Chinese human rights violations which is summarised in its reports.

11 A British parliamentary delegation visited China in the mid-1990s to examine human rights conditions, perhaps as part of the run-up to the hand-back of Hong Kong. Just before the hand-back this author ran a conference at Hong Kong University on the question of the universality of human rights, an idea that the Chinese present contested.

12 See the debate in *Prospect* magazine (February 1999) between A. C. Grayling and David Rieff on the idea of an International Criminal Court.

8. The Idea of Liberty and the Verge of Betrayal

1 Isaiah Berlin, *Liberty* (revised and expanded edition of *Four Essays On Liberty*) (Oxford, 2002).

2 Mill, *On Liberty*; see chapter 6 above.

3 One solution is to accept that there is no omniscient God, or that if there is a God it is not omniscient. Solutions to the dilemma for the theologically committed are to be found in St Thomas Aquinas and elsewhere in the literature of theology and philosophy of religion.

4 Kant, 'What is Enlightenment?', on Enlightenment.

5 Christopher Hill, *The Century of Revolution.*

6 See the discussion of Hobbes in chapter 4 above.

7 For H.L.A. Hart see his *The Concept of Law,* revised edition (Oxford, 2002).

8 The long debate about identity cards in Britain is comprehensively covered in media reporting, accessible online.

9 See A. C. Grayling 'In Freedom's Name', in *The Form of Things* (London, 2006).

10 See ACLU report online at www.aclu.org/safefree/resources/17343res20031114.html

11 *Ibid.*

12 '9/11' is the shorthand name of the atrocities committed on 11 September 2001 by Islamist terrorists in New York and Washington. The terrorists hijacked airliners full of people and crashed them into iconic buildings in the two cities, in New York the World Trade Center

twin towers, both of which were destroyed with the loss of thousands of lives, and in Washington the Pentagon, which was partly damaged. A fourth airliner was forced to crash in a field by the actions of courageous passengers on the aircraft.

13 See ACLU and other reports.

14 Abu Ghraib and Guantanamo Bay prisons are a standing indictment against US activity in these respects. The changes brought in after FBI activity against Vietnam War protestors in the 1960s and early 1970s as protection against arbitrary use of intelligence activity and coercion have effectively been reversed.

15 The degree to which the civil liberties regime of the US has been degraded even without these possible steps is insufficiently appreciated by public opinion in other democracies. But it is a striking fact that apart from the United Kingdom few others among these democracies have attempted anything so swingeing. The exception is the Netherlands, whose highly tolerant and open welcome of a large Muslim immigration population has led to some of those most severe tensions now; there the contrast between the once liberal nature of the society and recent proposals that strike many as deeply illiberal is shocking.

16 See ACLU report.

17 Examine any of the pronouncements of Mr Blair on the question of civil liberties, about which he is scathing.

18 Reference to Charles Clarke, *International Herald Tribune*, 14 July 2005.

19 Max Weber, *The Protestant Ethic and the Spirit of Capitalism* (London, 1930).

20 Churchill said this to the boys of his old school, Harrow School, on 29 October 1941.

Bibliography

Aaron, Richard I., *John Locke* (Oxford, 1971)

Acton, Lord, 'On Self Government and State Absolutism', in *Lord Acton and his Circle*, ed. Abbot Gasquet (New York, NY, 1968)

Acton, Lord, 'Inaugural Lecture on the Study of History', in *Lectures on Modern History* (London, 1906)

Acton, Lord, ed. J. Rufus Fears, *Essays in the History of Liberty: Selected Writings of Lord Acton* (Indianapolis, IN, 1985)

Alembert, J. d', 'Essay on the Elements of Philosophy' quoted in E. Cassirer, *The Philosophy of the Enlightenment* (Boston, MA, 1965)

Alembert, J. d', *Preliminary Discourse to the Encyclopaedia of Diderot* (1751), trans. R. W. Schwab (Chicago, IL, 1963)

Allen, P. S., *The Age of Erasmus* (Oxford, 1914)

Anchor, R., *The Enlightenment Tradition* (New York, NY, 1967)

Appiah, Kwame Anthony, and Henry Louis Gates, *Africana: Civil Rights* (Philadelphia, PA, 2005)

Archer, Leonie J., *Slavery and other Forms of Unfree Labor* (New York, NY, 1988)

Armistead, Wilson, *Anthony Benezet. From the original memoir* (London, 1859)

Atkinson, James, *The Great Light: Luther and the Reformation* (Grand Rapids, MI, 1968)

Aveling, J.C.H. *The Handle and the Axe: The Catholic Recusants in England from Reformation to Emancipation* (London, 1976)

Backhouse, R., *The Ordinary Business of Life* (Princeton, NJ, 2004)

Bacon, Francis, *The New Organon* ed. Lisa Jardine and Michael Silverthorne (Cambridge, 2002)

Bacon, Jacqueline, *The Humblest May Stand Forth: Rhetoric, Empowerment, and Abolition* (Columbia, SC, 2002)

Bagchi, D.V.N., *Luther's Earliest Opponents* (Philadelphia, PA, 1991)

Bagchi, David and David C. Steinmetz (eds), *The Cambridge Companion to Reformation Theology* (Cambridge, 2004)

Baillie, J., *The Belief in Progress* (London, 1950)

Bainton, R. H., *Erasmus of Christendom* (New York, NY, 1969)

Bainton, R. H., *Hunted Heretic: The Life and Death of Michael Servetus, 1511–1553* (Boston, MA, 1953)

Bainton, R. H., *The Reformation of the Sixteenth Century* (Boston, MA, 1952)

Bainton, R. H., *The Travail of Religious Liberty* (London, 1953)

Baker, H., *The Dignity of Man* (Cambridge, MA, 1947)

Balke, W., trans. W. J. Heynen, *Calvin and the Anabaptist Radicals* (Grand Rapids, MI, 1981)

Barker, E., G. Clark and P. Vaucher (eds), *The European Inheritance*, vols 2 and 3 (Oxford, 1954)

Barlow, Nora (ed.), *The Autobiography of Charles Darwin 1809–1882* (London, 1958)

Baron H., *From Petrarch to Leonardo Bruni* (Chicago, IL, 1968)

Barzun, J., *From Dawn to Decadence: 1500 to the Present: 500 Years of Western Culture* (London, 2001)

Bauman, M. M. Klauber (ed.), *Historians of the Christian Tradition* (Nashville, TN, 1995)

Becker, M. B., *The emergence of civil society in the eighteenth century* (Indianapolis, IN, 1994)

Beik, William, *Louis XIV and Absolutism: A Brief Study with Documents* (Boston, MA, 2000)

Benezet, Anthony, 'Caution and a Warning', in John Wesley, *Views of American Slavery taken a Century ago* (New York, NY, 1969)

Benezet, Anthony, *Some Historical Account of Guinea, its Situation, Produce and the General Disposition of its Inhabitants* (Kila, MT, 2004)

Bentham, Jeremy, *Collected Works* (London and Oxford, 1968)

Bentham, Jeremy, *A Fragment on Government*, ed. J. H. Burns and H.L.A. Hart (Cambridge, 1988)

Bentley, J. H., *Humanists and Holy Writ* (Princeton, NJ, 1983)

Berkhof, L., *The History of Christian Doctrines* (Edinburgh, 1969)

Berlin, I., 'Hobbes, Locke and Professor Macpherson', *Political Quarterly* 35 (1964), pp. 444–68

Berlin, I., *Liberty*, revised and expanded edition of *Four Essays on Liberty* (Oxford, 2002)

Besterman, Theodore, *Voltaire* (London and Harlow, 1969)

Bieber, Judy, *Plantation Societies in the Era of European Expansion* (Aldershot, 1997)

Blackburn, Robin, *The Overthrow of Colonial Slavery, 1776–1848* (London, 1988)

Blom, P., *Encyclopédie: The Triumph of Reason in an Unreasonable Age* (London, 2004)

Bossuet, Jacques, *Politics Drawn from the Very Words of the Holy Scripture*, ed. Patrick Riley (Cambridge, 1999)

Bouwsma, William J., *John Calvin: A Sixteenth Century Portrait* (Oxford, 1988)

Bouwsma, William J., 'Renaissance and Reformation: An Essay in Their Affinities and Connections', in *Luther and the Dawn of the Modern Era*, ed. Heiko Oberman (Leiden, 1974)

Bouwsma, William J., *The Waning of the Renaissance 1550–1640* (New Haven, CT, and London, 2000)

Brady, T. A., H. A. Oberman and J. D. Tracy (eds), *Handbook of European History 1400–1600*, 2 vols (Grand Rapids, MI, 1996)

Braudel F., *The Perspective of the World: Civilisation and Capitalism 15th–18th Century* (London, 1984)

Bredvold, L., *The Brave New World of the Enlightenment* (Ann Arbor, MI, 1961)

Breen, Quirinius, *Christianity and Humanism* (Grand Rapids, MI, 1968)

Brent, Margaret, *Archives of Maryland*, quoted in W. B. Chilton, *The Brent Family* (Alexandria, VA, 1981)

Brookes, George S., *Friend Anthony Benezet* (Philadelphia, PA, 1937)

Brown, S. C. (ed.), *Philosophers of the Enlightenment* (Brighton, 1979)

Brundage, A., *The Making of the New Poor Law: the Politics of Inquiry, Enactment and Implementation 1832–9* (London:, 1978)

Burke, E., *Reflections on the French Revolution* (London, 1790) (Oxford, 1999)

Burman, E., *The Inquisition: The Hammer of Heresy* (Wellingborough, 1984)

Bury, J. B., *The Decline and Fall of the Roman Empire* (New York, NY, 1977)

Bury, J. B., *History of the Freedom of Thought* (New York, NY, 1913)

Butler, Marilyn, *Burke, Paine, Godwin and the Revolution Controversy* (Cambridge, 1984)

Cameron, Euan, *The European Reformation* (Oxford, 1991)

Cameron, Euan, *The Reformation of the Heretics* (Oxford, 1984)

Canetti, Elias, *The Memoirs of Elias Canetti: The Tongue Set Free, the Torch in my Ear, the Play in my Eyes* (New York, NY, 1999)

Cargill-Thompson, W.D.J., *The Political Thought of Martin Luther* (Sussex, 1984)

Cassell, Christian Abayomi, *Liberia: History of the First African Republic* (New York, NY, 1970)

Cassirer, E., *The Philosophy of the Enlightenment* (Princeton, NJ, 1951)

Cassirer, E., *The Platonic Renaissance in England* (Austin, TX, 1953)

Chadwick, Owen, *Reformation* (New York, NY, 1964)

Chappell, Vere (ed.), *The Cambridge Companion to Locke* (Cambridge, 1994)

Christenson, Ronald, 'The Political Theory of Persecution: Augustine and Hobbes' in *Midwest Journal of Political Science*, vol. 12, no. 3 (August 1968), p. 419

Clayes, Gregory, *The Chartist Movement in Britain 1838–1856* (London, 2000)

Cole, G.D.H., *The British Co-Operative Movement in a Socialist Society* (London, 1951)

Collins, Gail, *America's Women: Four Hundred Years of Dolls, Drudges, Helpmates, and Heroines* (New York, NY, 2003)

Collins, Jeffrey R., *The Allegiance of Thomas Hobbes* (Oxford, 2005)

Collinson, P., *The Reformation* (London, 2003)

Colquhoun, P., *Treatise on the Wealth, Power and Resources of the British Empire* (London, 1814)

Condorcet, *Sketch for a Historical Picture of the Progress of the Human Mind* (1795), ed. Stuart Hampshire, trans. June Barraclough (London, 1955)

Cook, W., and R. Herzman, *The Medieval World View*, (Oxford, 2004)

Cooke, A., et al., *Modern Scottish History* (East Linton, 1998)

Copenhaver, B. P., and C. Schmitt, *Renaissance Philosophy* (Oxford, 1992)

Copernicus, *On the Revolving Heavenly Spheres*, ed. Stephen Hawking (Philadelphia, PA, 2005)

Correnti, Santo, *A Short History of Sicily* (Montreal, 2002)

Cragg, G. R., *The Cambridge Platonists* (London, 1968)

Crane, T., and S. Patterson, *History of the Mind–Body Problem* (London, 2006)

Cranston, Maurice, *John Locke, A Biography* (Oxford, 1957 and 1985)

Crocker, Lester G., *Diderot: The Embattled Philosopher* (New York, NY, 1966)

Cronin, Vincent, *Louis XIV* (London, 1996)

Cross, F. L., and E. A. Livingstone, *The Oxford Dictionary of the Christian Church*, 3rd edition (Oxford, 1997)

Cunningham, Andrew, and Ole Peter Grell, *The Four Horsemen of the Apocalypse: Religion, War, Famine and Death in Reformation Europe* (Cambridge, 2001)

Cunningham, William, *The Reformers and the Theology of the Reformation* (Edinburgh, 1967)

Curthoys, Mark, *Governments, Labour and the Law in Mid-Victorian Britain* (Oxford, 2004)

Davidson, Ian, *Voltaire in Exile* (London, 2005)

Davies, Godfrey, *The Early Stuarts 1603–1660* (Oxford, 1937 and 1963)

Davies, Godfrey, *Essays on the Later Stuarts* (London, 1976)

Davis, David Brion, *Inhuman Bondage: The Rise and Fall of Slavery in the New World* (New York, NY, 2006)

Davis, David Brion, *Problem of Slavery in the Age of Revolution* (New York, NY, 1975)

Dawkins, R., *The Selfish Gene* (Oxford, 1976)

Denifle, Heinrich, *Luther and Lutherdom*, trans. Raymond Volz (Somerset, OH, 1917)

Dickens, A. G., *The Age of Reformation and Humanism* (London, 1977)

Dickens, A. G., *The Counter Reformation* (London, 1968)

Diderot, Denis, *The Encyclopaedia* (selections), trans. S. Gendzier (New York, NY, 1967)

Diderot, Denis, *Selected Writings*, ed. Lester G. Crocker (London, 1966)

Dietz, F. C., *The Industrial Revolution* (London, 1973)

Douglas, J. D. (ed.), *New International Dictionary of the Christian Church* (Grand Rapids, MI, 1978)

Douzinas, C., *The End of Human Rights* (London, 2000)

Dowe, Dieter, *Europe in 1848: Revolution and Reform*, trans. David Higgins (New York, NY, and Oxford, 2001)

Drake, Stillman, *Galileo at Work* (Chicago, 1978)

Drescher, Seymour, *From Slavery to Freedom: Comparative Studies in the Rise and Fall of Atlantic Slavery* (New York, 1999)

Dunlop, Ian, *Louis XIV* (London, 2001)

Dunn, J., *Setting the People Free: The Story of Democracy* (London, 2005)

Edwards, Alistair, 'Hobbes', in *Interpreting Modern Political Philosophy: From Machiavelli to Marx*, eds. A. Edwards and J. Townshend (Basingstoke, 2002)

Emerton, E., *Humanism and Tyranny* (Gloucester, MA, 1964)

Erasmus, Desiderius, *The Praise of Folly, and other writings*, chosen, trans. and ed. Robert M. Adams (New York, NY, 1989)

Fasnacht, G. E., *Acton's Political Philosophy* (London, 1952)

Fears, Rufus J. (ed.), *Essays in the History of Liberty: Selected Writings of Lord Acton* (Indianapolis, IN, 1985)

Fellows, Otis, *Diderot* (Boston, 1977)

Filmer, Robert, *Patriarcha* (London, 1680)

Finocchiaro, Maurice A. (trans. and ed.), *The Galileo Affair: A Documentary History* (Berkeley, CA, 1989)

Fisher, H.A.L., *A History of Europe: Vol 2 1714–1939* (London, 1935)

Fleischer, M., *The Harvest of Humanism in Central Europe* (St Louis, MO, 1992)

Flexner, Eleanor, *Century of Struggle: The Women's Rights Movement in the United States* (Cambridge, MA, 1975)

Foot, Michael, and Isaac Kramnick (eds), *The Thomas Paine Reader* (London, 1987)

Frey, Sylvia R., and Betty Wood, *From Slavery to Emancipation in the Atlantic World* (Portland, OR, 1999)

Friend, W.H.C., *Martyrdom and Persecution in the Early Church* (London, 1965)

Furbank, P. N., *Diderot: A Critical Biography* (New York, NY, 1992)

Fussell, P., *The Rhetorical World of Augustan Humanism* (Oxford, 1965)

Gasquet, Abbot (ed.), *Lord Acton and his Circle* (New York, NY, 1968)

Gay, P., *The Enlightenment: An Interpretation*, 2 vols (New York, NY, 1966 and 1969)

Gebler, Karl von, *Galileo Galilei and the Roman Curia* (London, 1879; reprinted 1977)

Gilmore, M. P., *The World of Humanism* (New York, NY, 1952)

Gingerich, O., *The Book Nobody Read* (London, 2004)

Glendon, M. A., *The World made New: Eleanor Roosevelt and the Universal Declaration of Human Rights* (New York, NY, 2001)

Godwin, W., *Enquiry Concerning Political Justice* (London, 1793)

Goldstone, Lawrence and Nancy, *Out of the Flames* (New York, NY, 2002)

González, Justo L., *The Story of Christianity*, vols 1 and 2 (San Francisco, CA, 1985)

Goodway, David, *London Chartism 1838–1848* (Cambridge, 2002)

Gould, Andrew C., *Origins of Liberal Dominance* (Ann Arbor, MI, 1999)

Grant, A. J., *The Huguenots* (London, 1934)

Grant, Joanne, *Black Protest: 350 Years of History, Documents, and Analyses* (New York, NY, 1996)

Grayling, A. C., *Among the Dead Cities: Was the Allied Bombing of Civilians in World War II a Necessity or a Crime?* (London, 2006)

Grayling, A. C., *Descartes: The Life of René Descartes and its Place in his Times* (London, 2005)

Grayling, A. C., *The Heart of Things* (London, 2005)

Grayling, A. C., *The Meaning of Things* (London, 2001)

Grayling, A. C., *The Quarrel of the Age: The Life and Times of William Hazlitt* (London, 2000)

Grayling, A. C., *The Reason of Things* (London, 2002)

Grayling, A. C., *What Is Good?* (London, 2003)

Green, V.H.H., *Renaissance and Reformation* (London, 1952)

Greenleaf, W. H., *Order, empiricism and politics: two traditions of English political thought, 1500–1700* (Oxford, 1964)

Gregor, Mary J., *Immanuel Kant: Practical Philosophy* (Cambridge, 1999)

Gribbin, J., *Science: A History 1543–2001* (London, 2002)

Griffith, Elisabeth, *In Her Own Right: the Life of Elizabeth Cady Stanton* (New York, NY, 1984)

Halévy, Elie, *A History of the English People* (London, 1947)

Hamilton, Alexander, et al., ed. Jacob E. Cooke, *The Federalist* (Middletown, CT, 1961)

Hamilton, B., *The Medieval Inquisition* (London, 1981)

Hammond, J. L. and Barbara, *The Village Labourer 1760–1832* (London, 1920)

Hankins, T., *Science and the Enlightenment* (Cambridge, 1985)

Harmon, M. J., *Political Thought: from Plato to the present* (New York, NY, 1964)

Harris, I., *The Mind of John Locke: a study of political theory in its intellectual setting* (Cambridge, 1994)

Harris, R. W., *Reason and Nature in the Eighteenth Century* (London, 1968)

Harrison, Ross, *Hobbes, Locke, and Confusion's Masterpiece: An Examination of Seventeenth Century Philosophy* (Cambridge, 2002)

Hart, D. G., and M. Noll (eds.), *Dictionary of the Presbyterian and Reformed Tradition in America* (Downers Grove, IL, 1999)

Hart, H.L.A., *Concept of Law Revised Edition* (Oxford, 2002)

Hart, Trevor (ed.), The *Dictionary of Historical Theology* (Grand Rapids, MI, and Carlisle, 2000)

Hartwell, R. M., *The Industrial Revolution and Economic Growth* (London, 1971)

Hatton, R. (ed.), trans. W. Glyn-Jones, *A History of European Ideas* (Copenhagen, 1962)

Hazard, P., *European Thought in the Eighteenth Century* (London, 1954)

Heinze, Rudolph W., *Reform and Conflict: from the Medieval World to the Wars of Religion, A.D. 1350–1648* (Grand Rapids, MI, 2005)

Helm, Paul, *Calvin and the Calvinists* (Edinburgh, 1982)

Henderson, W. O., *The Industrialisation of Europe 1780–1914* (London, 1969)

Herbermann, C. G., et al. (eds), *The Catholic Encyclopaedia* (New York, NY, 1907–14)

Hill, Christopher, *The Century of Revolution, 1603–1714*, 2nd edition (London, 1961, 1980)

Hill, Christopher, *The English Bible and the Seventeenth-Century Revolution* (London, 1993)

Hill, Christopher, *The English Revolution, 1640* (London, 1940; 3rd edition, 1955)

Hill, Christopher, *Intellectual Origins of the English Revolution* (Oxford, 1965 and 2001)

Hill, Christopher, *Puritanism and Revolution: Studies in Interpretation of the English Revolution of the 17th Century* (London, 1958)

Hill, Christopher, *Turbulent, Seditious and Factious People: John Bunyan and his Church 1628–88* (Oxford, 1989)

Hill, Christopher, *The World Turned Upside Down: Radical Ideas During the English Revolution* (London, 1972)

Hillar, Marian, *The Case of Michael Servetus (1511–1553): The Turning Point in the Struggle for Freedom of Conscience* (Lewiston, Lampeter, 1997)

Hillar, Marian, *Michael Servetus: Intellectual Giant, Humanist, and Martyr* (Lanham, MD, 2002)

Hillerbrand, Hans J., *The World of the Reformation* (London, 1975)

Hillerbrand, Hans J. (ed.), *The Oxford Encyclopedia of the Reformation* (Oxford, 1996)

Himmelfarb, G., *Lord Acton* (Chicago, IL, 1952)

Hitler, Adolf, *Mein Kampf* (1925) (Reedy, WV, 2004)

Hobbes, Thomas, *Behemoth: or The Long Parliament*, ed. Ferdinand Tönnies (Chicago, IL, 1990)

Hobbes, Thomas, *De Cive* (London, 1642)

Hobbes, Thomas, *Leviathan* (1651) ed. Richard Tuck (Cambridge, 1996)

Hochschild, Adam, *Bury the Chains: The British Struggle to Abolish Slavery* (Basingstoke, 2005)

Höfer, J. (ed.), *Lexikon für Theologie und Kirche*, 10 vols (Freiburg, 1957–67)

Holcroft, Thomas, *The Life of Thomas Holcroft* (North Stratford, NH, 1968)

Holton, Sandra Stanley, 'To Educate Women into Rebellion: Elizabeth Cady Stanton and the

Creation of a Transatlantic Network of Radical Suffragists', in *American Historical Review* 99 (October 1994), pp. 1112–37

Houldon, Leslie, and P. Byrne, *Companion Encyclopedia of Theology* (London, 1995)

Hudson, W. S., 'John Locke, preparing the way for the Revolution', in *Journal of Presbyterian History* 42 (1964), pp. 19–38

Hulliung, M., *The autocritique of the Enlightenment: Rousseau and the philosophes* (Cambridge, MA, 1994)

Hulme, P., and L. Jordanova (eds), *Enlightenment and its Shadows* (London, 1990)

Hume, D., *An Enquiry concerning Human Understanding* (1748), ed. Tom L. Beauchamp (Oxford, 1999)

Hume, D., *Enquiries Concerning Human Understanding and Concerning the Principles of Morals* (Oxford, 1975)

Hume, D., *Essays, Moral, Political, and Literary* (London, 1862)

Hume, D., *Principal Writings on Religion, including Dialogues Concerning Natural Religion and the Natural History of Religion* (Oxford, 1998)

Hutchins, Robert Maynard (ed.), *Summa Theologica*, Encyclopaedia Britannica (London, 1952)

Ingram, A., *A Political Theory of Rights* (Oxford, 1994)

Ishay, M. R., *The History of Human Rights from Ancient Times to the Globalisation Era* (Berkeley, CA, 2004)

Israel, J., *Radical Enlightenment* (Oxford, 2001)

Jacoby, S., *Freethinkers: A History of American Secularism* (New York, NY, 2004)

James, C.L.R., *The Black Jacobins: Toussaint L'Ouverture and the San Domingo Revolution* (London, 1989)

Janik, A., and S. Toulmin, *Wittgenstein's Vienna* (London, 1973)

Jardin, André, trans. Lydia Davis with Robert Hemmingway, *Tocqueville: A Biography* (Baltimore, MD, and London, 1998)

Jardine, Lisa, and Alan Stewart, *Hostage to Fortune: the Troubled Life of Francis Bacon* (New York, NY, 2000)

Jeffrey, Julie Roy, *The Great Silent Army of Abolitionism: Ordinary Women in the Antislavery Movement* (Chapel Hill, NC, 1998)

Johnson, Charles Richard, and Patricia Smith, *Africans in America: America's Journey Through Slavery* (New York, NY, 1998)

Johnson, J. W., *A Profane Wit: The Life of John Wilmot, Earl of Rochester* (New York, NY, 2004)

Jones, Mark (ed.), with Paul Craddock and Nicholas Barker, *Fake? The Art of Deception* (London, 1990)

Jurieu, Pierre, *Lettres Pastorales Addressées sur Fidèles de France*, 3 vols (Rotterdam, 1689)

Jurien, Pierre, *Les soupirs de la France esclave* (Amsterdam, 1689)

Kamen, H., *Spain 1469–1714: A Society of Conflict* (3rd edition), (New York, NY, and London, 2005)

Kamen, H., *The Spanish Inquisition* (London, 1997)

Kant, Immanuel, *Critique of Pure Reason*, trans. P. Guyer and A. W. Wood (Cambridge, 1999)

Kaufmann, T. D., *Court, Cloister and City: the Art and Culture of Central Europe 1450–1800* (London, 1995)

Kelly, J. M., *History of Western Legal Theory* (Oxford, 1992)

Kidd, B. J., *The Counter Reformation 1550–1600* (London, 1933)

Kiernan, Michael (ed.), *The Oxford Francis Bacon XV: The Essayes or Counsels, Civill and Moral* (Oxford, 2000)

Kinder, A. Gordon, *Michael Servetus* (Baden-Baden, 1989)

Kitson, Peter, et al. (eds), *Slavery, Abolition and Emancipation: Writings in the British Romantic Period*, 8 vols (London, 1999)

Knapp, Bettina Liebowitz, *Voltaire Revisited* (New York, NY, 2000)

Knights, M., *Politics and opinion in crisis, 1678–81* (Cambridge, 1994)

Kristeller, P. O., *Eight Philosophers of the Italian Renaissance* (Stanford, CA, 1964)

Kristeller, P. O., *Renaissance Thought* (New York, NY, 1961)

Kristeller, P. O., *Renaissance Thought II* (New York, NY, 1965)

Langford, Jerome, *Galileo, Science and the Church*, 3rd edition (South Bend, IN, 1998)

Lanson, Gustave, *Voltaire* (Paris, 1906)

Laski, H. J., *Political Thought from Locke to Bentham* (London, 1920)

Latorette, Kenneth Scott, *History of Christianity, Volume 1: Beginnings to 1500 (Revised)* (San Francisco, CA, 1975)

Lauren, P. G., *The Evolution of International Human Rights* (Philadelphia, PA, 1998)

Lea, H. C., *A History of the Inquisition of Spain*, 4 vols (New York, NY, 1922)

Levey, M., *Early Renaissance* (London, 1967)

Levi, A., *Renaissance and Reformation: The Intellectual Genesis* (London, 2002)

Levi, A.H.T., *Louis XIV* (London, 2004)

Linder, Robert D., 'Calvinism and Humanism: The First Generation', in *Church History* 44 (1975), pp. 167–81.

Lindsay, J. and E. Rickword (eds), *A Handbook of Freedom: A Record of English Democracy Through Twelve Centuries* (London, 1939)

Lindsay, Thomas M., *A History of The Reformation*, 2 vols (New York, 1922)

Ling, Peter, and Sharon Monteith, *Gender in the Civil Rights Movement* (Crosscurrents in African American History) (London, 1999)

Littell, Franklin H., *The Origins of Sectarian Protestantism* (New York, NY, 1964)

Lloyd Thomas, David, *Routledge Philosophy Guidebook to Locke on Government* (London, 1995)

Locke, John, *An Essay Concerning Human Understanding*, ed. Roger Woolhouse (London, 1997)

Locke, John, 'A Letter Concerning Toleration' (1685), in David Wootton (ed.), *John Locke: Political Writings* (London, 1993)

Locke, John, *An Essay on Toleration* (1667), in Mark Goldie (ed.), *John Locke: Political Essays* (Cambridge, 1997)

Locke, John, *Some Thoughts Concerning Education and of the Conduct of the Understanding*, ed. Ruth W. Grant and Nathan Tarcov (Cambridge, MA, 1996)

Locke, John, *Two Treatises of Government*, ed. Peter Laslett (Cambridge, 1988)

Lohse, Bernhard, *Martin Luther: An Introduction to His Life and Work* (Edinburgh, 1986)

Lossky, Andrew, *Louis XIV and the French Monarchy* (Piscataway, NJ, 1994)

Louis XIV, *Memoirs for the Instruction of the Dauphin*, trans. P. Sonnino (New York, NY, 1970)

Lyon, T., *The Theory of Religious Liberty in England* (Cambridge, 1937)

Machamer, P. (ed.), *The Cambridge Companion to Galileo* (Cambridge, 1998)

Machiavelli, Niccolò, *The Prince*, trans. G. Bull (London, 1961)

Macpherson, C. B., *The Political Theory of Possessive Individualism: Hobbes to Locke* (Oxford, 1962)

Madison, James, *Writings 1772–1836* (New York, NY, 1999)

Maland, D., *Europe in the Seventeenth Century* (Hong Kong, 1966)

Mandrou, R., *From Humanism to Science: 1480–1700* (London, 1978)

Manent, P., *An intellectual history of liberalism* (Princeton, NJ, and Chichester, 1987)

Manuel, F., *The Eighteenth Century Confronts the Gods* (Cambridge, MA, 1959)

Marlow, Joyce, *The Tolpuddle Martyrs* (London, 1971 and 1985)

Martin, Jane Roland, *Reclaiming A Conversation: the Ideal of the Educated Woman* (New Haven, CT, and London, 1985)

Martin, K., *French Liberal Thought in the Eighteenth Century* (London, 1929)

Marty, Martin E., *Martin Luther* (New York, NY, 2004)

Marx, Karl, and Friedrich Engels, *Collected Works* (London, 1975)

Marx, Karl, and Friedrich Engels, *The Communist Manifesto* (1848) (London, 1998)

McGiffert, A. C., *History of Christian Thought*, 2 vols (New York, NY, 1954)

McGrath, Alister E., *The Intellectual Origins of the European Reformation* (Oxford, 1987)

McKim, D., and D. Wright (eds), *Encyclopedia of the Reformed Faith* (Louisville, KY, 1992)

McLellan, D., *The Thought of Karl Marx* (London, 1971)

Mettam, Roger, *Power and Faction in Louis XIV's France* (Oxford, 1988)

Mill, J. S., *Autobiography* (London, 1873)

Mill, J. S., *Considerations on Representative Government* (1861) (Whitefish, MT, 2004)

Mill, J. S., *On Liberty and Utilitarianism* (London, 1864)

Mill, J. S., *Three Essays on Religion* (London, 1874)

Miller, John, *Bourbon and Stuart: Kings and Kingship in France and England in the Seventeenth Century* (London, 1987)

Milton, John, *The Complete Prose Works of John Milton*, 8 vols, gen. ed. D. M. Wolfe (New Haven, CT, and London, 1959)

Mitchell, B. G., *Morality: Religious and Secular* (Oxford, 1980)

Moncure, Conway, *The Life of Thomas Paine* (London, 1908)

Monk, Ray, *Bertrand Russell 1872–1921* (London, 1996)

Montesquieu, Baron de, *The Spirit of the Laws*, trans. Thomas Nugent (New York, NY, 1949)

Morley, Lord, T. Smollett, W. Fleming and O. Leigh (eds), *The Works of Voltaire, A Contemporary Version* (New York, NY, 1901)

Morrow, J., *A History of Political Thought* (New York, NY, 1998)

Newton, Isaac, *The Principia: The Mathematical Principles of Natural Philosophy*, trans. Bernard Cohen, Anne Whitman and Julia Buden (Berkeley, CA, 1999)

Nussbaum, F. L., *The Triumph of Science and Reason* (New York, NY, 1953)

Oberman, H. A., *The Dawn of the Reformation* (Edinburgh, 1986)

Oberman, H. A., *Luther: Man Between God and the Devil*, trans. Eileen Walliser-Schwarzbart (London, 1993 (reprint))

Oberman, H. A., *Masters of the Reformation: The Emergence of a New Intellectual Climate in Europe*, trans. D. Martin (Cambridge, 1981)

Offen, Karen, 'Women and the Question of "Universal" Suffrage in 1848: A Transatlantic Comparison of Suffragist Rhetoric', in *NWSA Journal* 11 (Spring 1999), pp. 150–178

Ogg, D., *Europe in the Seventeenth Century* (Edinburgh, 1925)

Olson, R., *The Story of Christian Theology* (Downers Grove, IL, 1999)

Osler, William, 'Michael Servetus', in *A Way of Life* (London, 1946)

Outka, G., and J. Reeder, *Religion and Morality* (Garden City, MI, 1973)

Owen, Robert, *The Book of the New Moral World* (1841) (London, 1970)

Paine, Thomas, *Common Sense*, ed. Isaac Kramnick (Harmondsworth, 1976)

Paine, Thomas, *The Rights of Man* (London, 1791)

Parker, G., *Europe in Crisis: 1598–1648*, 2nd edition (Oxford, 2001)

Parker, William Riley, *Milton: A Biography Volume 1: The Life* (Oxford, 1968 and 1996)

Passmore, J. A., *The Perfectibility of Man* (London, 1970)

Patterson, Orlando, *Freedom in the Making of Western Culture* (New York, NY, 1991)

Patterson, Orlando, *Slavery and Social Death: A Comparative Study* (Cambridge, MA, 1982)

Pauck, W., *The Heritage of the Reformation* (Oxford, 1961)

Payne, H. C., *The Philosophes and the People* (New Haven, CT, 1976)

Persico, J. E., *Nuremberg: Infamy on Trial* (London, 1994)

Plato, *Apology*, in *The Last Days of Socrates*, trans. H. Treddenick (London, 2003)

Podmore, Frank, *Robert Owen: a Biography* (Honolulu, HI, 2004)

Pole, J. R., *The Pursuit of Equality in American History* (Berkeley, CA, 1978)

Pollock, John, *Wilberforce* (New York, NY, 1978)

Popkin, Richard H. (trans. and ed.), *Pierre Bayle Historical and Critical Dictionary: Selections* (Indianapolis, IN, and Cambridge, 1991)

Porter, R., *Enlightenment: Britain and the Creation of the Modern World* (London, 2000)

Proclamation of Papal Infallibility (1870)

Randall, J. H., *The Making of the Modern Mind* (Cambridge, MA, 1940)

Ranum, Orest, *The Fronde, A French Revolution* (New York, NY, 1993)

Rayner, R. M., *European History 1648–1789* (London, 1949)

Rees, Martin, *Before the Beginning: Our Universe and Others* (London, 1997)

Reid, Alistair J., *United We Stand: A History of Britain's Trade Unions* (London, 2005)

Remini, Robert V., *Andrew Jackson and the Course of American Empire 1767–1821* (New York, NY, 1977)

Remini, Robert V., *Andrew Jackson and the Course of American Freedom 1822–1832* (New York, NY, 1981)

Ricardo, David, *On the Principles of Political Economy and Taxation* (London, 1819)

Richter, Peyton, *Voltaire* (Boston, MA, 1980)

Roosevelt, Eleanor, *Courage in a Dangerous World: the Political Writings of Eleanor Roosevelt*, ed. Allida M. Black (New York, NY, 2000)

Roosevelt, Eleanor, *The Autobiography of Eleanor Roosevelt* (New York, NY, 1992)

Roth, C., *The Spanish Inquisition* (New York, NY, 1964)

Rousseau, J. J., *Confessions*, trans. J. M. Cohen (London, 1953)

Rousseau, J. J., *Emile*, trans. A. Bloom (London, 1911)

Rousseau, J. J., *Profession of Faith of a Savoyard Vicar* (1782), trans. M. Cranston (London, 1987)

Rousseau, J. J., *The Social Contract*, trans. M. Cranston (London, 1974)

Rule, John C. (ed.), *Louis XIV and the Craft of Kingship* (Columbus, OH, 1969)

Rummel, E., *The Humanist-Scholastic Debate* (Cambridge, MA, 1995)

Sabatini, R., *Torquemada and the Spanish Inquisition* (New York, NY, 1924)

Sambrook, J., *The Eighteenth Century*, 2nd edition (London, 1993)

Sawyer, Roger, *Children Enslaved* (New York, NY, and London, 1988)

Schama, S., *Citizens: A Chronicle of the French Revolution* (London, 1989)

Schnucker, R. V., *Calviniana: The Ideas and Influence of John Calvin* (Kirksville, MO, 1988)

Schoules, P., *Reasoned Freedom: John Locke and Enlightenment* (Ithaca, NY, 1992)

Schuettinger, R. L., *Lord Acton: Historian of Liberty* (La Salle, IL, 1976)

Scott, Jonathon, *England's Troubles: Seventeenth-Century English History in European Perspective* (Cambridge, 2000)

Scribner, R., and G. Benecke, *The German Peasant War* (London, 1979)

Shackleton, Robert, *Montesquieu: A Critical Biography* (New York, NY, 1961)

Sharp, Andrew, *The English Levellers* (Cambridge, 1998)

Sharratt, Michael, *Galileo: Decisive Innovator* (Cambridge, 2006)

Singer, C., *From Magic to Science* (New York, NY, 1958)

Skorupski, J., *Why Read Mill Today?* (London, 2006)

Smith, A., *An Inquiry into the Nature and Causes of the Wealth of Nations* (Dublin, 1776)

Smith, P. (ed.), *Bagehot: The English Constitution* (Cambridge, 2001)

Smith, P., *A History of Modern Culture Vol. 2: The Enlightenment* (New York, NY, 1934)

Smolin, L., *The Trouble with Physics* (London, 2007)

Soderland, Jean R., *Quakers and Slavery: A Divided Spirit* (Princeton, NJ, 1989)

Sorrell, Tom (ed.), *The Cambridge Companion to Hobbes* (Cambridge, 1996)

Sorrell, Tom, *Hobbes* (London, 1986)

Spater, George, *William Cobbett: The Poor Man's Friend* (Cambridge, 1982)

Spender, D., *Women of Ideas* (London, 1982)

Sperber, J., *The European Revolutions 1848–1851 2nd edition* (Cambridge, 2007)

Spinoza, Benedict de, *A Theological-Political Treatise*, trans. R.H.M. Elwes (Toronto, 1951)

Stanton, Elizabeth Cady, *History of Woman Suffrage* (New York, NY, 1881)

Steele Commager, H., *The Empire of Reason* (London, 1978)

Stephens, W. P., *The Theology of Huldrych Zwingli* (Oxford, 1984)

Strauss, Leo, *The Political Philosophy of Hobbes: Its Basis and Its Genesis* (Oxford, 1936)

Strachey, Lytton, *Queen Victoria* (London, 2000)

Taylor, H. O., *Thought and Expression in the Sixteenth Century* (New York, NY, 1920)

Terborg-Penn, Rosalyn, *African American Women in the Struggle for the Vote, 1850–1920* (Bloomington, IN, 1998)

Thomas, J.A.C., *Textbook of Roman Law* (Amsterdam and Oxford, 1976)

Thomas, K., *Religion and the Decline of Magic* (London, 1980)

Thompson, E. P., *The Making of the English Working Class* (London, 1991)

Thucydides, *The Peloponnesian War*, trans. R. Warner (London, 1954)

Thurlow, R., *Fascism in Britain* (Oxford, 1987)

Thurner, Manuela, ' "Better Citizens Without the Ballot": American Anti-Suffrage Women and Their Rationale During the Progressive Era', in *Journal of Women's History* 5 (Spring 1993), pp. 33–61

Torek, P., 'Liberties, not rights: Gauthier and Nozick on property', in *Social Theory and Practice* 20 (1994), pp. 343–61

Tracy, J., *Erasmus: The Growth of a Mind* (Geneva, 1972)

Trevor-Roper, H. R., *Religion, the Reformation and Social Change*, 2nd edition (London, 1972)

Tuck, R., *Natural Rights Theories: Their Origin and Development* (Cambridge, 1979)

Vaux, Roberts, *Memoirs of the life of A. Benezet* (Philadelphia, PA, 1817). *See* Wilson Armistead 1859 revision with notes

Venturi, F., *Utopia and Reform in the Enlightenment* (Cambridge, 1971)

Voltaire, *Philosophical Dictionary* (1764), trans. P. Besterman (London, 1979)

Voltaire, *Treatise on Toleration* (1764) (Cambridge, 2000)

Wade, Ira O., *The Intellectual Development of Voltaire* (Princeton, NJ, 1969)

Waldron, J., 'John Locke – social contract versus political anthropology', in *The social contract from Hobbes to Rawls*, ed. D. Boucher and P. Kelly (London, 1994)

Waller, A. R., and A. Glover, *The Collected Works of William Hazlitt* (London, 1902)

Walvin, James, *Slavery and the Slave Trade: a Short Illustrated History* (Jackson, MS, 1983)

Warfield, Benjamin B., *Calvin and Calvinism* (New York, NY, 1931)

West, J. F., *The Great Intellectual Revolution* (London, 1965)

Westfall, R. S., *Essays on the trial of Galileo* (Vatican, 1989)

Wheen, Francis, *Karl Marx: A Life* (London, 1999)

Wilbur, Earl Morse, *A History of Unitarianism: Socinianism and its Antecedents* (Cambridge, MA, 1945)

Wilkinson, Richard, *Routledge Historical Biographies: Louis XIV* (London, 2004)

Willey, B., *The Eighteenth Century Background* (London, 1953)

Willey, B., *The English Moralists* (London, 1964)

Willey, B., *The Nineteenth Century Studies* (London, 1955)

Willey, B., *More Nineteenth Century Studies* (London, 1956)

Williams, G. H., *The Radical Reformation* (Philadelphia, PA, 1962, and Kirksville, MO, 1994)

Williams, W., *Saint Bernard of Clairvaux* (London, 1952)

Wilson, A. N., *The Life of John Milton* (Oxford, 1984)

Wilson, Arthur M., *Diderot: The Testing Years 1713–1759* (New York, NY, 1957)

Wise, Steven M., *Though the Heavens May Fall: The Landmark Trial that Led to the End of Human Slavery* (Cambridge, MA, 2006)

Wollstonecraft, Mary, *A Vindication of the Rights of Women*, ed. Carol H. Poston (Toronto, 1975)

Woodward, Sir Llewellyn, *The Age of Reform 1815–70* (Oxford, 1938)

Woolhouse, R. S., *Locke: A Biography* (Cambridge, 2007)

Yates, F. A., *Collected Essays* (London, 1982–4)

Yolton, J. (ed.), *Philosophy, Religion and Science in the Seventeenth and Eighteenth Centuries* (New York, NY, 1990)

Yolton, J., et al., *The Blackwell Companion to the Enlightenment* (Oxford, 1991)

Zakaria, F., *The Future of Freedom: Liberal Democracy at Home and Abroad* (London, 2003)

Zweig, Stefan, *Castellio gegen Calvin, oder, Ein Gewissen gegen die Gewalt* – 'The Right to Heresy: How John Calvin Killed A Conscience: Castellio against Calvin' (Vienna, 1936)

Index

A NOTE ON THE AUTHOR

A. C. Grayling is one of Britain's leading intellectuals. Reader in Philosophy at Birkbeck College, University of London, a fellow of St Anne's College, Oxford and the author of the best-selling *The Meaning of Things, The Reason of Things* and most recently *The Mystery of Things*, he believes that philosophy should take an active, useful role in society, rather than withdrawing to the proverbial ivory tower. He is a columnist for *The Times* and a regular contributor to the *Financial Times, Observer, Independent on Sunday, The Economist, Literary Review, New Statesman* and *Prospect*, and a frequent and popular contributor to radio and television, including CNN, *Newsnight* and for BBC Radio 4, *Today, In Our Time* and *Start the Week*. He was a Man Booker judge in 2003, is a Fellow of the World Economic Forum and an adviser on many committees ranging from Drug Testing at Work to human rights groups.

A NOTE ON THE TYPE

The text of this book is set Adobe Garamond. It is one of several versions of Garamond based on the designs of Claude Garamond. It is thought that Garamond based his font on Bembo, cut in 1495 by Francesco Griffo in collaboration with the Italian printer Aldus Manutius. Garamond types were first used in books printed in Paris around 1532. Many of the present-day versions of this type are based on the *Typi Academiae* of Jean Jannon cut in Sedan in 1615.

Claude Garamond was born in Paris in 1480. He learned how to cut type from his father and by the age of fifteen he was able to fashion steel punches the size of a pica with great precision. At the age of sixty he was commissioned by King Francis I to design a Greek alphabet; for this he was given the honourable title of royal type founder. He died in 1561.